In this book Bo Rothstein seeks to defend the universal welfare state against a number of important criticisms which it has faced in recent years. He combines genuine philosophical analysis of normative issues concerning what the state *ought* to do with empirical political scientific research in public policy examining what the state *can* do. Issues discussed include the relationship between welfare state and civil society, the privatization of social services, and changing values within society. His analysis centres around the importance of political institutions as both normative and empirical entities, and Rothstein argues that the choice of such institutions at certain formative moments in a country's history is what determines the political support for different types of social policy. He thus explains the great variation among contemporary welfare states in terms of differing moral and political logics which have been set in motion by the deliberate choices of political institutions. The book is an important contribution to both philosophical and political debates about the future of the welfare state.

D1164172

JUST INSTITUTIONS MATTER

THEORIES OF INSTITUTIONAL DESIGN

Series Editor
Robert E. Goodin
Research School of Social Sciences
Australian National University

Advisory Editors
Brian Barry, Russell Hardin, Carole Pateman, Barry Weingast,
Stephen Elkin, Claus Offe, Susan Rose-Ackerman

Social scientists have rediscovered institutions. They have been increasingly concerned with the myriad ways in which social and political institutions shape the patterns of individual interactions which produce social phenomena. They are equally concerned with the ways in which those institutions emerge from such interactions.

This series is devoted to the exploration of the more normative aspects of these issues. What makes one set of institutions better than another? How, if at all, might we move from a less desirable set of institutions to a more desirable set? Alongside the questions of what institutions we would design, if we were designing them afresh, are pragmatic questions of how we can best get from here to there: from our present institutions to new revitalized ones.

Theories of institutional design is insistently multidisciplinary and interdisciplinary, both in the institutions on which it focuses, and in the methodologies used to study them. There are interesting sociological questions to be asked about legal institutions, interesting legal questions to be asked about economic institutions, and interesting social, economic, and legal questions to be asked about political institutions. By juxtaposing these approaches in print, this series aims to enrich normative discourse surrounding important issues of designing and redesigning, shaping and reshaping the social, political and economic institutions of contemporary society.

Just institutions matter

The moral and political logic of the universal welfare state

BO ROTHSTEIN

CAMBRIDGE
UNIVERSITY PRESS

PUBLISHED BY THE PRESS SYNDICATE OF THE UNIVERSITY OF CAMBRIDGE
The Pitt Building, Trumpington Street, Cambridge CB2 1RP, United Kingdom

CAMBRIDGE UNIVERSITY PRESS
The Edinburgh Building, Cambridge, CB2 2RU, United Kingdom
40 West 20th Street, New York, NY 10011–4211, USA
10 Stamford Road, Oakleigh, Melbourne 3166, Australia

First published 1998

Printed in the United Kingdom at the University Press, Cambridge

Typeset in 10½/12 pt minion [CE]

A catalogue record for this book is available from the British Library

Library of Congress Cataloguing in Publication data

Rothstein, Bo, 1954–
Just institutions matter : the moral and political logic of the universal welfare state / Bo Rothstein.
    p.   cm. – (Theories of institutional design)
Includes bibliographical references and index.
ISBN 0 521 59121 X (hb). – ISBN 0 521 59893 1 (pb)
1. Welfare state.   2. Public welfare.   3. Social policy.
I. Title.   II. Series.
HV31.R765   1998
361.6′5 – DC21   97–2700   CIP

ISBN 0 521 59121 X hardback
ISBN 0 521 59893 1 paperback

To the memory of Rosa and Samuel Rothstein

Contents

Figures

Tables

Preface

In the spring of 1986, I worked in Copenhagen while remaining a resident of the city of Lund in Sweden. I was therefore classified by the Swedish state – or by the tax authorities more precisely – as a *boundary-crosser*. This was a designation which, after a time, I came to like very much, for it gave concise expression to my wish to regard myself as a person accustomed in different contexts to crossing boundaries. This book is itself of just such a character, an attempt to cross a number of intellectual (and personal) boundaries.

I wish I could say this is the conclusion of a research project, but according to my experience such things never end. As with one's other old heroes and relations, perhaps, they just gradually fade away. It is likewise difficult to say when it actually began. The idea of writing such a book developed successively while I was occupied with other things. Yet it was Jörgen Hermansson who, I think without knowing it, once gave me the idea of putting together a book such as this one. The degree to which I have able to make decisions which are both autonomous and good (in the sense of well-considered) falls now to others to judge.

The book is my report to the project on the future of the public sector conducted at the Swedish Institute for Future Studies. A special thanks to the Institute and to its director Åke E. Andersson, for providing me with the rare combination of generous intellectual *and* economic support. The Swedish version of this book, which was published in 1994, was the final report of a project begun in 1992, financed by the Swedish Research Council on the Humanities and Social Sciences. The council also provided generous funding for the translation of the book into English.

Many persons and institutions have contributed to making it possible

to complete this project. For a period of three months, Hans-Ingvar Roth
was an uncommonly skillful and efficient research assistant. I have had
many rewarding discussions concerning these things over the years with
Jens Hoff, Tim Knudsen, Sven E. Olsson-Hort, Sven Steinmo, Christina
Bergqvist, Torsten Svensson, and AnnChristin Rothstein. Peter Mayers
has been invaluable for this project. Not only did he make the initial
translation of the text into English, but he also provided me with many
substantial comments and ideas. Frank Castles did his very best to cure
me from my Swedish ethnocentrism and to show that there are other
ways of being a welfare state than I (then) understood.

My thanks to Peter Hall, who made it possible for me to spend the first
semester I worked on the project as a guest researcher at the Center for
European Studies at Harvard University (CES). My discussions at the
Center, especially in the working group on "Social Policy and Citizenship" – together with, among others, Margaret Weir, Rosemary C. R.
Taylor, Andrew Martin, and Paul Pierson – gave me many and valuable
impluses and ideas. Both the basic idea of the project and an early version
of chapter 6 were presented at CES.

A hearty thanks as well to Margaret Levi, who invited me to stay as a
guest researcher at the University of Washington in Seattle in the spring
of 1993. Our many discussions about the possibilities and limits of
"contingent consent," and about the importance of political institutions,
have been critical for getting this book in order. Margaret's intellectual
and personal generosity has proved to me that the laws of dialectics still
apply, and that hard-headed rationalists can have an uncommonly big
heart.

Lennart Lundquist has offered constructive comments on the first two
chapters, and from the beginning has encouraged me in my approach.
Johan P. Olsen's invitation to visit the Norwegian Research Center in
Organization and Management at the University of Bergen gave me,
besides the opportunity to discuss the disposition of the project, contact
with the working group on "The Moral Foundations of the Welfare
State," and with its initiator, Erik Oddvar Eriksen. At two subsequent
meetings with this group, moreover, I have received valuable comments
on various parts of the manuscript.

Colleagues at the Department of Government at Uppsala University
have offered comments on various sections of this book. As my opponent
when I presented the basic proposal, Sverker Gustavsson was as enthu-
siastic as he was constructive. Shirin Ahlbäck's penetrating comments on
chapters 3 and 4 inspired me with altogether different and more
constructive ideas. Mikael Axberg and Mats Lundström, generously
shared their knowledge in political philosophy.

Robert E. Goodin, Jörgen Hermansson, Jens Hoff, Sven E. Olsson-Hort, and Per Molander have all read an earlier version of this manuscript in its entirety, ventured many valuable opinions, and saved me from a great many fatal mistakes.

A number of persons in my immediate vicinity have done what they could to divert my attention and energy from the research. To just you I extend my very greatest thanks, for without you I would have succeeded in repressing some essential things in life.

This book is dedicated to my paternal grandparents, Rosa and Samuel Rothstein, who lived and worked in the village of Güssing in Austria until 1940. For them, the relation of the state to the citizens was not just a theoretical problem. Their fate, first in Lodz and then finally in Auschwitz, in November 1941, has been with me throughout the writing of this book. So long ago, and yet still so near.

1

Speculation and discipline

My aim in this book is to unite two incompatible ambitions: speculation and discipline. Let us begin with the former. In several ways, this book is a speculative one. Firstly, because it tries to say something about the shape of the future, an always daring (not to say foolhardy) enterprise.[1] The future I make so bold as to describe, moreover, is that of a phenomenon which today is both contested and in the midst of change: the universal welfare state. As Sweden is perhaps the most prominent example of such a welfare state, I will mostly use Swedish data in this study.

A second speculative feature inheres in the fact that, in contrast to most social scientific research undertaken today, this book is both openly normative *and* empirical. I do not restrict my efforts to describing and explaining the characteristic features of the universal welfare state; I also submit arguments for how this policy should be framed in the future, and I attempt to justify these proposals. This approach is not (or at least not only) dictated by a need to air my political values and social prejudices. I write this book, rather, in the conviction that the discussion of welfare policy must always remain incomplete until the normative problems raised by the question of social justice are confronted. Empirical analysis is, needless to say, central to such a project as this, but if my efforts to

---

[1] During the autumn of 1968, a group of Swedish sociologists visited the mining areas in Kiruna and Malmberget to study the miners' working conditions. Their investigations revealed that discontent with working conditions was minimal, and that satisfaction with life was in general very high. Some months later, these workers went on a strike which shook both the dominant ideology of consensus and the country's political leadership to their roots. On this episode in Swedish social research, see Larsson (1984), pp. 9f.

peer into the future are to yield anything more than simple extrapolations of today's trends, then the normative arguments for different models and solutions must be put on the table. This book represents, in other words, an attempt to combine empirical and normative concerns in one and the same theory.[2]

David Ricci supplies us with good reasons for such a project in his book written in 1984, *The Tragedy of Political Science.* In this work, Ricci points out that classical political science was dominated by such normatively charged concepts as "justice," "nation," "rights," "patriotism," "society," "virtue," and "tyranny." The tragedy of political science today, according to Ricci, lies in the fact that such concepts have largely disappeared and been replaced – in the brave new world of mass data and policy analysis – by sexless and technical concepts like "attitude," "cognition," socialization," and "system." Ricci argues that this shift in interest – from critical, normatively charged questions about the foundations of politics and democracy to the empirically manageable and the politically useful – helps to explain the crisis in which, he claims, modern political science finds itself. Political scientists have turned away, that is, from such questions as the members of society consider relevant and important. Yet it is precisely the reflection on such matters that grants the scientific study of politics a degree of importance for the world outside the protected preserves of academic specialization. One may summarize Ricci's critique of contemporary political science in the following manner: it has sacrificed its political relevance and urgency on the altar of empirical precision and statistical generalization.[3]

Ricci's description may be exaggerated (I think it is), but still it captures something central about developments in the field. For the attempt to separate normative questions from empirical ones in social science does indeed raise considerable problems. To begin with, normative premises – if only implicit ones – underlie every analysis of welfare policy, and these should, as a matter of intellectual propriety, be stated plainly. Moreover, the social welfare programs examined here are not just instrumental arrangements; they are also, and in a high degree, expressions of definite moral conceptions. They cannot be understood unless their normative foundations are laid bare.[4] As the Norwegian political

---

[2] Lundquist (1988), p. 18, and Lundquist (1993), pp. 84ff. For an argument against the wisdom of such a project, see Westerståhl (1993). Perhaps he is right, but it happens to amuse me to undertake just such things as are declared forbidden. Or to quote Westerståhl himself: "All research should of course be critical in the basic sense of being free from belief in authority" (1993), p. 382.

[3] Ricci (1984), p. 296; cf. D. Held (1987), p. 273.

[4] This is one of the main theses of March & Olsen (1989).

scientist Johan P. Olsen argues, it has been and remains a central task of political science to "clarify which ideals, values, and interests should be safeguarded through public action."[5]

The social sciences have undergone an unprecedented expansion during recent decades. One consequence of this has been a high degree of specialization, both within and between branches of the discipline. The American Political Science Association, for instance, is now divided into no less than thirty-eight different sections, and communication between them is often minimal. This simplest way for a scholar to master a field, of course, is to make it as narrow as possible. The minimization of risk, the preference for the safe over the unsafe, and the limitation of analytical scope – these are the natural choices. A high degree of specialization entails the risk, however, of so narrowing the scope of analysis as to make it impossible to say anything of interest about the urgent questions facing society. One scholar may know something about the moral-philosophical bases of solidarity and the welfare state, another might perform mathematically advanced cost-benefit analyses of different welfare programs, a third is perhaps an expert on statistical analyses of public attitudes towards various welfare questions, a fourth may study problems of bureaucracy in social policy, and a fifth, finally, might have some interesting things to say about the historical course of welfare policy in different countries. If we are to be able, however, to say anything about the future of universal welfare state(s) *as a whole,* we must combine insights and analyses from all of these five areas (and others besides). Scientific specialization deepens our knowledge, certainly, but narrows it as well. What above all else is lost through excessive specialization is the possibility of a more synthetic and overarching analysis of how the phenomena falling under the various analytical domains affect each other. To take just one example: a given social welfare program may be designed according to principles thought by the best moral philosophers to express the very soul of social justice, and might furthermore enjoy public confidence and strong electoral support. If, however, the implementation of this program is assigned to an administrative apparatus which is badly organized for the task, and if the result is waste, corruption, and the abuse of power, then the philosophers (but nobody else) will be surprised that their theories turned out not to fit the need. The holistic perspective to which I mean to adhere will necessarily force us into speculative discussions about how the various areas relate to each

---

[5] Olsen (1993), p. 4, cf. Fischer (1995).

other. The only defense I can offer in this matter is that speculation inheres in the subject under review.

It may at this point be appropriate to take up the second of this book's ambitions – discipline. Discipline, according to the dictionary, is the same as orderliness. It is my purpose in this book to be orderly, insofar as this is possible. This ambition has an important corollary: the normative analysis conducted here is *not* to be a mere exercise in airing my views. It is not so much that I stand under a scholarly obligation to state my innermost values in these matters openly,[6] so that, for example, my readers might gather why I find the problem I have selected to be interesting. Such underlying values have obviously in some manner conditioned my theoretical premises and choice of problem;[7] this, however, is something for my critics to occupy themselves with. I wish rather to emphasize that, by normative analysis, I do not here mean mysticism, or the airing of personal opinions, or the simple stipulation that certain values are obviously much better than others.[8] I shall present, accordingly, a small selection of the great debate within modern political philosophy about the nature of social justice (which has enjoyed a renaissance in the social sciences since the early 1970s). This portion of the book will seek to demonstrate how good arguments can be found within this political-philosophical discourse for particular positions on the question of social justice. The best formulation I have seen regarding the place of philosophical discourse in the discussion of public policy is that of Sidney Hook:

> the most important contribution the philosopher can make to the discussion of public affairs is to make explicit the ethical issues behind conflicting public policies and then relate them to the kind of society in which we want to live and to the kind of men and women we wish to see nurtured in such a society.[9]

Let me immediately stress that I share the view, held by most, that it cannot be scientifically demonstrated that certain normative standpoints are more correct (in the sense of closer to the truth) than others. It is rather a question of tracking down, as far as this is possible, persuasive arguments that certain conclusions follow logically from certain basic

---

[6] If indeed I know what they are myself, and could present them in a reasonably intelligible and coherent manner. Cf. Herméren (1972), pp. 211ff.
[7] Cf. Lundquist (1993), p. 89.
[8] See Therborn (1973), pp. 25–47.
[9] Hook (1980), p. 11.

principles – principles over which, we can reasonably hope, far-reaching agreement can be reached.[10] It is presumably the case, as John Rawls has claimed, that

> in philosophy questions at the most fundamental level are not usually settled by conclusive argument. What is obvious to some persons and accepted as a basic idea is unintelligible to others. The way to resolve the matter is to consider after due reflection which view, when fully worked out, offers the most coherent and convincing argument.[11]

The object of intellectual discipline is to render such argumentation – in respect of both basic and derivative principles – as clear, open, and logical as possible, and thereby to grant potential critics ready access to the object of their assaults, by exposing it to plain view. The scientific character of this discourse resides in its logical method for the giving and taking of arguments, rather than in any rules regarding the presentation of evidence. In this normative discourse, then, we "subject ourselves to the scientific ideal which goes under the name of the supremacy of argument,"[12] that is, we undertake to consider the arguments of others, and to submit rational reasons for our own. The requirements of logical consistency, rationality, and open discussion (the rules of scientific disputation, in other words) set limits upon which standpoints we can present if we wish to continue to take legitimate part in the discussion. It may be said, then, that the purpose of this book is to speculate in a disciplined manner.[13]

---

[10] N. P. Barry (1981), p. 92. Cf. Westerståhl (1993), who claims, on p. 282, that one can build a bridge over the chasm separating normative and empirical analysis by framing the operationalization of normative concepts in such a manner that they "must be accepted by the majority of those most closely affected."

[11] Rawls (1993), p. 53.

[12] Hermansson (1995). See also Björklund (1977) and Fischer (1983).

[13] Such a thesis – of scientific logic and rationalism as the binding cement in this discussion – is of course altogether meaningless from a postmodernist viewpoint. There must be some limits, however, on how intellectually chic one can be. In this matter and at this time, therefore, I have chosen to renounce my ambition to keep up with the latest trend. These questions are simply too important to be sacrificed on the altar of intellectual fashion. The reason I find it meaningless to conduct a discussion about these things on the postmodernists' terms is that they do not recognize any common point of reference from which a discussion can proceed. The postmodernists must finally end up at a point where all scientific and political values are equally good or bad, except of course rational ones, which by definition are the worst. After that there is, as I see it, nothing to discuss. For an overview of this genre, see Dewes (1987), Rorty (1993), and Premfors (1993).

On the need for a constructive political theory

I shall illustrate the consequences of academic specialization in this area by considering the relation of modern political philosophy to empirical analysis. The background is the following. Beginning in the 1970s, the social sciences (and political science among them) have seen a sharply increased interest in normative analysis and debate. This renaissance of political philosophy began with the publication in 1971 of John Rawls' *A Theory of Justice*, and the publication a few years later of Robert Nozick's *Anarchy, State, and Utopia.* Both Rawls and Nozick broke with the utilitarianism and moral relativism that dominated political philosophy, and demonstrated the significance of a pronouncedly normative discourse, in which such concepts as justice, equality, and rights again took center stage. Rawls' project was to specify the distributive principles on which reasoning individuals would agree, if – as the thought experiment went – they were placed in a hypothetical *original position* in which they (a) formally and substantively were of equal standing to make decisions, and (b) lacked information about their own social, physical, and economic resources in the future, and about the shape of society as well.[14] From an analysis of how the actors in such a situation could be expected to reason, Rawls derives two lexically ordered principles (i.e., the first has priority over the second). The first principle states that "each person is to have an equal right to the most extensive basic liberty compatible with a similar liberty for others," while the second prescribes that inequality in the distribution of resources can only be accepted to the extent that the situation of everyone (thus including the worst-off) is thereby improved.[15]

Rawls' great impact probably reflects – besides the originality and quality of his work – his attempt to combine, in one and the same theory, the liberal idea of the inviolate rights and freedoms of the individual with the notion that such freedoms must be restricted in order to achieve social justice. Or, as Alan Goldman writes of Rawls' two principles: "The first reaffirms the foundations of Western liberal, capitalist democracies; the second accepts the validity of much of the socialist critique of capitalist freedoms."[16]

The works of Rawls and Nozick have provoked great attention, to put it mildly, also outside the traditional domains of political philosophy, and not least within political science. Their contributions have called forth a tidal wave of books, and a couple of altogether new journals as well.

[14] Rawls (1971), pp. 136f.
[15] Ibid., pp 60f.   [16] Goldman (1980), p. 431.

Even if this philosophical discourse is (naturally) rather complicated and inaccessible, the essential problem with which it grapples is fairly simple. It can be summarized in the following brief question: what should the state do? The matters addressed in this discourse are thus central to the debate on welfare policy. The problems are perennial ones of both politics and philosophy: How far should collective responsibility for the individual extend? What should be the responsibility of the individual alone (independently of how he exercises this responsibility)? The question of what the state should do – that is, of what the moral framework for collective political action should be – is designated below as *normative state theory.*[17]

At about the same time as this renaissance of political philosophy took place, a new and exciting branch emerged within political science. This field, which goes under the name of *implementation research,* examines what occurs in the administrative process when programs of political reform are carried out, that is, when policy becomes "reality." The interest of political scientists in public administration had previously been confined largely to formal-legal and organizational questions, and to the problem of bureaucracy as a power factor in its own right. The innovative element in implementation research is that it places operative action at the center, and asks under what conditions the measures decreed by a democratic political system will be realized out in the field. This is the moment of truth for public policy – when it takes concrete form for the citizen. Implementation research thus broke with earlier administration research, which was either of a juridical and formalistic character or concerned itself with organizational and decision-theoretical models. Implementation research poses the question of how different ways of organizing public administration affect the prospects for carrying out programs successfully.

The breakthrough of implementation research can also be regarded as a reaction to the very great confidence – which had earlier prevailed – in the possibility of remedying social problems through political action. This faith was widespread throughout the Western world in the decades following the Second World War, and it culminated in the 1960s. In the United States, it was expressed in the Johnson administration's drive to create "The Great Society," while in Sweden it inspired the Social

---

[17] I should emphasize here, for the sake of clarity, that throughout this book I use the term "state" to encompass the full range of political order, independently of level. The term as used here thus embraces municipalities, county councils, the nation-state, supranational collective organs, or any of these in conjunction.

Democrats to adopt a program called "Increased Equality" (largely written by Alva Myrdal) at the end of the decade.

The question posed in this research is why certain public programs have failed to achieve their objectives. The subtitle of the book which introduced this current – *Implementation,* by Jeffrey Pressman and Aaron Wildavsky – is revealing: *How Great Expectations in Washington are Dashed Out in Oakland.* As with the renaissance of modern political philosophy, Pressman and Wildavsky's book gave rise to a new current of research, in which scholars have investigated the preconditions for directing society's development by political and administrative means.[18] What makes this current interesting here is that it tries to answer a question parallel to that posed by political philosophy, namely: what *can* the state do? I take this question as the point of departure below for an attempt to reconstruct an empirical theory of the state.

I must hasten to add, however, that the greater number of scholars within this current seldom pose the problem in such general terms. On the contrary, much of what is written consists of rather myopic and detailed case studies – with limited theoretical ambitions – of what happens during the implementation of different individual programs. The interest in synthesis, that is, in viewing the analysis in which one is engaged as a contribution to an empirical state theory, is (as far as I have been able to discover) almost nonexistent.[19] Nevertheless, I believe that more than twenty years of research in this genre have greatly enhanced our ability to judge which types of programs have better or worse chances of success. Some attempts have been made to summarize this research; these will be cited later on. It should therefore be possible – it is the ambition of this book, at any rate – to reach some conclusions of a synthetic and rather general nature concerning the prospects for political management in Western democracies.

These two branches of political science have generally been regarded as far apart. Communication between them, for example, is as good as nonexistent.[20] This book proceeds from the premise that this is an unfortunate state of affairs. For attempts to analyze the future represent

---

[18] Implementation research is part of the broader current usually termed policy analysis. The goal of policy analysis may be said to offer "conditional recommendations" to political decision-makers, i.e., to specify the conditions requisite for converting the intentions of policy-makers into practical policy. However, policy analysis also examines other parts of the chain of political decision-making, as in the case of evaluation analysis. Cf. Premfors (1989).

[19] For an exception see Goggin, Bowman, Lester, and O'Toole (1990).

[20] Lundquist (1993), p. 88; cf. Fischer (1980), pp. 40ff. Goodin (1988) is an important exception.

an exercise in constructive theorizing, an attempt to make predictions concerning what is both possible and good. Such an enterprise requires a combination of empirical and normative analysis. If one is to say something about the future, both "can" and "should" must be addressed. It is meaningless in this context to discuss what the state *should* do separately from what in fact it *can* do, and wholly inappropriate and unethical to try to answer what it *can* do without reflecting as well on what it *should* do.[21]

Since Rawls' theory was published, political philosophers have shown an increasing interest in public policy.[22] One sign of this was the founding of several journals: *Philosophy and Public Affairs* (1971), *Social Justice* (1989), *Social Philosophy and Politics* (1983), and *The Journal of Political Philosophy* (1993). In an article summarizing the field, however, Dennis Thompson claims that this newly awakened interest in social reality has not led philosophers further – to the study of "actual public policies."[23] They have instead contented themselves, according to Thompson, with analyzing the principles on which public policy rests, and have shown no interest in the specific experiences of the actual programs run by the state. The preferred method of political philosophers for handling the need for concreteness – not least in the above-mentioned journals – is to devise hypothetical cases. With a certain acerbity, Robert Goodin has criticized this approach for its unrealistic assumptions and general lack of relevance:

> First we are invited to reflect on a few hypothetical examples – the more preposterous, the better apparently. Then, with very little further argument or analysis, general moral principles are quickly inferred from our intuitive responses to these "crazy cases" . . . Whatever their role in settling deeper philosophical issues, bizarre hypotheticals are of little help in resolving real dilemmas of public policy.[24]

I shall follow Goodin's recommendation in this book: instead of devising "crazy cases," therefore, I shall attempt to formulate a constructive political theory by confronting the normative discourse with concrete studies of public policy.[25] David Held stresses this point as well, from the

---

[21] Lundquist (1991), pp. 223ff. The question of "should" is in fact almost always present – if only implicitly (and therefore unanalyzed) – in studies of the question of "can." See, e.g., Lundquist (1993), p. 84.

[22] See Michelman (1976).

[23] D. Thompson (1985).   [24] Goodin (1982), p. 8.

[25] Cf. Malnes (1992). Malnes' approach to constructive theory is different from mine, however. Malnes proposes that, to achieve greater concreteness, political philosophy should take up a dialogue with "the moral convictions of everyday life," in order to try to find out "what is really right." The problem is that, as

perspective of democratic theory: "if a theory of the most desirable form of democracy is to be at all plausible, it must be concerned with both theoretical and practical issues, with philosophical as well as organizational and institutional questions." Without this double focus, Held argues further, the discussion of democracy amounts to no more than a debate – as abstract as it is endless – over philosophical principles chosen on a completely arbitrary basis.[26]

The debate over social justice within political philosophy proceeds, as David Miller emphasizes, on two fundamental assumptions. The first is that political actors can direct social processes consciously, or at any rate influence them heavily (as regards their essential shape), "so that it makes sense to try to reshape society deliberately." The second premise is that "it is possible to find a source of power – usually in government – sufficient to carry out the reshaping."[27] The latter question, however, is one which political philosophers usually disregard. To cite Miller again: "almost without exception political theorists have failed to consider the bearing that empirical findings might have on their formulations."[28]

An example of what the weak interest among political philosophers in confronting empirical evidence can lead to may be found in the primer that the English philosopher Norman Barry has written on the subject. In common with many others, he allows that there is a tension between political philosophy and empirical analysis, in that, however expertly the normative argumentation for a policy is carried out, such a policy may be impossible to implement nonetheless. However, instead of arguing that the appropriate conclusion is to try to formulate a constructive political theory, Barry concludes his argument by noting that this is simply "one of the unfortunate consequences of the political realist's approach." In the next breath, however, he emphasizes that "one of the interesting tasks for the political theorist is to formulate appropriate institutional devices for the implementation of policy on the assumption that there is *some*

---

compared to the case in empirically oriented policy analysis, our grounds for drawing conclusions about people's everyday conceptions of moral propriety are much less certain. Research in experimental psychology has furnished us, however, with new and valuable insights in this matter. I shall consider some of the results of this research later on.

[26] D. Held (1987), p. 273. He argues further that: "A consideration of principles, without an examination of the conditions for their realization, may preserve a sense of virtue, but it will leave the actual meaning of such principles barely spelt out at all."

[27] D. Miller (1987a), p. 261. One important question concerns the freedom of maneuver political actors enjoy in relation to the existing socio-economic structures within which they must work. See Rothstein (1988) and (1990).

[28] D. Miller (1992), p. 555. This section builds on Rothstein (1992b).

agreement on principles."[29] One might reasonably ask how this can be done without explicitly integrating normative and empirical theory.

Milton Fisk makes a good point when he argues that the entire idea of reasoning our way to general principles of justice – on the basis of some universal rationalism, and independently of the surrounding material world – is a vain and hopeless enterprise. The discussion should rather, according to Fisk, take its starting point in the principles of justice which actually exist and are used in society. Philosophers who reason in a fashion unconnected to the real world open up a wide gap between the real and the ideal, with the result that "true" justice becomes something wholly separate from the prevailing political order. The danger with this, in Fisk's view, is that it leads to a cynical attitude towards existing politics.[30]

That there is much to Fisk's claim can be seen in the way in which another established political philosopher, G. A. Cohen, argues regarding principles of equality. Cohen takes the view that state responsibility for the welfare of citizens should be restricted to compensating for such differences as have not arisen from citizens' own choices. Accordingly, the state should only assist citizens to surmount such difficulties as have been beyond their power to influence (like inborn physical handicaps).[31]

All who have occupied themselves even a little with the actual conditions facing social-policy programs know well that distinctions of this kind often are almost impossible to make. Should, for example, an unemployed person be deemed responsible for his condition – for not having acquired an adequate education, or for not seeking work effectively, or for not having foreseen in time the impact of international economic downturns and structural shifts on the demand for his labor, etc.? Or does unemployment instead depend on macroeconomic circumstances which its victims cannot reasonably be expected to influence or to foresee?[32] Should persons suffering an illness caused by a frivolous and dissipated lifestyle be treated differently (i.e., be forced to face the consequences of their actions) from those who, despite good character and clean living free of every conceivable vice, nevertheless end up suffering some affliction, apparently through no fault of their own?

Making correct choices here is not, I think, so simple. To take a concrete example – according to available statistics, excess mortality from alcohol-related diseases can be observed among alcoholics (naturally), but also among teetotallers. The curve is U-shaped, and moderation seems, as usual, the best policy; the question, however, is what constitutes modera-

---

[29] N. P. Barry (1981), p. 92.   [30] Fisk (1989).   [31] G. Cohen (1989).
[32] See M. D. Jacobs (1986) and R. Dworkin (1977), pp. 208f.

tion, and how this should be judged. The empirical evidence here is plain: a clear negative correlation may be observed between low social class and good health.[33] On the other hand, Helena Rivière has recently turned the discussion of health and class upside down: "It was formerly a mark of high status among middle-class people to sit at the pub and have an ale. Now they invest in good health, just as they invest in a lengthy education and a beautiful house." She compares this with the more debauched lifestyle of the working class: "They smoke, drink, and eat delicious greasy sausages . . . They enjoy the good life while they have it." As she rightly points out, moreover, this reverses the readings on the quality-of-life scale: "Suddenly, a light touch of neurosis becomes visible in the upper and middle classes, who push life in front of them, so to speak, until some such time as they think themselves able to pinch some of the capital."[34] Finding the right time is probably as delicate as it is difficult.

The more serious side of the matter concerns whether we are morally responsible for our preferences, or whether instead these should be classified as inborn handicaps. Cohen as well recognizes that the attempt to make such distinctions "subordinates political philosophy to metaphysical questions that may be impossible to solve." Yet this furnishes no reason, according to this noted political philosopher, to look more closely at attempts made in concrete social programs to solve this question. It is simply a matter of "tough luck. It is not a reason for not following the argument where it goes."[35]

John Rawls' theory has also come in for criticism of this type. His so-called difference principle means that only such inequalities in the distribution of resources as work to the maximal benefit of the least-favored can be justified. The problem, however, is that he thereby disregards the distinction between such inequalities as arise from what might be called fundamental resources (which reflect genetic and social circumstances over which individuals can exert no control) and those reflecting individuals' conscious choice of differing levels of ambition, that is, their varying levels of exertion. The question, of course, is whether the inclination to exert oneself should also be seen as an innate resource (in which case the state should compensate those who lost out in the natural lottery). It must be stressed that this proposition denies the

---

[33] Kjellström & Lundberg (1984), p. 78.

[34] Rivière (1993), p. 49.

[35] G. Cohen (1989), p. 934. There are, however, legal theorists who think more clearly about this question. One is Ronald Dworkin, who argues that "it is impossible to discover, even in principle, exactly which aspects of any person's economic position flow from his choices and which from advantages or disadvantages that were not matters of choice." R. Dworkin (1985), pp. 208f.

responsibility of individuals for their own actions, and moreover calls democracy into question, for the latter is based on the notion that citizens are capable of making well-considered decisions and of taking responsibility for their choices. If citizens are not so equipped, the idea of universal and equal suffrage is, as I see it, without foundation.

John Roemer, an innovative and philosophically oriented Marxist economist, furnishes a further example. In an analysis of the idea of egalitarianism, he asks why it is usual to limit the discussion of justice to the distribution of material resources, and to neglect the distribution of personal attributes, such as diligence or talent. True equality demands, in Roemer's view, that the latter resources be distributed fairly as well. For his theory to work, however, the following conditions must apply: "It will be assumed that inalienable assets possessed by people are precisely known; there is no problem in getting the person to reveal what assets he possesses. This assumption is appropriate to the present context, as I wish to study equality theories independently of implementation problems."[36] As Jon Elster points out, however, sorting out such questions in a just manner would, in practice, "be hopelessly complex and costly."[37]

Yet another example may be seen in the work of the American legal philosopher Bruce C. Ackerman, who, in his oft-cited book *Social Justice and the Liberal State,* frankly declares that he proceeds on the assumption of "a polity possessed of a *perfect technology of justice.*" He bids the reader assume, that is, that "you live in a place where *there never is any practical difficulty implementing the substantive conclusions.*"[38] One last example is Richard J. Arneson who discusses the problem of whether welfare distribution should be tailored to people's preferences. First, he recognizes that this would be very expensive and administratively difficult, "perhaps impossible", because we could not imagine public authorities with the capacity to collect and use the amount of information necessary to accomplish such a task. Secondly, he states that he will "ignore these practical feasibility problems" and instead "assume that correct and full information regarding people's preferences is available at no cost whatsoever to whatever institutions we establish to implement the principles of distributive justice that we accept."[39]

Now, if need be one could accept this virtually demonstrative neglect of empirical analysis were it the case that these philosophers were only interested in carrying on a debate within the strict bounds of their discipline. This is not the case, however; rather, they take the view that their analyses have, and should have, significance for the concrete

---

[36] Roemer (1985), p. 154. [37] Elster (1992), p. 134.
[38] Ackerman (1980), p. 21. [39] Arneson (1990b), pp. 158f.

formulation of policy.[40] As Sidney Hook points out, however, the problem is that "the philosopher is initially out of his field when he discusses questions of public policy."[41] It is natural enough, then, that in his study of how medical districts in the United States choose principles of distribution in such a critical case as organ transplantation (in which there are more needy patients than available organs), Jon Elster finds that current philosophical models are unusable on the whole.[42] In sum, the idea that it is possible to move from normative to constructive theory directly, without an intermediate empirical stage, is at best futile and at worst downright dangerous.[43]

Calls for greater concreteness have also been heard within the philosophical field. In his contributing article (on political theory) to a recently published encyclopedia of philosophy, the English philosopher David Miller concludes with the following words:

> Although there have been some important contributions to political theory in the last two decades – for instance the work of Oakshott, Rawls, Nozick and Dworkin – it is noticeable that none of these combines the philosophical analysis of political principles with an empirical understanding of political processes in a wholly successful way. Their work is philosophically sophisticated but poorly-grounded empirically, and highly vulnerable to criticism by social scientists. Further progress in the field must involve rectifying this imbalance, a task that is, however, easier set than to achieve.[44]

Alan Weisbard argues that this anti-empirical orientation has had negative consequences for philosophy as a discipline as well. Weisbard has evaluated the effects of the participation of political philosophers in various governmental commissions in the United States under the Reagan administration (these commissions were assigned the task of solving ethically problematic questions in public policy). He concludes that "philosophical analysis tended to invoke standards for justification

---

[40] Rapaport (1981).
[41] Hook (1980), p. 10; cf. Kymlicka (1990), p. 89.
[42] Elster (1992).
[43] Lundquist (1988), pp. 17ff. The list of famous philosophers' sins on this point is long. Alfred North Whitehead, Bertrand Russell, John Dewey, and George Santayana all supported the Munich agreement of 1938 as a guarantee for peace. Martin Heidegger's support for Hitler, Jean-Paul Sartre's and Jacques Merleau-Ponty's refusal to condemn the Gulag economy in the Soviet Union, Santayana's excuses for Stalin and Mussolini, and Russell's proposal for a preventive nuclear war against the Soviet Union are among the cases mentioned by Hook (1980), p. 13.
[44] D. Miller (1987b), p. 385; cf. D. Miller (1991).

that few real world policy initiatives . . . could meet."[45] This lack of constructive theorizing is a significant problem, according to Weisbard – and not just for the possibility of supplying usable recommendations, but for the development of political philosophy itself as well.

Things are not much better, be it noted, in the empirically oriented field of policy research that I have here termed empirical state theory. We are frequently presented with what might be described as long "laundry lists," which enumerate the requisites for a successful implementation of policy.[46] Such research raises the critical problem, as does all policy analysis, of how to handle the normative implications.[47] Scholars in this field often proceed directly from empirical analysis based on concepts of rationality and efficiency to recommendations for action, without showing due regard for the normative aspects of the case. This can lead to catastrophic results.[48] Accordingly, in an article reviewing the relation between policy analysis and philosophy, Ethan Fischerman argues that the study of "public policy remains essentially isolated from the history of Western political philosophy."[49]

A central premise of this study is that empirical analysis based on notions of rationality and efficiency should not be the sole basis of policy recommendations – not, at any rate, when fundamental moral principles are at stake (as in the case of welfare policy).[50] It is, to quote Charles Anderson, "only when you take your ethics for granted that all problems emerge as problems of technique."[51] Thus does one search in vain for such concepts as "justice," "democracy," and "equality" in the indices of standard volumes on public policy implementation.[52]

That economic cost-benefit analysis alone does not supply an adequate basis for policy recommendations is illustrated by a recent report from the Swedish National Audit Bureau. The report in question sought, through the use of economic analysis, to determine how the state should allocate its resources in order to save lives (by improving roads, for example). The method proposed – which focused on individuals' will-

---

[45] Weisbard (1987), p. 781. [46] See ch. 4. [47] Olsen (1993), p. 6.
[48] Lundquist (1993), pp. 88f; Fischer (1980), pp. 40ff. For an excellent account of a particularly frightening example, see Mason (1988) on Nazi Germany's implementation of the extermination of its Jewish citizens. For an analysis of the morally problematic character of teleological reasoning, see M. Lundström (1993).
[49] Fischerman (1991), p. 720. For an exception, see Fischer (1995).
[50] See Majone & Gretschmann (1986), and Lundquist (1988), pp. 17f., and literature cited therein.
[51] Anderson (1990), p. 2. For an example of such an amoral discussion of welfare policy, see I. Hansson (1993).
[52] Palumbo & Calista (1990); Mazmanian & Sabatier (1981 and 1983).

ingness to pay – proved inadequate, however, partly because such concepts as "justice" were not considered in the analysis. It proved difficult, moreover – even for economists – to accept that certain groups should be exposed, on account of their inability or unwillingness to pay, to greater risks than others.[53]

The future of the universal welfare state, which is an altogether concrete matter, cannot be analyzed only in the ethereal terms in which political philosophers conduct their exercises. Formulating principles of justice without considering what is possible typically results in a remote intellectual game – inspiring for its practitioners perhaps, but of limited relevance for the problems under consideration here. On the other hand, we must dare to raise our sights above the empirical ground and to draw some conclusions of a general nature about the possibilities and limits of public policy. An analysis of welfare policy – and especially of its future – must combine normative and empirical discourses into a constructive discourse. Deciding what the state can do, and what it should do, are in other words matters of equal importance.[54]

Figure 1.1 illustrates how I aim to do this. The question is if it is possible to do it. That it is not altogether simple is clear from the gloomy situation report in a recently published textbook by Lundquist:

> There is a very sharp division of labor according to which political science (empirical theory) and political philosophy (normative theory . . .) are treated each in themselves, with the result that the practitioners of each specialty are often unacquainted with each other's work. *The result is that proper conditions are lacking within the discipline for achieving a constructive theory.*[55]

One critical point of departure for this study bears mentioning here: the importance in politics of institutional conditions. By institutional conditions I understand, in this context, various formal systems of rules, such as constitutions, systems of taxation, and – critically for this analysis – social welfare programs. These are not to be seen merely as rule-systems determining which strategies of action are rational, but as established

---

[53] Riksrevisionsverket (1991).

[54] I am uncertain at present as to whether the sort of constructive theory referred to here is, strictly speaking, an independent type of social scientific theory, or whether it should rather be seen as amounting to a collection of various portions of empirical and normative theories which, in one way or another, overlap each other. My thanks to Lennart Lundquist and Mats Lundström for their valuable (if wholly opposed) viewpoints on this.

[55] Lundquist (1993), p. 88.

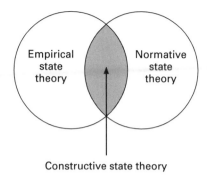

Constructive state theory

Figure 1.1   Empirical, normative and constructive state theories

normative arrangements as well. According to this view, political conditions result in more than just rules (such as those specifying the
mechanisms of political decision-making). They also affect what values
are established in a society, that is, what we regard as a common culture,
collective identity, belonging, trust, and solidarity.[56] The Norwegian
social scientist Jon Elster, for instance, has argued that "one task of
politics is surely to shape social conditions and institutions so that people
behave honestly, because they believe that the basic structure of their
society is just."[57]

Thus, analyzing established institutions makes it possible for us to link
the study of political philosophy (the question of what the state *should*
do) with an investigation of how "actually existing" political institutions
operate (the question of what the state *can* do). John Rawls has therefore
argued, in a partly self-critical article on his theory of justice, that the
basic principles on which he built his theory should *not* be regarded as
metaphysical postulates. They should rather be understood as based
"solely upon basic intuitive ideas that are embedded in the *political
institutions* of a constitutional democratic regime and the public traditions of their interpretations."[58] The explanation Rawls offers is critically
important for this study, for it indicates that normative discourse need
not be tantamount to metaphysical speculation (as, e.g., in discussions of
natural law) or other arbitrary reasoning, in which any viewpoint is as
good as another. By analyzing the principles forming the basis of
established and generally accepted institutions, it should be possible,

---

[56] March & Olsen (1989), p. 126. See also R. Dworkin (1977), pp. 160ff and
Rothstein 1996.
[57] Elster (1987).   [58] Rawls (1985); my italics.

through analogous reasoning, to come to general normative principles for the framing of social policy.

Universal versus selective welfare policy

From a comparative and historical perspective, the welfare state poses an interesting puzzle. Today, advanced industrial nations differ greatly in the amount of public spending (of which social programs are a major part) as a share of GDP. In the 1990s, the large European counties spend about 50 percent more than the United States, while the Scandinavian countries spend about twice as much as the United States. This was, however, not always the case. In the 1960s, the difference between these countries in total public spending was much smaller – the level in the United States was about 28 percent compared to a mean of 29 percent for the Scandinavian countries. And while the United States spent about 7 percent of GDP on social insurance and social assistance, the Scandinavian countries spent only about 2 percent more.[59] Thus, despite an enormous internationalization of trade, the globalization of financial markets, and the increased internationalization of values through mass media, the differences in government spending in this area have increased dramatically since 1960.

The empirical subject of this study is the future of the universal welfare state of which Sweden is perhaps the most prominent case.[60] This policy may be said to consist, in the main, of three parts. Firstly, publicly produced and universally available services such as health care, basic education, care of children and of the elderly, and publicly regulated and subsidized housing. Secondly, a system of universal flat-rate benefits tied to citizenship, such as basic pensions and child allowances. Thirdly, a mandatory social insurance system, in which benefits reflect earnings on the labor market and are designed to provide income security up to a relatively high level. Examples include the supplementary (earnings related) pensions scheme, sickness pay, and parental insurance.[61]

Many scholars have sought to describe what distinguishes a social policy of the Swedish (or Scandinavian) type from that of other Western

---

[59] Moene & Wallerstein (1996). "Large European countries" are Britain, France, Germany, and Italy. "Scandinavian countries" are Denmark, Norway, and Sweden.

[60] Esping-Andersen (1990), cf. Sainsbury (1996), ch. 1. Another term that has been used is "institutional welfare state." Other countries which are considered to have a universal social policy are Norway, Denmark, Finland, and to some extent the Netherlands.

[61] Sainsbury (1996), p. 19, Stephens (1996), p. 34.

nations.[62] It is not so easy, certainly, to find any uniform principles in the structure of Swedish welfare policy. I shall employ a fairly coarse distinction here, namely that between *universal* and *selective* welfare policies. What distinguishes social policy in Sweden (and the other Scandinavian countries as well) in an international comparison is its high degree of universal coverage.[63] This means, simplifying somewhat, that benefits and services are intended to cover the entire population throughout the different stages of life, and on the basis of uniform rules.

What more precisely should be included in the concept of universal welfare policy is often unclear in the debate, for the concept contains several dimensions. One such dimension concerns the proportion of the citizenry covered by the policy. Naturally, the extremities consist of a policy embracing the entire population (universal welfare policy) and one restricted to certain delimited groups (selective welfare policy). Another dimension has to do with how benefits and services are allocated. We may distinguish here between support taking the form of specified rights (universal allocation), and that granted according to some type of needs-testing (discretionary allocation).

These distinctions are based on Axel Hadenius' analysis in *A Crisis of the Welfare State? Opinions about Taxes and Public Expenditure in Sweden.*[64] A tricky problem in this account, however, is that Hadenius does not distinguish between the different criteria according to which needs-testing can be done. If, however, the role of welfare policy in establishing social justice is the concern, then it is critically important to distinguish between needs-testing that represents an application of professional norms (as when a physician prescribes a certain treatment for a patient) and needs-testing done in order to determine the individual's ability to pay, i.e., *means*-testing. Since welfare policy is aimed at correcting market outcomes (in the form of citizens' varying ability to pay), it is inappropriate to subsume these different types of needs-testing in a single category (as Hadenius does). This difference becomes clear if we compare the consequences of failing the two different types of needs-test in question. It is, for example, quite a different thing to be denied a

---

[62] The term "welfare state" does not adequately describe social programs in Sweden. As Theda Skocpol (1987: 38) has argued, the word "welfare" – at least in the United States – implies targeted means-tested programs and connotes stigmatization of the persons receiving it. In Sweden, these programs comprise a small part of social policy. Most programs are instead universal and not means tested, and are provided either in kind (e.g., health care) or in cash (e.g., child allowances). The "social insurance state" would be a more accurate term, but I will nonetheless (with this protest) follow common usage.

[63] Stephens (1996), p. 36.   [64] Hadenius (1986).

certain medical treatment because the responsible physician deems it medically unsuitable, and to be denied a certain public service because the responsible official judges one to possess sufficient means to purchase it on the open market. Only social policies employing the latter type of needs-test, that is, that performed to ascertain the individual's ability to pay, should be classified as selective welfare policies, since they select in relation to individuals' economic standing. Equating these two types of needs-test, as Hadenius does, has the consequence of erasing the main distinction on which the basic logic of the universal welfare policy is based.

In what follows, I use the term universal welfare policy to refer both to programs embracing the entire citizenry and to those allocating benefits or services without the application of economic needs-testing (or means-testing). Needs-testing is a rather complicated concept, however, and it requires further specification. In a great many welfare programs, needs-testing is applied because the program is of such a character that the need can only be ascertained locally, and/or by investigating each individual case.[65] It is often necessary to adjust the concrete measures to the situation if the overarching goals of the program are to be achieved. This means, however, that the program's local administrators must be granted a considerable discretionary power to decide which measures are the most suitable.[66] Only such patients as require a particular treatment for a certain illness should receive it, only students possessing the intellectual requisites for a given theoretical training should be offered it, only persons who are jobless should be offered relief work, and so on. This kind of needs-testing follows from the relation of the program to the situation of the citizen, but it is *not* coupled to the latter's private economic circumstances.

By selective social policies, then, I mean only those applying the latter type of needs-testing, that is, in which the criterion for receiving support is an insufficient ability to pay for services or social insurance. Selective policies thus target assistance on the economically weakest part of the population – those unable to purchase essential goods, insurance and services on the market for themselves. Such a system supports only those considered to be, as the common usage has it, the "truly needy."[67]

---

[65] Elster (1992), p. 2 and pp. 63ff.

[66] I have developed this perspective in Rothstein (1992a), ch. 3.

[67] The research on social and welfare policy is very extensive, and many different concepts and systems of classification are used. Instead of *universal* welfare policy, for instance, some scholars speak of *institutional* welfare policy. In similar fashion, some researchers refer to *residual* rather than *selective* welfare policy. Among the more important works on the organization of welfare policy may be

In practice, this means that every existing welfare state contains both universal and selective programs and that specific programs also can vary greatly on this dimension. The notions "universal" and "selective" welfare state(s) are here used as Weberian ideal-types. This means that they are constructed as analytical instruments describing what, according to the theoretical applications, are the specific characteristics of the object under study. Although not empirical objects, ideal-types are nonetheless constructed from empirical observations but contains as such no normative value. "Ideal" here does not mean good; an empirical "real" object may be closer to or further from a specific ideal-type, but it is not by virtue of that being better or worse. The methodological point in using such theoretically informed ideal-types is that they are used to "measure" empirical cases (be they specific programs or the total set of a state's social program) to see if they are "more or less" universal or selective.[68]

The challenges faced by the universal welfare state

It is natural, for one seeking to ascertain the universal welfare policy's normative and political foundations (and thus its future prospects), to begin by examining the strength of its political support. In the Swedish case, the four-party bourgeois[69] government which was in office from 1991 to 1994 proclaimed its support for the principles of the universal welfare policy in the following terms:

> Welfare policy in Sweden is in large part universal . . . The alternative to the welfare state is a selective system aimed at supporting only those suffering the worst conditions. Such a system has many drawbacks. It requires more testing and control. Someone has to decide who has the right to assistance and who does not. This leads easily to bureaucracy and to investigations that violate integrity. A selective system also creates marginal effects. Benefits fall as income rises. Many people risk falling into

mentioned Gøsta Esping-Andersen (1990), Castles (1989), Olofsson (1979), Korpi (1981), Kuhnle & Solheim (1991), Olsson (1993), and Titmuss (1968). For a critique from a feminist perspective of the idea that Swedish welfare policy can be regarded as general in character, see Bergqvist (1990). For a neo-liberal critique, see Borg (1992).

[68] Weber [1922] (1971), p. 199.

[69] The Swedish translation for "bourgeois" – *borgerlig* – is typically used in a political context simply as a synonym for "non-socialist." The usage refers, moreover, primarily to ideological orientation rather than social-class background. The term has, finally, no derogatory connotations.

the poverty trap. The fundamental ideology of the welfare state, based on universalism, shall serve as guidance in the future as well.[70]

The four-party bourgeois government, accordingly, declared its support for the universal welfare policy in fairly unequivocal terms. The cutbacks decreed by the Social Democrats since they came back to power in 1994 have certainly entailed reduced compensation in various programs such as unemployment and sickness insurance, a higher retirement age, lower state subsidies to municipal services, and a reduced number of vacation days. These cuts, made necessary by the deterioration in public finances since 1991, have made Swedish social policy somewhat less universal.[71] Individual voices have been heard calling for more drastic changes, but the overall picture is that, except for the Conservatives, no party has seriously challenged the basic principles of the universal welfare state.

The Social Democrats, who took office following the election in 1994, have historically been closely associated with the creation of the universal welfare policy, even if they have by no means been alone in carrying it out.[72] The party's political identity is closely bound up with the preservation of this policy and it must be deemed unlikely that any fundamental challenge to its principles will emerge from that quarter. Logically enough, then, the party has portrayed itself in the political debate as the foremost defender of the universal welfare policy.[73]

Nor is it only among the political elite that support for the universal welfare policy remains largely unchanged. It appears as well to be the case, judging from interview studies of the opinions held by Swedish citizens, that the universal welfare policy enjoys a strong and stable support in public opinion. The ideological changes of market liberal character which swept over the political debate during the 1980s have had no impact at all on the level of popular support for those parts of the welfare system that are organized on a general basis (at any rate, no

---

[70] Records from the Swedish Parliament, Regeringens proposition 1991/92, no. 100, appendix 6, p. 5.

[71] Olsson (1993), pp. 292ff.

[72] See Olsson (1993). See also Uddhammar (1993a), who has demonstrated the relatively broad agreement in Sweden between the bourgeois parties and the Social Democrats as regards their view of the state.

[73] This should not be allowed to obscure the fact, however, that the concrete policy the Social Democrats conducted during their time in power from 1982 to 1991 and also after coming back to power in 1994 has undermined the universal welfare policy in certain areas. Two elements bear mentioning in this regard: firstly, it was during this period that expenditures on means-tested social assistance were allowed to increase dramatically – see Salonen (1993); and secondly, the Social Democratic government introduced a system characterized by decentralization and management by goals – see Rothstein (1993a).

erosion of support can be detected by means of interview studies).[74] The question, accordingly, is whether the apparently broad support for the universal welfare policy in Sweden – among both the political elite and the population at large – renders its future reasonably secure. If the answer to this question were yes, this book could be concluded here. I would like, however, to call attention to some economic and political challenges to the universal welfare policy which make it necessary to examine, once again, the arguments for and against.

The *first* challenge is public finances. In 1994, the Swedish budget deficit reached an unprecedented 13 percent of GNP. Even if this was caused not by the welfare state, but by major mistakes in macro-economic policy leading to a dramatic increase in unemployment, the deficit forced the Social Democrats to make some drastic cutbacks in services and allowances. Even if these cutbacks have greatly improved public finances (the budget is likely to show a surplus in 1997 and Sweden is now one of the few members of the European Union (EU) that has a chance to meet the stern demands for entering into the European Monetary Union), the deficit showed the financial vulnerability of the system.

Universal welfare states require a relatively high tax level – this for the simple reason that, if all citizens are to receive subsidized benefits and services, the result is necessarily expensive for the public purse.[75] Inasmuch as the Swedish tax level is, viewed in an international perspective, already very high, there is reason to assume that increased demands of services and benefits cannot, at least in their greater part, be solved by raising taxes. The increasing number of retired citizens is for example, likely to put further financial strain on any welfare state in the near future. This being said, it should also be underlined that leading Swedish economists inspired by the Chicago school in their discipline have so far, despite quite substantial efforts, not been able to show that high public spending and high taxes are likely to create a less efficient economy. There may be many reasons to avoid high public spending and high taxes, but economic efficiency is not one. From this perspective, the choice between a universal and a selective welfare state must be made for other reasons than pure economic ones.[76] Another economic challenge against the universal welfare state con-

---

[74] Svallfors (1991 and 1996).
[75] Problems with the financing of welfare policy are by no means restricted to Sweden. On the contrary, they seem to be legion in most welfare states, regardless of the level of taxes or of public expenditure. See Dogan (1988), especially pp. 201–218.
[76] Agell, Lindh, & Ohlsson (1994), Korpi (1997), Esping-Andersen (1996).

cerns the effects of globalization. The argument is that the dramatic increase in the integration of markets, and especially the market for capital, has eroded the possibility of keeping tax levels high enough for sustaining a universal welfare state. In a recently published work, however, Geoffrey Garrett has, with considerable empirical backing, refuted this idea. He concludes that "the relationship between the political power of the left and economic policies that reduce market-generated inequalities, has not been weakened by globalization; indeed it has been strengthened in important respects."[77]

A *third* challenge to the universal welfare state may be found in the fact that, in today's social policy debate, the deeper moral aspects of welfare policy have come under scrutiny once again. Many commentators and researchers argue that, if the welfare system grows too large, it risks perverting incentive structures in both working life and society in general.[78] In the case of working life, scholars have pointed to (what they consider to be) excessively generous sickness benefits, and to the manifold opportunities for drawing disability pensions, and they claim that this excessive generosity has resulted in various forms of over-utilization. In respect of society in general, these authors maintain that the assumption by the state of far-reaching responsibilities for the well-being of citizens leads to a moral weakening of the various networks of civil society – families, neighborhoods – and that the persons receiving assistance are relieved of responsibility for their own actions.[79] They claim, not without empirical grounds, that social policy if anything worsens the problems it sets out to solve.[80] This critique is by no means new, of course; quite the contrary. The debate over the "spirit of welfare dependency" raged already in the dawn of social policy, both in Sweden and elsewhere.[81] What is new is the renewed energy with which this critique is put, together with the fact that those expressing it may now be found on the left of the political spectrum as well as on the right.[82]

This critique is partly based, in its left-wing variant, on the work of the German social philosopher Jürgen Habermas. Habermas argues that the market dependence of citizens under pure capitalism has simply been replaced, through the welfare state, by dependence on arbitrary and impenetrable administrative bodies. By combining the individual programs into a comprehensive network, the state seeks to satisfy all the

---

[77] Garrett (1997), p. 1.

[78] See Isaksson (1992), Rivière (1993), and Borg (1992).

[79] Wolfe (1989).

[80] Murray (1984). For an overview of neo-liberal and neo-conservative critiques, see Offe (1988).

[81] See Salonen (1993), p. 179f.   [82] See, e.g., Rosanvallon (1988).

needs which citizens might experience in the various stages of life. It colonizes ever more of civil society thereby. It also undermines what Habermas considers to be a kind of natural (by definition non-public) solidarity between citizens.[83] Bonds of family and of friendship become – on account of this comprehensive social policy – less and less necessary. Natural social relations wither, while the welfare state grows.

In its larger part, this critique of the welfare state is not new either. Quite the contrary. It is a faithful old companion which has followed along ever since the first rudimentary social protections were established. Even so, this critique is an important one and deserves to be taken seriously. A universal welfare state can be seen as an experiment in solidaristic behavior on a massive scale. If benefits are widely and systematically abused, this solidarity comes under severe stress.[84] That is, the solidarity necessary for the system's preservation is not absolute but *conditional.*

A *fourth* challenge to the universal welfare state consists in the marked pessimism widespread at least since the late 1970s regarding the possibility of managing social development by political means. This applies not least in the area of social policy. A number of social problems – marginalization, criminality, social segregation, etc. – seem to be exceedingly difficult to solve, notwithstanding that considerable resources have been expended in the attempt. The possibility of political management has come under increasing question, not least as a result of the implementation research mentioned above. The realization that the state cannot do everything has taken hold in both the academic and political spheres. The managerial optimism in social policy which characterized the decades following the Second World War seems to have given way to its opposite at some point during the 1970s.[85]

Fifthly, there are clear signs – observable in a series of studies – that the values held in Western societies have undergone a considerable shift during the last decade. This change, which exists in many other Western countries as well, may be roughly described as a shift from *collectivism* to *individualism.* In Sweden, citizens' traditional loyalty to established organizations and authorities has clearly weakened.[86] The view of oneself

---

[83] Habermas (1987), pp. 357ff. See also Cohen & Arato (1993), ch. 9, and Wolfe (1989). Cohen & Arato (1993) claim, on pp. 284f., that Michel Foucault's works may also be counted among critiques of the welfare state, something about which I am rather less certain.

[84] Lindbeck (1993).

[85] See Lindensjö (1987) for an overview. Cf. also Therborn (1991).

[86] Pettersson & Geyer (1992), Petersson, Westholm & Blomberg (1989). Cf. also Inglehart (1990) for a comparative international study of such changes in value patterns.

as part of a larger collective with a common historical mission has diminished, not least in the industrial working class.[87] The willingness to acquiesce in central decisions and collective solutions seems to have declined as well. Demands for personal autonomy have come to the fore instead, and a conception of life as a project to be planned and pursued individually has come increasingly to predominate. The decisions of public authorities and organs are called into question more frequently, and citizens are also generally more competent in pressing their demands. The individual stands more at the center, and demands to be allowed to decide for oneself over such matters as public services and care are stronger than before.[88] The question is how well this new individualism – or anticollectivism – in Sweden as well as in other Western societies matches the universal welfare policy. The one problem concerns the relation between the increased individualism and the abstract solidarity on which especially the universal type of welfare state is based.

The other problem has to do with the qualititative manner in which welfare policy has usually been framed in universal welfare systems. To a great extent, this policy has been built on the basis of what may be termed *uniform, standardized solutions.* This is true both of the social insurance system and of the public services. The prospects for individualized treatment in the system of social insurance, or of free choice between different service alternatives within, for example, education or care have been very limited up until now. The question is whether this increased individualism leads to problems for the universal welfare state as practiced in Sweden, and if so how. Can the demands for individualized treatment within the social insurance system and the public services be solved within the framework of the universal welfare state?

A *sixth* problem is that, despite the unanimous backing of the dominant political parties for the universal welfare state,[89] a very sharp increase in needs-tested programs has occurred since the early 1980s in Sweden. The number of persons receiving means-tested public assistance (what Americans call "being on welfare") has increased sharply. The proportion of persons receiving this benefit has reached 12–13 percent in some of the larger cities. According to Salonen's estimate, fully 20 percent of the Swedish population received public assistance at some point or other during the 1980s. In one of the larger cities in the study, the figure

---

[87] Åberg (1990).   [88] Offe (1988), especially p. 217.

[89] There are great differences, however, in what the different parties include within the concept of universal welfare policy. The new program of the Conservative Party may signal a shift to advocacy of a more selective system.

was 25 percent. It bears noting that this increase took place during a period of economic expansion and very low unemployment.[90]

It is especially striking how dramatic this increase in the receipt of means-tested public assistance has been among youth. During the postwar period the proportion of persons from sixteen to twenty-nine years of age receiving means-tested public assistance has quadrupled; moreover, this group has replaced the sick and the elderly as the predominant group among such recipients.[91] Viewed over time, this means that almost 40 percent of young citizens (those born in 1965 and after) had at some point received public assistance by the time they had reached twenty-four years of age.[92] I hasten to add that the greater number of these recipients draw such benefits only temporarily, but as Salonen points out this nevertheless means that means-tested public assistance is no longer primarily a selective form of welfare policy targeted on a relatively small and vulnerable part of the population.[93] There is doubtless a certain limit beyond which the needs-tested elements loom so large that one can no longer say that the principle of universality predominates within Swedish social policy. The importance of this fact should be understood against the conclusion drawn by Paul Pierson in his study about welfare retrenchment policies in the United States and the United Kingdom: "If conservatives could design their ideal welfare state, it would consist of *nothing but* means tested programs."[94]

A *seventh* challenge to the universal welfare state lies in the fact that public provision within the public care and service sector has been reduced. Partly for ideological reasons, and partly on account of straitened economic circumstances, municipalities and county councils have begun – in a higher degree than formerly – to contract the provision of public services out to private companies in the areas of education and care. The four bourgeois parties that were in power between 1991 and 1994 saw the privatization of public service production as one of their primary recipes for the public sector – the "freedom of choice revolution," as they called it. It must immediately be said that there is no direct or obvious contradiction between the private production of public services and the pursuit of a universal welfare state. The following question must be put, however: under what conditions are competition and private production compatible with the universal welfare state? A distinction must be made between public production of services and public financing of services.

---

[90] Salonen (1993), p. 223 and pp. 81ff.
[91] Ibid., p. 91.   [92] Ibid., p. 103.
[93] Ibid., p. 83; cf. pp. 188ff.   [94] Pierson (1996) p. 6.

In sum, these seven challenges to the universal welfare state make it urgent to try to say something about its future. The traditional way in the social sciences to accomplish such a task would be to identify the major causes behind the establishment of different welfare states, that is, the eternal hunt for the independent variable(s) with the most explanatory power. A number of scholars have presented various such "master explanations," for example, the political strength of the left (however measured), or the character of the state apparatuses, or the effects of economic modernization. This has been a large and fruitful research industry and I humbly recognize my great intellectual debt to this type of research.[95] One problem, however, with many of these explanations is that it is often difficult to see which is actually the dependent variable and which the independent one. To take one example, there is definitively a strong relationship between the strength of the labor movement and universalism in social policies, as for example in the Scandinavian countries. However, as I have shown in an earlier book, the strength of the labor movement can to a large extent be explained by the character of social policy initiatives at an earlier stage.[96] Patterns of political mobilization influence social policy, but the design of social policy also has an influence on political mobilization.[97] The implication is that what is the independent and the dependent variable changes in the historical context as certain social policy initiatives strengthen the organizational capacity of the labor movement. Another problem is that the statistical analysis tends to hide important exceptions. In this case there are important "outliers" such as for example, Australia and the Netherlands, which indicate that you can have a strong labor movement that does not create universalism in the welfare state, and you can have a universal type of welfare state without a strong labor movement.[98]

As stated above, the differences in spending between the selective and the universal types of welfare state have increased dramatically since 1960. From a rational choice perspective, this can be understood as the establishment of two different political equilibria: one in which low taxes are combined with a predominantly means-tested system, and one in which high taxes are combined with a predominantly universal system.[99]

---

[95] For a recent summary and analysis see Stephens (1996).

[96] Rothstein (1992c), cf. Pierson (1996).

[97] This is very much a discussion of "society-centered" versus "state-centered" explanations. Cf. Svensson (1994) and Tarrow (1996).

[98] About Australian exceptionalism see Castles and Mitchell (1992).

[99] Moene & Wallerstein (1996). In common language, this means that "once the system gets there, it stays there."

Bearing in mind that policies have effects on political support as well as the other way around, this implies that the development to these different systems has been path-dependent. Path-dependency, however, is not only another word for saying that "history matters." The idea is that (a) small early changes in institutional arrangements, be they deliberate and rational or not, can have great implications at much later stages; (b) that certain courses of action once established are almost impossible to reverse; and (c) that cause becomes effect which, in the next historical sequence, strengthens the "original" cause (i.e., you have increasing returns or positive feedback).[100] The idea of path-dependency is how I understand that independent and dependent variables sequentially change places. That is, depending on your ideological preferences, the development of these different political equilibria in social policy is to be understood as a result of history at certain "formative moments" changing track into virtues or vicious circles. The argument in this book is that the type of welfare state is to be explained by the existence of such a "circle," what I here call the moral and political logic of the universal welfare state. The term "logic" refers to the idea of history being path-dependent, so that to reason about the future of the universal type of welfare state, instead of finding the "master independent variable," we must capture the ongoing logic of the relation between its type of policies and its political and moral support.

[100] Pierson (1996).

2

The universal welfare state and the question of individual autonomy

How should the relation between citizens and the welfare state be described? The various answers offered to this question lie, in general, between two polar extremes. The one extreme regards the universal welfare state as a political system which has succeeded, by means of ever more refined public programs, in meeting the greater number of citizens' needs for economic security and social care. By representative and parliamentary means, a kind of service democracy has been created, in which citizens collectively organize the benefits and services they – or the majority of them, at least – desire. The system is solidaristic and just, moreover, for it ensures equal treatment according to centrally standardized norms.

The opposite ideological extreme portrays the advanced welfare state as a new Leviathan, a despotic master which orders citizens about at will, and which severely limits the prospects for individual freedom and self-determination. Welfare provisions cultivate, moreover, a sort of learned helplessness in the citizenry. Furthermore, the welfare state deprives citizens of much of their economic autonomy – through the heavy taxes it levies. "The welfare state thus deprives the needy of the ability and authority to decide their own affairs, and hands over decisions that should express the individual's autonomy to paternalistic officials," writes Avishai Margalit.[1] The bureaucracy in charge of this monstrosity, finally, lives a life of its own, and the possibility of directing its operations by means of parliamentary decision is, in actuality, extremely limited.[2]

---

[1] Margalit (1996), p. 238, cf. King & Waldron (1988), p. 416f.
[2] Cf. Culpitt (1992) and Rothstein (1983).

Both of these pictures – which, be it granted, I sketch here in somewhat simplified fashion – raise the question I shall try in this chapter to answer, a question which moreover is decisive for the discussion thereupon following, namely: how should we frame the basic normative principles governing the relation of the state to the citizens? In other words, what should the state do? In seeking an answer, I shall consider the contributions of some ʘmodern political philosophers who have addressed these issues. A general welfare policy of the Swedish type involves a very heavy commitment on the part of the state, as symbolized in the expression "from the cradle to the grave." One picture related above portrays this state commitment as stifling for individual freedom, and as conducive to an unsound dependence on the state besides. The other regards this state commitment as precisely the factor that makes it possible for the broad masses of the population – and not just a small minority – to realize their autonomously chosen life projects. In this view, the prominent role of the state enhances the freedom of citizens. This opposition between collectivist and individualist views of democracy has supplied a fundamental line of political division in Sweden, and indeed throughout the West.[3] As the Italian philosopher Norberto Bobbio puts it: "The entire history of political thought is riven by the great dichotomy between organicism (holism) and individualism (atomism)."[4]

In seeking to devise appropriate principles for governing the relation of the state to the citizens, we face an interesting quandary. For most citizens want the state to follow two basic principles, and these are fundamentally incompatible. The first, which I refer to here as the principle of state neutrality and individual autonomy (also known as political liberalism), calls on the state to allow citizens to pursue such life projects as they wish.[5] The state should assume a neutral posture, that is, vis-à-vis individuals' choice of life project.[6] In the formulation of the legal theorist Ronald Dworkin, the state should treat citizens not just with "concern

---

[3] Olsen (1990).

[4] Bobbio (1990), p. 41 and ch. 9; cf. Olsen (1990). The critical work on Sweden is Lewin (1967). See also Goldman (1980).

[5] By "autonomy" I mean what John Rawls (1993) calls "rational autonomy" which is "citizens' capacity to form, to revise, and to pursue a conception of the good, and to deliberate in accordance with it" and also "capacity to enter into an agreement with others" (p. 72). This type of autonomy should be differentiated from "full autonomy" which is a specific ethical ideal that is not always compatible with the principle of neutrality, cf. Rawls (1993), p. 78 and Lindley (1986), p. 3.

[6] The first section of this chapter builds in large part on Lehning (1990).

and respect, but with equal concern and respect."[7] This principle finds expression, according to Dworkin, in Rawls' theory of justice, notwithstanding that the latter contains no explicit premise supporting the principle of "equal concern and respect." This principle forms, rather, the very basis of Rawls' theory, for justice is "owed to human beings as moral persons."[8] In other words, the right to be treated in accordance with the precepts of justice is "a right . . . [which persons] possess not by virtue of birth or characteristic or merit or excellence but simply as human beings with the capacity to make plans and give justice."[9]

The principle of equal concern forbids the state to apply any principle stating that some persons are worth more than others; it may not, for example, distribute resources unequally on such grounds. Furthermore, equal concern entails a view of individuals as "creatures capable of suffering and frustration."[10] The principle of equal respect, in turn, prohibits the state from restricting citizens' freedom to choose and to pursue such life projects as they themselves see fit; in particular, this freedom may not be confined just because the majority takes the view that the life projects of certain citizens are morally or socially superior to those of others.

Equal respect further enjoins the state to treat citizens as creatures capable of formulating their own opinions – in a considered manner – of what is fitting and appropriate for achieving their goals in life, and as persons capable of acting on these choices independently. In this respect, however, the principle of state neutrality is based on one specific idea about the good life, namely that citizens are capable of autonomy. i.e. that people are capable of forming opinions of their own. To use Will Kymlicka's argument: "state neutrality is required to respect people's self-determination."[11] Essential to this position is the view that citizens as autonomous individuals have the capacity to form different conceptions

---

[7] R. Dworkin (1977), pp. 180ff. and pp. 272ff.

[8] Ibid., p. 181, cf. Barry (1995), p. 129.

[9] Ibid. For a critique of this universalistic approach, see Fisk (1989).

[10] Langton (1991). Langton's article is both an excellent summary and a sharp critique of Dworkin's theory (or, more strictly, of Dworkin's application of his own theory).

[11] Kymlicka (1990), p. 207 and Ackerman (1980), p. 11. For a contrary argument see Barry (1995), pp. 129ff. My argument would be that the very idea of a democratic state is meaningless without the existence of autonomous citizens. Why should people be given the right to vote if they have, as e.g., in Marxism, "false consciousness." Rawls' theory is thus built on the idea that individuals have the capacity for "reason" and "rational autonomy" which I believe is a capacity that non-autonomous individuals cannot possess. Cf. Rawls (1971), p. 213 and (1993), p. 98.

of what is right and good in life. Moreover, the state should not intervene in such choices, or even try to encourage some such conceptions – or life projects founded on these – over others.[12] This type of what Jean Hampton labels "rights-based liberalism" is founded on the Kantian idea about the "equal worth and moral autonomy of all human beings" which is used to "justify a political society that recognizes rights of autonomy for its citizens."[13] The state, Dworkin argues, may "impose no sacrifice or constraint on any citizen in virtue of an argument that the citizen could not accept without abandoning his sense of his equal worth."[14] The only thing the state may do is see to it that citizen A's pursuit of his life project does not hinder citizen B's pursuit of his.

It should be noted that the principle of *equal concern and respect* does not say anything about the appropriate level of state ambition in regard to economic distribution and social security. This principle can be combined either with a highly comprehensive welfare policy or with a minimal one. The right to equal treatment is, rather, "simply the right to treatment *as an equal:* the right to have one's interest treated as fully and sympathetically as the interest of anyone else."[15] It is, one might say, a matter of regarding all citizens as possessed of *equal worth* in relation to the state, and of treating them as responsible for their actions (at least until the opposite has been proved).[16]

The central point with this injunction is that it does not imply an equal distribution of the burdens and benefits allocated by the state. It bears noting that the right to "equal concern and respect" does not imply that the state should treat everyone the same, if by that is meant that all citizens have the right to an equal share of resources at all different points in life. The universal welfare state is in one respect of course about equality, but it should not be understood as an idea about "equal treatment". Suffice it to say that certain persons may, for example, require more medical attention than others. Giving more to some persons than to others need not imply a view that the life projects of the former are worth more than those of the latter. It could rather reflect the

---

[12] Dworkin's views on this point can be traced back to the principle – which John Stuart Mill ascribed to Jeremy Bentham – of all citizens' equal worth: "everybody is to count, nobody to count for more than one." See Mill (1863/1910), p. 58.

[13] Hampton (1997), p. 175.   [14] R. Dworkin (1985), p. 205.

[15] Langton (1991), p. 315. As Langton shows, the simplicity which seems at first glance to characterize Dworkin's theory is an optical illusion. Upon closer inspection, the principle of equal concern and respect proves to be quite complicated – when, that is, it must be applied to different areas.

[16] The idea of "equal worth" as used here presumably has much the same content as the "equality of status" which, according to David Miller, occupies a central place in Michael Walzer's theory of justice. See D. Miller (1990), p. 95.

judgment that, if the former are not allocated extra resources (e.g., dialysis treatment), their suffering will be greater than the latter's. For the principle of "equal concern and respect," as used here, requires that such inequalities be rectified.

A strictly liberal society of this kind implies a state that does not take positions in questions of value. All citizens must enjoy the right to pursue their life projects, and the task of the state is to guarantee this, neither more nor less. The majority may not impose any particular view of what constitutes a worthy life project on minorities. For the individual has certain rights which the majority may not infringe, however persuasive the grounds for so doing may seem to be.[17]

Political liberalism of this kind also entails defending the right of citizens to make mistakes. The principle that the individual has the right freely to choose his goals in life cannot be set aside even when the majority has good grounds for believing the person in question is making a mistake, and will likely live to regret it.[18] Not just the authoritarian state, but also the *benevolently* authoritarian state must be rejected if the principle of neutrality is to apply.[19] The right to autonomy proscribes the state from seeking to prevent citizens from living in a manner that (it may reasonably be assumed) will not to lead to their happiness and prosperity (or whatever else it is that autonomously choosing citizens may desire). This principle takes precedence over the utilitarian dictum of "the greatest good of the greatest number." According to Dworkin, when the goals of the state – that is, its reforms or policies in some area – come into conflict with the individual's right to be treated with *equal concern and respect*, the latter functions as a kind of moral trump, i.e., the rights of the individual take precedence over the objectives of the state or collective. *No* individual's right to *equal concern and respect* may be violated, not even if the "greatest good" of ever so many other citizens would be dramatically furthered thereby. The doctrine that the supreme goal of politics and ethics is the "greatest good of the greatest number" – otherwise known as utilitarianism – long dominated political philosophy. A critical weakness of utilitarianism, however, is that it does not take the differences between citizens, as regards their views of what constitutes well-being, with sufficient seriousness.[20]

Dworkin justifies this position by reference to a distinction between "external" preferences (what one considers best for others) and "per-

---

[17] R. Dworkin (1985), ch. 17; cf. Raz (1986), pp. 395f.; Bobbio (1990), pp. 42f.; and Phillips (1993).

[18] R. Dworkin (1989), pp. 484ff.   [19] V. Held (1984), p. 17.

[20] Hart (1979), p. 77.

sonal" preferences (what one desires for oneself). Preferences of the former sort – such as those reflected in racist doctrines that some citizens are worth more than others – cannot be accepted, for they set the principle of equal concern and respect at nought. If external preferences are counted, the result is a sort of double reckoning, that is, the state must take account not only of what I want for myself, but also of what I think others should want for themselves. Rights as trumps – which expresses the idea of equal concern and respect – provide a reason for avoiding such double counting.[21]

A contrary ideal – contrary to that of the principle of neutrality – enjoins the state (in practice, the majority of citizens) to take a stand in favor of certain collective moral principles, and thus to hold out certain life projects as more desirable than others. The state should not, in other words, be neutral in questions of value but have a more or less perfectionist idea about how its citizens should structure their lives. One important such idea is the *communitarian* principle, that portrays the relation between citizens and the state as organic in character. Its corollary is that the collectivity, that is, the state, is duty-bound to assert the superiority of certain values, and thus of certain life projects, over others. It portrays the citizenry as a community bearing certain common values – above and beyond the value of equal concern and respect – values which are worth defending. The state should therefore act, according to this perspective, to further equality between the sexes, or Christian morality, or solidaristic values, or (various forms of) social equality, or the national culture, or ethnic homogeneity, or other good things.[22]

In its concrete actions in many areas, moreover, the state tries to influence our values and to hold out certain life projects as more desirable than others – for example, by subsidizing organizations which are thought to work for admirable values and practices (temperance, soli-

---

[21] As Langton (1991) demonstrates, however, it is not in fact always so easy to determine between which preferences are external and which are personal. See also Axberg (1993).

[22] See, e.g., Sandel (1982) and MacIntyre (1981). Between neo-Kantian liberalism and full-fledged communitarism are also various forms of perfectionist accounts of civil liberties. The argument is that the various liberal freedoms can only be motivated by their contribution to some form of conception of the human good. Cf. Raz (1986) and George (1993). But as Hardin has argued, "it is untenable to claim to community is simply good. When it is good, it is good; but it can be bad, and when it is, it can be horrid beyond measure" (1996), p. 216.

darity with the Third World, peace, sports activities, equality between the sexes, healthy eating habits, etc.).

A particular case is when the state, on (more or less) good grounds, views a citizen's chosen life project as ill-advised, perhaps because the person in question lacks information about, and/or knowledge of, the future consequences of his actions. Or the state may take the view that certain groups of citizens tend to make less-than-judicious choices. Maybe the state should openly declare, for instance, that the so-called *carpe diem* strategy in the choice of lifestyle (also known as the James Dean strategy: drive fast, die young) is ill-advised, at any rate if it involves the consumption of dependency-creating substances and other scabrious habits.[23] A state seeking to guarantee a reasonable measure of welfare to all its citizens generally introduces sanctions against life projects of this sort.

In any case, the political liberalism/neutrality and communitarian/ perfectionist principles are from one point of view in clear and undeniable opposition to one another, that is, they relate to each other as two communicating vessels.[24] From another point of view, however, these two principles do not bear such a one-dimensional relation to one another. For it can be argued that, if the state is to remain neutral in respect to citizens' choice of life project, it must also create equivalent opportunities for citizens to realize these varying choices.[25] To quote Ronald Beiner, for this type of liberalism "considerable state intervention is required in order to distribute to every individual an equitable share of the total aggregate of social resources, in order to give each individual a fair opportunity to give play to his or her conception of his or her own personal good."[26]

Generally, the Swedish welfare state has been understood as resting on some form of communitarian principles.[27] This goes back to a famous speech in Parliament in 1928 by the Social Democratic Prime Minister P.-A. Hansson where he launched the idea of building a "people's home" as the central metaphor for the welfare state. An often-cited sentence of this speech reads: "The basis of the home is togetherness and common feeling. The good home does not consider anyone as privileged or unappreciated; it knows no special favorites and no step-children."[28] My argument in this book (see especially chapter 7) is that such a commu-

---

[23] Arneson (1990a), p. 449.
[24] Cf. Olsen (1990) and Mulhall & Swift (1992), p. 294.
[25] Rawls (1985); cf. Rawls (1987), p. 7.
[26] Beiner (1996) p. 191; cf. R. Dworkin (1977), p. 180 and Raz (1986), p. 124.
[27] See, e.g., Rivière (1993).   [28] Quoted from Tilton (1990), p. 126.

nitarian understanding of the ideas behind the Swedish welfare state is wrong, both from a normative and from a historical perspective.

The whole idea of achieving justice through individual rights has in Scandinavia been regarded at times as an obstacle to a left-oriented welfare policy.[29] Individual universal rights, according to this argument, tend to emphasize the freedom of the individual, and may be supposed to block welfare projects of a more (Scandinavian) collectivist and egalitarian character.[30] However, as I shall seek to demonstrate later on (in ch. 8), this connection is not a logically necessary one; the concrete political impact of rights-based principles of justice is not tied to the principle of individual rights. For if that were the case, a great many rights to which all citizens are entitled – universal and equal suffrage, equality before the law, and other rights and freedoms besides – would in themselves constitute impediments to the achievement of egalitarian objectives. The political content of the concept of rights is determined, rather, by what kinds of rights the state guarantees to the individual.

All the same, the principle of neutrality and communitarian principles do come into conflict with each other, for equal opportunity requires the state to provide at least some citizens with resources, in order that their prospects for realizing their life goals are at least tolerably equal to others'. Deciding just what these resources should be – for example, health care, basic education, social insurance, freedom of speech and of the press, economic freedom, equality before the law – requires the state to take a position in questions of value. This is because it is impossible to determine which resources are critical for pursuing different kinds of life goals without also influencing thereby which life projects are thought better than others.[31] Dworkin has tried to solve this problem by differentiating between two types of paternalism, "volitional" and "critical." The former is an argument that the state can use coercion to help people "achieve what they already want to achieve." For example forcing

---

[29] Note that in the United States, however, the situation is the reverse. Civil rights forced through by the courts have been a left-wing project there.

[30] Campbell (1990), p. 38. Some variants of feminist theory also dismiss the idea of universal (non-sexist) rights as a viable option; cf. Lister (1995).

[31] Edwards (1988). Edwards, who takes the view that this can be determined objectively, concludes his article with the following words: "It has avoided specifics and no doubt when the details are filled in, many difficulties would surface, and many compromises would have to be made – particularly over the specifications of need" (pp. 150f.). The best he can propose is that the meaning of "objective needs" be established by "welfare practitioners and administrators" (p. 146). That it would pose any problems of democracy or legitimacy whatsoever to grant such power over citizens' welfare to local officials seems not to have struck the author.

people to use seat-belts to protect them from physical injuries which is something the state presumes that citizens are interested in.[32] Still the question remains, how does the state know and where, in the practical world of public policy, to draw the line?

Furnishing an education in classical literature to someone who does not regard such knowledge as in any way important for his life project – who even regards it, maybe, as a hindrance thereto – is of course pointless. It assumes, moreover, that a knowledge of classical literature amounts to a moral good in itself. It may thus be impossible to carry on public activities aimed at supplying citizens with resources without thereby affecting which values come to prevail in society. The principle of the neutral state, however fine it may be in itself, is perhaps untenable at bottom. Guaranteeing basic resources to all citizens may mean, further-more, that the state – by collecting taxes from the citizens – prevents some individuals from carrying out their autonomously chosen goals in life.

The communitarian critique of political liberalism

I shall argue, later on in this book, for a slightly modified form of political liberalism. Before so doing, however, I shall present, and attempt to refute, a certain critique of the principle of state neutrality (and of the associated right of citizens to *equal concern and respect* as regards their choice of life project). Charles Larmore summarizes the contrary prin-ciple, that is, the communitarian idea, in the following fashion:

> Because no one can determine with full autonomy how he shall see the world and what goals he shall pursue, but instead can come to understand himself only through participating in shared traditions and social forms – because in some areas he should not even strive for autonomy, the primary role of the state must not be to sustain a kind of neutrality, but rather to embody and foster some particular conception of the good life.[33]

In the communitarian view, the state should express a collective moral order. It should take a stand for certain definite values, such as those originating in a common ethnicity, nation, history, or culture. Its role is to embody the shared fate of those encompassed by a collective identity.[34] Communitarian doctrine thus charges the state with cultivating and

---

[32] R. Dworkin (1989), p. 484.

[33] Larmore (1987), p. 92; cf. B. Barry (1965), pp. 38f.; and Beiner (1992), ch. 2.

[34] An earlier tradition in Swedish political science – the foremost representative of which was Rudolf Kjellén, Skytteanum Professor of Rhetoric and Political Science from 1916 to 1922 – took such a view of the state. Kjellén's organicist state

maintaining a particular set of cultural values in the citizenry – with acting, in other words, on the view of the collectivity/majority that certain life projects are better, that is, morally more correct, than others.[35]

Communitarianism need not be based, however, on any presumption of moral superiority. It can as well express a separatist attitude, that is, that different ethnic groups should have different political orders, the task of which is to promote their particular values. An individual state can favor a certain set of values without thereby insisting that some values are superior to others. This notion – that the various communities are "separate but equal" – is embodied in states which proclaim themselves to be more than just political orders, for example, the Christian state, the Jewish state, the Serbian state, the (fe)male state, the proletarian worker and peasant state, etc.

In the communitarian view (as articulated by Michael Sandel, for instance), the principles of a neutral state rest on altogether mistaken assumptions about human nature, about what it is that forms our values and character as persons. The principle of political liberalism and individual autonomy is founded, that is, on a series of unrealistic and metaphysical postulates about "the true nature of man." Most critically, it is well-nigh impossible for proponents of political liberalism to handle the empirical fact that citizens achieve their identity through participating in various collectivities. There cannot ultimately be such a creature as an autonomous individual. For human beings are social animals, and their notions of the nature of the good life are governed by their social affiliations.[36]

The Rawlsian idea of justice through fair procedure assumes, in the view of its communitarian critics, an individual shorn of all such affiliations. If we accept the proposition that our individual personalities are created through the particular social and political contexts of which we are a part, then the political order upon which we agree should reflect a *particular* conception of the good life.[37] The political order should at any rate be able, in the view of the communitarians, to discard certain types of life project as morally less desirable than others.

Michael Walzer has tried to stake out something of a middle position in this debate. He argues that justice cannot be founded on the universal

theory closely resembles the communitarian view. See Falkemark (1992) and Tingsten (1971), p. 138ff.

[35] A case in point is the prohibition against sodomy (including between consenting adults) in the state of Georgia, which the US Supreme Court declared in 1986 to be fully compatible with the constitution. See R. Dworkin (1989).

[36] For an extreme but thought-provoking position, see Douglas (1988).

[37] Sandel (1982), pp. 179ff.

precepts upheld by the champions of the political liberalism. Rather, the requirements of justice vary between the different social spheres, in accordance with the nature of the good to be distributed. The principles appropriate to the distribution of voting rights differ, for example, from those which ought to govern the allocation of job opportunities, and the distribution of health care should follow other principles still. According to Walzer, the principles appropriate to the different spheres of society are socially and historically conditioned. Liberal distributive principles cannot therefore be applied across the board, because what is accepted as just within the different spheres has arisen through a communitarian process.[38] The principle of equal concern and respect does not forbid the rules of distribution from varying between the spheres: all that is prescribed is that individuals be treated with differing degrees of concern and respect when they find themselves in the same sphere.

In my view, the communitarians commit a classical mistake here: confusing "is" with "ought." While communitarianism makes sense as an epistemological theory, this need not have any implications for its value as a normative theory.[39] Even if it is empirically true that our values are formed by the social networks in which we take part, it does not at all follow from this that the political order also *should* take a stand on behalf of certain specific moral principles. Even if we are all to be regarded as more or less drugged by the cultural and structural conditions which produced us,[40] it does not logically follow that certain individuals have the right – just because they happen to be in the majority – to prescribe for others which life projects are fitting.

At a more empirical level, furthermore, the communitarian position is less than persuasive. For even if it portrays the social formation of the individual correctly, it does not show sufficient regard for the fact that citizens in one and the same state can exhibit plural social affiliations.[41] This point finds an obvious illustration, moreover, in the case of states encompassing a range of ethnic and/or religious groups, social classes, etc. We should therefore, according to those advocating the principle of neutrality, make a sharp distinction between our social and cultural affiliations on the one hand, and the political order on the other.[42] In the former sphere, it is altogether legitimate to promote – individually or through associations of various kinds – our notions of what constitutes a correct life project. The crucial thing is that we do not use our political

---

[38] Walzer (1983).   [39] Hardin (1996), ch. 7.
[40] Cf. Giddens (1979), pp. 49ff.   [41] Cf. Olsen (1993), p. 14.
[42] My own view is that the great misery breaks out the moment this distinction is not maintained. The examples are many: Northern Ireland, Nazi Germany, Bosnia, Rwanda, etc.

influence to see to it that *the state* favors our own particular values (or those of the group to which we belong); it is furthermore critical that we do not (which is more usual) employ the coercive power of the state to hinder those life projects we consider to be less worthy. A person or association may oppose abortion, for example, and propagate for this standpoint in various settings, and yet hold the opinion that the state's coercive power should not be employed to discourage or forbid this practice. An adherent of a particular religious or political philosophy may devote the larger part of his life to trying to win converts to his views, and even so not wish to enlist the power of the state on behalf of his doctrine. One can, in the same way, be opposed to pornographic products (or heavy motorcycles, or alcoholic drinks, or promiscuity among youth, or a certain type of culture), yet take the view nonetheless that the state should not intervene in how citizens choose to travel, or what they pour down their throats, or how they entertain each other in bed, or what they choose to look at.[43] The principle of neturality means according to Rawls that

> citizens think of themselves as free in three respects: first, as having the moral power to form, to revise and rationally to pursue a conception of the good; second, as being self-authenticating sources of valid claims; and third, as capable of taking responsibility for the ends. Being free in these respects enables citizens to be both rationally and fully autonomous.[44]

To argue that the state should be organized so at to promote citizens to be "fully autonomous," is also to argue against a morally indifferent state.[45] The principle of neutrality should not be confused with moral relativism, that is, the view that all values are equally good or bad. A person who espouses the idea of the neutral state can be as strongly committed in various moral questions as his communitarian counterpart.

---

[43] R. Dworkin (1977), pp. 256ff. and pp. 180f. Dworkin's view is that communitarianism portrays the political order as a metaphysical entity. For example, arguing that the state should forbid or obstruct certain kinds of sexual activity "supposes that the political community also has a communal sex life. It supposes that the sexual activities of individual citizens somehow combine into a national sex life" R. Dworkin (1989), p. 497. It is fully possible that Rudolf Kjellén – who developed, as mentioned above, an organicist theory of the state in Uppsala during the early part of this century – would have thought such a notion wholly in order. For Kjellén knew that the state propagated itself by means of a kind of spore. See Falkemark (1992) and Tingsten (1971), pp. 133ff.

[44] Rawls (1993), p. 72.

[45] There is a debate on how "anti-perfectionist" Rawls is, arguing that his writings can be interpreted in a more pragmatic way corresponding to the ideas of John Dewey. See George (1993), pp. 139f.

The crux of the matter lies not in our position on moral questions, but rather in our view of where the boundaries to the coercive power of the state should be drawn. The principles prevailing in the political sphere need not apply elsewhere.[46] The principle of neutrality is compatible with the existence of common social values and norms, as long as these apply narrowly to the political order. The state should not, on the other hand, favor any particular religious, moral, or ideological conceptions. In their more recent writings, Ronald Dworkin and John Rawls have both been careful to stress that their theories of justice – based as they are on the idea of the neutral state – are limited to the political order. Their theories do not oblige us to disregard, or abstain from propagating, the moral values which we consider *in other contexts* to be crucial. Rawls, for instance, writes as follows:

> Justice as fairness assumes . . . that the values of community are not only essential, but realizable, first in the various associations that extend across the boundaries of nation-states, such as churches and scientific societies. Liberalism rejects the state as a community because, among other things, it leads to the systematic denial of basic liberties and to the oppressive use of the state's monopoly of (legal) force.[47]

Rawls argues as well that the communitarian critique is based on a failure to understand that "the original position" is meant as a hypothetical representative and discursive forum, into which we enter whenever we wish to discuss and deliberate upon the principles of a just social order. In no way does it imply that we step outside of our personalities: "When, in this way, we simulate being in the original position, our reasoning no more commits US to a particular metaphysical doctrine about the nature of the self than our acting a part in a play, say of Macbeth or Lady Macbeth, commits us to thinking that we are really a king or a queen engaged in a struggle for political power."[48] The original position functions, then, as a discursive setting in which we are able to imagine ourselves, whenever our purpose is to ascertain how we would choose – after deliberating under the veil – to act in a given question.

The point, according to Rawls, is that our *political* institutions should

---

[46] Cf. Larmore (1987), p. 70.

[47] Rawls (1985), p. 10, note 17. To what extent Rawls' argument in this article from 1985 amounts to a genuine change from his original position in *A Theory of Justice* from 1971, or whether it just reflects a change in emphasis, is discussed in Mulhall & Swift (1992), ch. 5. Cf. R. Dworkin (1989), pp. 489f. Wise as an owl, Walzer (1990) writes on p. 21: "The central issue for political theory is not the constitution of the self but the connection of constituted selves."

[48] Rawls (1993), p. 27; cf. Kymlicka (1989), ch. 4 and King & Waldron (1988), p. 441.

be designed in such a manner that they are generally accepted, notwithstanding the fact that citizens hold fundamentally divergent opinions about what constitutes a morally correct way to live. Therefore, the political institutions should not take a stand on behalf of any particular view of the good life, but should rather ensure that all citizens enjoy, as far as this is possible, equal opportunities of fulfilling what they themselves regard as morally correct life projects. This is not to deny the cultural, social, and religious affiliations of different individuals and groups; it is only to insist that such affiliations do *not* have any bearing on the political order, that is, the state. The Rawlsian goal is an order marked by tolerance, a society in which an overarching consensus prevails on the principles of justice to which the political institutions should conform – a consensus which in no way is undermined by the fact that different groups and individuals hold fundamentally divergent views as regards cultural, religious, and ideological questions.[49] The Rawlsian principles of justice and fair procedure apply, in other words, over a limited field – in respect to our role as citizens. In view of Western societies' historical development towards ever greater pluralism, a theory of justice must "allow for a diversity of general and comprehensive doctrines, and for the plurality of conflicting, and indeed incommensurable, conceptions of the meaning, value and purpose of human life."[50]

One might as stated above object that the idea of the neutral state is itself a moral principle: that also a neutral state must take the view that some values are better than others.[51] The neutral state must attempt, that is, to implant the conviction in its citizens that they should not employ the coercive power of the state to impose their own views of what constitutes a correct way of life on others. The neutral state must also try to bring about a society in which it is possible for individuals to settle on their values autonomously, and to choose their life projects independently.[52] One could say that the neutral state must at any rate defend, as a minimum principle, the idea of the neutral state itself.[53] Now this does not in fact pose any fundamental problem for the advocates of political liberalism. On the contrary. Rawls, for example, concedes in his later writings that his principles apply only to democracies of a Western type.

---

[49] Rawls (1993), pp. 131–172.

[50] Rawls (1985), p. 4. Cf. Mulhall & Swift (1992), pp. 174ff.

[51] Nagel (1987), p. 16: "liberals ask of everyone a certain restraint in calling for the use of state power to further specific, controversial moral or religious conceptions – but the result of that restraint appears with suspicious frequency to favor precisely the controversial moral conceptions that liberals usually hold."

[52] V. Held (1984).

[53] Cf. Petersson (1989), p. 91: "Only the intolerance of intolerance is justified."

In other words, his theory of justice is a logical consequence of the principles of Western democracy.[54] One could, as Aryeh Botwinick does, interpret this development in Rawls' thinking as meaning that he now "is recommending his liberal theory to US on communitarian grounds." I believe this interpretation to be mistaken, however, at least if one means by it that Rawls' theory could only apply in societies which, on account of their inherent nature, create citizens with democratic values. Rawls' aim is rather, by designing just political institutions, to "shape the character and aims of the members of society, the kinds of person they are and want to be."[55] It is not, then, a democratic "community" which, by virtue of its creation of democratically minded people, results in a democratic political order. The causal connection works instead in the opposite direction; it is, as I read Rawls, just (i.e., democratic) political institutions which create democratic citizens who are interested in justice.

The neutral state's neutrality

The democratic state does not consist only of procedures; it also produces, by means of majority decision, rules of a material kind (such as the law providing for free abortion). This does not require, however, that the majority advocating a given rule is animated by a shared ideological norm. It is altogether possible, for example, to favor legislation on women's freedom to choose abortion for many different reasons.[56] One can justify it, for instance, by reference to a woman's absolute right to control her own body. A more consequentialist argument is that a state prohibition would lead, in practice, to greater suffering, and thus would be morally more objectionable than abortion itself (objectionable though the latter in itself may be).

One can take this line of argument a step further, moreover. Ronald Dworkin contends that it is precisely the principle of neutrality which can serve as a basis for the social integration sought by communitarianism; the latter, by contrast, can only provide such a foundation by referring to metaphysical principles, or by appealing to pure majority paternalism (i.e., that the majority decide what is right for the minority also). A citizen can perfectly well regard himself as an integral part of the common political system, as long as it is restricted to specifying how the political institutions shall operate, that is, how its representative, legisla-

---

[54] Rawls (1980), p. 519; cf. Rawls (1988), p. 252. See also Rorty (1991b), pp. 185ff.
[55] See Rorty (1993), pp. 47f.; and Rawls (1980), pp. 538f. On Rawls' constructivism, see B. Barry (1989), pp. 264ff.
[56] Gutman & Thompson (1990), pp. 134ff.

tive, executive, judicial, and other such functions shall be performed. A citizen who is integrated into this order (in the communitarian manner) "accepts that the value of his own life depends on the success of his community in treating everyone with equal concern."[57] If this communitarian (but strictly limited) line of thought prevails in society,

> then the community will have an important source of stability and legitimacy even though its members disagree greatly about what justice is. They will share an understanding that politics is a joint venture in a particularly strong sense: that everyone, of every conviction and economic level, has a personal stake – a *strong* personal stake for someone with a lively sense of his critical interests – in justice not only for himself but for everyone else as well.[58]

Individuality and community, then, are not necessarily antinomous.[59] Even if the principle of neutrality puts strict limits on what we can allow the state to entertain moral views about, this principle is in no way empty of moral substance. On the contrary, Dworkin argues: precisely because these notions are restricted in the fashion indicated above, they are stronger than they would be if they grew out of a common social and ideological base. If political conflicts turn on which notions of the good life should be favored over which others (on account of the fact that a temporary majority can be mobilized on their behalf), then the political discourse will be poisoned by the suspicion and logrolling associated with the construction of such majorities. This, in the long run, will prove morally destructive.[60]

If the principle of state neutrality is interpreted as meaning that no particular moral conception should be favored by state policy, then in my view it holds good in the face of the above critique. A neutral state is not the same as an indifferent state, in which everything is equally legitimate. On the contrary, there is a large body of law – the criminal code, for example – which must be interpreted as meaning that the state has highly definite notions on certain moral questions, notions which it is prepared, moreover, to back up with force.[61] The principle of neutrality must be interpreted with sufficient generosity as to permit the state to combat lifestyles which reduce other citizens' possibilities of pursuing their own autonomously chosen life projects, and which violate the principle that the state should treat all citizens with equal concern and respect.

The principle for which I settle here is that the neutrality of political

---

[57] R. Dworkin (1989), p. 500.
[58] Ibid., p. 501; cf. Mulhall & Swift (1992), p. 218.
[59] Olsen (1993), p. 17.   [60] R. Dworkin (1989), p. 502, cf. Hardin (1996).
[61] George (1993), cf. Hampton (1997), p. 174f.

institutions must be relative rather than absolute. This relativity is dictated by two conditions. The first is the value of preserving the neutrality of the state, and the need for an open and tolerant society consisting of citizens endowed with a capacity for deciding independently over, and taking responsibility for, their lives. The second has to do with resources. As mentioned above, the state must distribute resources so as to make it possible for citizens to be autonomous. With this modification, then, we can handle the tension between the principles of individual autonomy and state neutrality.[62]

As regards the specific problem of state policy towards *carpe diem* lifestyles (see above, pp. 36–37), a conflict with the principle of state neutrality clearly arises. The question is whether the neutrality principle means that the state should not try to prevent citizens from choosing manners of living which one can on good grounds assume will place them in a future position they will find unacceptable, and which they would have avoided had they understood the consequences of their choices beforehand. The answer to this quandary, in my view, should be as follows. The choice of life project, as this is envisioned in the principle of neutrality, places demands on citizens' capacity of independent decision. Such a choice cannot take place under conditions which under-mine the possibility of arriving at an independent decision – for example, conditions characterized by inaccurate or absent information about consequences. When it comes to lifestyles of this type, then, we should regard the state as standing under two obligations: to furnish citizens with the best possible information, on the one hand; and to observe the greatest restraint in the use of compulsion, on the other. For as Arneson points out, even a person who is pale and drawn with the bitter wisdom gained from having gambled and lost with a *carpe diem* lifestyle can conclude in the end – when all the results are in – that he would have done it all over again.

It is far from certain that the citizen in question truly regrets, in retrospect, the kinds of life experiences which were not directly enjoyable. The coercive power of the state should therefore be restricted, in Arneson's view, to preventing "egregiously irrational ways of arriving at commitments, so that these commitments would be abandoned with further knowledge and reflection and with high probability would not be reaffirmed."[63] On the grounds that this type of life project cannot be

---

[62] This corresponds to Rawls' notion, if I understand it aright, of an overarching consensus on the political order (which, be it noted, is limited precisely to the political sphere).

[63] Arneson (1990a), p. 449.

considered autonomously chosen, then, we may conclude that the use of state power in this case does not violate the principle of neutrality. Paternalism this certainly is – that cannot be denied – but it is paternalism subject to severe constraints.[64] Those wishing to employ the coercive power of the state to hinder *carpe diem* lifestyles have been saddled thereby with a relatively heavy burden of proof.

Seen from an implementation point of view, however, it must be granted that this is a balancing act performed on a very slack rope. Arneson argues that the state should be used to prevent certain life projects if "nobody would affirm that conception once she had passed a certain point of progress toward ideal deliberation with full information."[65] Sticklers for intellectual detail might here put the question of how reasonable criteria can be found for determining when this "certain point" has been reached, or for deciding what qualifies as "full information," or for identifying which instances of deliberation are "ideal."

Some scholars have objected to Rawls' theory on the grounds that it amounts to an idealized and sophisticated defense of the principles of Western liberalism, as these find expression in, for example, the constitution of the United States. If one holds more egalitarian notions, therefore, one can dismiss Rawls' argument as a rationalization for liberal democracy. As Dworkin shows, however, this reasoning is untenable, for Rawls' theory of justice is not based on the right of citizens to certain specific freedoms, but rather on their right to treated by the political institutions with equal concern and respect. This right may be contested, certainly, by those

> who believe that some goal, like utility or the triumph of a class or the flowering of some conception of how men should live, is more fundamental than any individual right, including the right to equality. But it cannot be denied in the name of any more radical conception of equality, because none exists.[66]

If we look to the public policies which have actually been implemented in a country such as Sweden, however, we find that the principle of neutrality has not been applied so very often. On the contrary, one could say that modern Swedish politics has been stamped in an unusually high degree by strong perfectionist and/or communitarian principles. The Swedish state has granted support to a multitude of organizations and associations precisely because they have been thought to stand for high moral principles. Examples include the temperance movement, the peace

---

[64] Cf. R. Dworkin (1989) o\ "volitional" versus "critical" paternalism.
[65] Ibid., p. 450.   [66] R. Dworkin (1977), p. 182.

movement, the sports movement, various producer groups (such as trade unions and farmers' cooperatives), the state church, and (in more recent years) other religious associations.

In addition, large parts of the public service sector have been constructed on the basis of standardized solutions, that is, the same type of child care, schools, and old-age care for all citizens, regardless of their particular wishes. The determination of what constitutes high-quality service in these programs has been made centrally, at the municipal or national political levels, and citizens have enjoyed but limited possibilities of affecting such determinations. It is thus no exaggeration to say that, historically at least, the Swedish ideal of democracy has been more communitarian than neutral in character.[67] As general ideas, the principles of neutrality and state neutrality are perhaps uncontroversial; as a matter of practical politics, quite the reverse is true. As I shall demonstrate later on (see pp. 188–198), moreover, these principles have decisive consequences for the organization of welfare policy.

The neutral state and the question of equal opportunity

The justification for the principle of neutrality and individual autonomy can be found, as mentioned earlier, in the idea of equal concern and respect. If we do not observe the principle of neutrality, but instead regard ourselves as entitled to use the state to force our values on other people, then we have no guarantee that others will not do the same to us.[68] If, on the other hand, we embrace this principle of what the state should and should not do, the question immediately arises of how the state should act so as to ensure that all citizens can, on tolerably equal terms, realize their various autonomously chosen life plans. Let me state at the outset that the fundamental complication here has to do with the *variation* of life projects.[69] A more communitarian state, which views itself as entitled to induce citizens to embrace certain definite moral values and goals, clearly has an easier task on this point.[70] The problem arises when we attempt both to safeguard the principle of neutrality and to ensure all citizens reasonably equal chances of choosing their moral principles autonomously, and of realizing the life projects founded thereon. Simply put, how can we create conditions for the realization of something when we do not know what it is?

The first question is: what are the resources which all citizens must be guaranteed if they are to enjoy reasonable prospects of making "informed

---

[67] SOU (1990: 44), pp. 12ff.; Olsen (1990), ch. 4.   [68] Cf. Hardin (1996).
[69] Cf. Bell (1985).   [70] Cf. Rawls (1993), pp. 179f.

and reasoned judgments about alternative modes of conduct, free from undue manipulation by others?"[71] What, in other words, do citizens need in order to be capable of acting with good judgment? One answer is given by Barbara Misztal: "to be able to participate in democratic processes individuals need resources enabling them to be autonomous subjects."[72] The second question is: what is the correct distribution of these resources, given that we do not wish to violate the principle of equal concern and respect? These are obviously sensitive political questions. They touch on the fundamentals of every discussion of welfare policy. Moreover, any attempt to find, by means of scientific argumentation, any definite answer to these questions is of course vain. Still, it bears noting that scarcely any political grouping, save perhaps one espousing pure anarchism, does not take the view that there are critical resources with which every citizen must be provided – and, moreover, that there is a fitting distribution of such resources. Even a (formerly) neo-liberal theorist like Robert Nozick insists that all citizens be furnished with the resource of "state protection for property," and that this resource be distributed equally, that is, that no one should be better protected than anyone else.[73] All democrats, moreover, hold the view that the resource of "voting rights for elections to political assemblies" should be guaranteed to all citizens on an equal basis. This list may of course be indefinitely lengthened (health care, basic education, etc.) according to what we regard as the necessary fundamental and sufficient resources for enjoying reasonably equal prospects of realizing one's life project, and of forming independent views in political questions. My purpose here is simply to call attention to the fact that there is no democratic political position in which the provision of state-guaranteed resources – for the purpose of guaranteeing equal opportunities to all – is not central.

If we now, for reasons which in my view are persuasive, embrace the (moderately modified) principle of neutrality, the question immediately arises of whether there is any way for the state to guarantee the resources mentioned without violating this very principle.[74] Rawls' well-known solution to this problem is based on the idea of "primary goods." These

---

[71] Bell (1985), p. 179, cf. Lehning (1990).   [72] Misztal (1996), p. 234.

[73] Nozick has on critical points abandoned the position he took in 1974 in *Anarchy, State, and Utopia*. See Nozick (1989), ch. 25.

[74] Cf. Fishkin (1983). Fishkin claims that this is not the case. He argues that, when the state attempts to distribute something neutrally (whatever it may be), it has already – by choosing what is to be distributed – set the principle of neutrality aside. This is an absurd position, however, since it would mean that a neutral distribution of democratic rights and freedoms is impossible. The rest of this section draws on Lehning (1990).

are "goods" whose possession Rawls considers necessary for the individual to be capable of autonomously forming, and of carrying out, a conception of a morally correct and good life.[75] A politically determined distribution of primary goods does not, according to Rawls, conflict with the principle of state neutrality, for these are goods which every rationally acting citizen desires more and not less of, independently of his views on the nature of a morally correct life. In this conception, "primary goods" consist of the things we usually associate with the basic rights and freedoms of modern democracy: the right to choose occupation and residence freely, the right to vote and to run for public office, etc. A more problematic matter, however, is that Rawls also counts income, wealth, and "the social bases of self-respect" among the primary goods. If it is possible to specify the "primary goods" to which every citizen is entitled, we should be able – according to this notion – to distribute these goods to the citizens without thereby violating the principle of state neutrality. The reason for this, Rawls argues, is that such primary goods do not in themselves favor or facilitate the adoption by citizens of any particular moral conception.[76]

Regardless of what we think this list of primary goods should include (and Rawls is not especially concrete here), there is another and more critical problem with Rawls' principle of an equal distribution of primary goods. As the economist and philosopher Amartya Sen has noted, Rawls' principle has the consequence that gravely handicapped persons will receive exactly as much (or as little) as persons free of any handicap. The question of handicapped citizens (to whom Americans for some reason refer as "hard cases") reveals some important difficulties; that is, an equal distribution of primary goods does *not* create equal opportunities for all citizens, *because their initial situation differs.* Sen describes this problem as follows:

> If people were basically very similar, then an index of primary goods might be quite a good way of judging advantage. But, in fact, people seem to have different needs varying with health, longevity, climatic conditions, location, work conditions, temperament, and even body size . . . So what is involved is not merely a few hard cases, but overlooking very widespread and real differences. Judging advantage purely in terms of primary goods leads to a partially blind morality.[77]

---

[75] Rawls (1982).   [76] For a critique, see Fishkin (1975).

[77] Sen (1982), p. 366. Sen's critique of the idea of resource equality is not – despite the stir it has created – especially original. Aristotle himself, according to Martha Nussbaum's interpretation (1990), criticized the idea of resource equality in like fashion.

The list of citizens who require compensation – because their initial situation deprives them of prospects equal to those enjoyed by a majority of their fellow citizens – could be made long indeed. It is not impossible that an ambitious policy in this respect might lead to a situation in which an overwhelming majority of citizens receives special support in some area, in order that their prospects for realizing their life prospects will be equal to those enjoyed by the majority.

One problem concerns what to do with citizens who, through no obvious fault of their own, just happen to have very expensive tastes, that is, for whom life seems meaningless if they are not able to carry on exceedingly expensive pursuits.[78] Another difficulty is that the idea of primary goods disregards the fact that our possibilities vary when it comes to converting such goods into usable personal resources, that is, it makes it appear that these goods are goals in themselves, instead of just means to self-realization. Sen argues that Rawls, with his primitive notion of equality as measured in primary goods, commits a fundamental fallacy here, one presumably reflecting the psychological impact of a long life spent in the capitalist market economy: the fallacy of commodity fetishism.[79]

Another questionable feature of the idea of primary goods has to do with the fact that different people have different conceptions of welfare, as well as varying notions of what is required to realize their life plans. This is not just a difference in quantity; there is also a qualitative dimension, that is, different citizens' conceptions of welfare may be of such a nature as to exclude any comparison based on a single index. No distribution of primary goods which is genuinely neutral between different conceptions of the good life can therefore be designed. Accordingly, Dworkin argues, we should think not in terms of primary goods but rather in terms of resources. The notion of resource equality, however, runs up against much the same problem as the Rawlsian idea of primary goods; that is, it does not take into account citizens' sharply varying capacities to convert material goods (which are the only goods the state is able to distribute) into actual personal power. Such a distribution favors those citizens whose personal constitution is such as to equip them with a greater capacity than that possessed by others to convert the resources (or primary goods) supplied by the state into personal power. None of these ideas fulfills, then, the (slightly modified) principle of state neutrality. The question is: must we discard this

---

[78] Cf. G. Cohen (1989).

[79] Ottomeyer (1977), p. 42. Rawls has since engaged in self-criticism on this point, see Rawls (1988).

principle, however lovely it may be, on the grounds that no adequate method can be found for implementing it?

The critic of Rawls and Dworkin mentioned above – Amartya Sen – offers a possible way out of this quandary with his notion of *basic capability equality*.[80] Sen argues that every form of egalitarianism capable of being combined with political liberalism – whether the egalitarianism in question is of a political, social, or economic character – must take into account the differences between citizens (partly in ability, partly in moral conceptions). Sen criticizes Rawls and Dworkin for neglecting the question of citizens' capabilities. These have to do with what is usually termed "positive freedom," that is, the freedom to achieve (with the help of the state) certain things. Examples include the opportunity to change one's residence, to acquire sufficient nourishment, and to take part in the social and economic functions of society.[81] The critical thing is that the resources distributed by the state play a role in reducing or eliminating the disabilities suffered by those with physical, social, or economic handicaps. (By "handicaps" is simply meant such conditions, personal or social, as prevent citizens from living such lives as they will.) An equal distribution of either primary goods or resources cannot accomplish this objective, because these conceptions of equality confound goods or resources with what people *are able to accomplish* with these. Instead, a principle of compensating ability is suggested.

The principle of neutrality and individual autonomy does not just mean that the state should assume a neutral stance *vis-à-vis* citizens' choice of life project. It also means that the state should seek to achieve, as far as this is possible, equal opportunities for citizens to realize their ideas and plans. Whether citizens then make use of these opportunities, or squander them rather, is their own affair. The idea of equal basic capabilities is central here. What more precisely should be comprised within this notion is largely a political question, which is impossible to answer in any definitive fashion on the basis of political philosophy. For the purpose of political philosophy is not to empty the democratic process of all significant questions, but only to seek a common view of what the discussion should concern.

In seeking to answer the question of how to distribute basic capabilities, we cannot avoid addressing the problem of what citizens need in order to be able to realize their autonomously chosen life projects. This question is inevitably political, for the simple reason that different life projects

---

[80] Sen (1982), p. 368.   [81] Sen (1988).

require different kinds of resources.[82] Nevertheless, the idea of basic capabilities remains central, because it indicates that, in order to achieve this basic level – assuming we can agree on what it is – different citizens must be furnished with varying resources of different amounts.

The critical thing is that, with this approach, we have focused attention on the fact that there is a logically consistent possibility, at least in theory, of combining the principle of neutrality (that all citizens have an equal right to choose their life goals independently) with that of state neutrality (that the state should not specify which ways of living are morally superior to others).

Where, then, can we find a common denominator for what should included among the "basic capabilities" with which the state is duty-bound to furnish all citizens? We could keep the matter simple by resorting to the United Nations Declaration on Human Rights. Its 25th paragraph states that:

> Everyone has the right to a standard of living adequate for the health and well-being of himself and his family, including food, clothing, housing and medical and necessary social services.

This paragraph, short though it is, must be interpreted as meaning that the capabilities enumerated are critical for the ability of citizens to function in society, and that it is the obligation of the state to furnish them. Martha Nussbaum has developed a theory which may be relevant here. She interprets Aristotle in the light of modern welfare policy, and arrives at the following premise. The state cannot content itself just with allowing citizens to choose different life projects, because some citizens – on account of a lack of educational and other capabilities – possess such inadequate information and knowledge that their prospects for making good (in the sense of well-informed) choices are limited. Furthermore, persons living under difficult conditions tend, according to Nussbaum, gradually to accept their fate, in part because they cannot imagine any reasonable alternative. Instead of accepting this situation, it is the duty of the state, with due respect for citizens' right to choose different ways of life, to see to it that citizens are in a position to make "good" (in the sense of well-considered) choices. Nussbaum writes:

> The Aristotelian takes desires seriously as one thing we should ask about, in asking how well an arrangement enables people to live. But she insists that we must also, and more insistently, ask what the people involved are actually able to do and be and, indeed, to desire. We consider not only whether they are asking for education, but how they are being educated;

---

[82] Nussbaum (1990), p. 212.

not only whether they perceive themselves as reasonably healthy, but how long they live, how many of their children die, how, in short, their health is.[83]

The problem is that, once again, we can hardly take a position on this without violating the neutrality principle (at least in part), since we must answer such questions as: "What human functions are important? What does a good human life require?"[84] Nussbaum argues, as does Amartya Sen, that it is citizens' capabilities which are crucial, but she makes so bold as to specify the meaning of these capabilities much more precisely. Instead of proposing, as does the social liberal John Rawls, a precise and narrow theory – that is, an exact enumeration of what types of "goods" citizens should be furnished with – she opts for an imprecise but broad principle. In Nussbaum's view, Aristotelian principles, which are usually thought to express a more communitarian ideal, actually supply good arguments for political liberalism. This line of reasoning is very appealing. To begin with, it is advantageous that the state should supply a broad range of resources, since it cannot know in any exact fashion which resources are critical for ensuring that citizens possess the capacity to realize their life goals. In addition, it is appropriate that the state should refrain from specifying what these resources should be used for, since it should not hold out certain ways of living (with a few exceptions as mentioned above on pp. 46f.) as more desirable than others. "The Aristotelian proceeds this way in the belief that it is better to be vaguely right than precisely wrong; and that, without the guidance of the thick vague theory, what we often get, in public policy, is precise wrongness."[85] The purpose, as mentioned earlier, is to place citizens in such a position – by means of a politically determined distribution of capabilities – that they are able to make good (in the sense of well-considered) choices. Is this not then an expression of paternalism all the same, since it is based on the idea that the state/collective knows what the individual requires in order to make good choices? And have we not violated the principle of neutrality thereby?

Not at all, I would argue. For the principle of neutrality requires precisely that citizens are truly in a position to make autonomous choices. For this to be a reality, they must have access to certain basic resources/capabilities.[86] They need not use these resources, or indeed

---

[83] Ibid., p. 213. Cf. Raz (1986), pp. 416ff. for a similar (and even less accessible) discussion.

[84] Nussbaum (1990), p. 212.   [85] Ibid., p. 217.

[86] Cf. G. Dworkin (1988), pp. 31f.; Raz (1986), pp. 133f.; and Nussbaum (1990), p. 238.

even acquire them, but they must have the possibility of obtaining them should they so desire.[87]

Excursus. On the moral status of market interventions

We have concluded that the state must furnish citizens with certain basic resources, so as to enable them to carry out their autonomously chosen life projects. This means, obviously, that the state must extract resources from the surrounding society. Libertarians have criticized taxation as an iniquitous intervention into the rights of private ownership, rights which occupy a virtually metaphysical (not to say holy) status in their thinking.[88] It is not so easy to find defenders of this standpoint in its pure form today, for the exponents of this doctrine have painted themselves into a corner. The fundamentally insoluble dilemma in which they have been trapped is that even if the state is to defend the rights of ownership, *and only these,* it clearly cannot do so free of charge. Police forces, courts, professorships in penal, procedural, and civil law, debt-collection agencies, prisons, tank battalions (and other defense and correctional institutions of a still more Draconian nature) – these are by no means cost-free.[89] The ironic result is that even a minimal state devoted solely to defending the rights of property must end up violating precisely these, for there will always be free riders who try to obtain protection for their property while refusing to contribute solidaristically to defraying the costs of such protection. It has proven impossible to escape from this logical labyrinth, and so the neo-liberal project has, theoretically speaking, run aground.[90]

This critique of the supremacy of property rights can be developed further. It is clear, for example, that the market and the political system are not rightly regarded as dichotomous. In an analysis of Rawls' theory, Söderström argues that the participants in the original position would probably choose to leave certain decisions to the market. But they would also, in all likelihood, wish to regulate certain things through collective decision, partly in order to moderate the consequences of market solutions in the area of distribution, but also, I am inclined to add, in order to bring about conditions of fair competition on the market. For the market and the political system, in Söderström's words, are "two inseparable components in a single system of resource

---

[87] Rawls (1993), p. 189.   [88] See, e.g., Berthu & Lepage (1988).
[89] Beuchamp (1980), p. 146. See also Gray (1993), p. 101.
[90] Fishkin (1992), pp. 71f. See also Gray (1993), pp. 77ff. and p. 101.

distribution, and the one component cannot be seen as an 'intervention' in the other."[91]

In order to achieve what economists call market-conforming regulations, then, some form of taxation must be instituted, and this can only be done by restricting the absolute rights of ownership.[92] From a contract-theoretical standpoint, therefore, there is no cause to claim that taxation aimed at guaranteeing to all citizens the capabilities specified by Amartya Sen should run afoul of any moral problems. On the contrary, the moral burden of proof should rather be placed, in accordance with the idea of equal concern and respect, on those arguing that the state has no obligation to furnish citizens with the fundamental capability of realizing their autonomously chosen life projects, or to use Dworkin's words: "people must not be condemned, unless this is unavoidable, to lives in which they are effectively denied any active part in the political, economic, and cultural life of the community."[93] This appears to be Rawls' opinion on the subject as well, as when he contends that a system founded solely on voluntary market relations is "not, in general, fair, unless the antecedent distribution of income and wealth as well as the structure of the system of markets is fair."[94]

[91] Söderström (1977). Söderström writes further: "Those claiming that societal intervention in 'free' markets involves a lack of respect for the freedom of the individual are not necessarily right. The question is: is it the individual's freedom of action under the rules, or the individual's freedom to influence the rules, that should be respected?"

[92] A growing interest may be observed among economists in the role of political institutions in bringing about properly functioning, efficient markets. Among the more important contributions here may be mentioned that of North (1990). Cf. Myrdal (1969), who called attention to this factor early on.

[93] R. Dworkin (1977), p. 211.   [94] Rawls (1977), p. 160.

3

Is governance possible?

Implementation research: a short background

In the last chapter, I explored some recent contributions to political philosophy, in the hope of finding some assistance in determining what the state should do, and what its responsibilities *vis-à-vis* the citizens should be. We must now join battle with our other central question, namely: what *can* the state do? As mentioned earlier, my purpose here is to consider what lessons can be drawn from the empirical research of the last two decades on the implementation of public programs in the area of welfare policy. This will take us, in no uncertain terms, away from the beautiful and often elegant analysis of principle characteristic of political philosophy to the harshly empirical analysis of a world not always free from blemish – that of public policy. Sensitive readers, especially those who find political reality to be disagreeably bereft of principle, at times irrational, and therefore insignificant, are hereby warned.

Research on the implementation of public policy began in connection with the launching of "The Great Society" by the Johnson Administration in the United States during the 1960s. The discovery of massive and enduring poverty in the world's richest country, together with the very great confidence – characteristic of the time – in the ability of public policy to change society, set off a social policy offensive unprecedented in the modern history of the United States. Optimism was rife, the country that had crushed the (previously) greatest war machines on earth should find it a simple matter to eliminate poverty, illiteracy, and other social miseries at home. "The War on Poverty," accordingly, was declared.[1] Faith in the possibility of solving all manner of social ills by means of public measures was enormous during this period; as one of the participants later said: "for every problem there is a policy."[2] It should be noted that the programs receiving the bulk of the monies were directly targeted on particularly exposed and needy population groups, ethnic minorities not least. The Great Society programs were thus mainly selective rather than general in nature.[3]

This reformist optimism was by no means restricted to the United States. Similar large-scale public programs were established throughout the Western world.[4] In Sweden, for example, a social policy offensive was launched in the late 1960s, inspired in large part by the Social Democratic program for "increased equality," which a working group under the leadership of Alva Myrdal had presented at the party congress of 1967. Poverty and social misery were rediscovered in Sweden as well, and faith in public policy as a means of promoting social change was very widespread, here as elsewhere.[5] "The Strong Society" (in the words of a Social Democratic slogan of the time) would now be realized at last, and the cracks in the social policy wall would be sealed.[6]

The American government decided, in contrast to its Swedish counterpart, that all federal programs launched during "The War on Poverty" would be assessed. The US Congress wanted to know what effect the programs had – it wanted some idea, quite simply, of what the American people got in return for their money. A small army of social scientists – many with left-liberal political views – was therefore dispatched to investigate the impact of the programs. Thus was implementation research born, together with its cousin, evaluation research.

In general, these investigations into the impact of the Great Society programs yielded rather disheartening results. The researchers discovered small positive effects, if any, and reported as well inadequate coordination between organizations and among the various levels of government, unforeseen and often negative side-effects, all manner of waste and incompetence, and sometimes outright corruption and abuse

[1] Zarefsky (1986).   [2] Glazer (1988), p. 3.
[3] Zarefsky (1986), pp. 161f. and pp. 199f. See also Dionne (1991) and Skocpol (1987).
[4] See, e.g., the four-volume collection edited by Peter Flora, *Growth to Limits. The West European Welfare States Since World War II* (1986 and 1987).
[5] See, e.g., Inghe & Inghe (1967). This book made a very great impact, and almost 50 000 copies were printed in Sweden – an almost unbelievable figure for a book of this sort. The American counterpart was Harrington (1962).
[6] Now this was not just a Social Democratic notion. For an interesting empirical analysis of the broad faith in public measures characteristic of Swedish politics, see Uddhammar (1993).

of power.[7] Proceeding as they did on the basis of left-liberal assumptions, most of these pioneers within implementation and evaluation research drew the conclusion that what was needed was more resources, bolder programs, better organization, and a clearer division of responsibility.

Ironically, however, the outcome proved quite different. The conservative forces in US politics – in the Republican Party most especially – drew wholly different conclusions from the evaluation reports authored by the left-liberal social scientists. Instead of agreeing that more resources and better coordination were needed, the conservatives concluded that programs of this type could not work, that they led to waste, that they put recipients in a position of helpless dependence, and that in many cases they did more harm than good. This social-policy pessimism is intimately associated, moreover, with a larger crisis for rationalism as a fundamental political idea. A typical expression of this view is the following statement from a well-known implementation researcher:

> Intervention has been thought of as the deliberate, rational use of central authority to alter the structure of political, social, and economic relationships. This view grew out an essential optimism about central government's ability to know what causes social problems, to translate that knowledge into binding prescriptions, and to use beneficent coercion to implement its prescriptions. Furthermore, so long as a case could be made for intervention, by an appeal to data or political argument, the prevailing assumption was that the government would provide the resources necessary to make intervention work. The story of social policy over the past fifteen or twenty years has been the story of the unraveling of these assumptions. They have proven to be wrong on all accounts, or at least sufficiently problematic to make them an unreliable basis for policy. The notion of cumulative progress, directed from the center with scientific know-how, orchestrated through the systematic rational use of beneficent coercion, seems less plausible the more we know about the effects of past intervention. Our confidence in the center declines, as does its authority to provide benefits and coerce. Things fall apart. The center, it seems, cannot hold.[8]

One conservative American scholar in particular, Charles Murray, has left an imprint on conservative thinking in the United States on these issues.[9] In his book, *Losing Ground*, he argues that the more reformers in the United States have expanded this type of targeted program, the worse the situation has become for those groups whom the measures were intended to help (African Americans most especially). By means of a rather

---

[7] See Fox (1987).   [8] Elmore (1983), p. 213.
[9] Murray (1984). See also Glazer (1988).

debatable and since highly criticized statistical comparison of the situation before and after "The Great Society," Murray claims to show that the programs aimed at improving the situation of the worst-off have not done any palpable good.[10] On the contrary, these programs have led to a sort of learned helplessness among their already troubled beneficiaries. Murray's book had a great impact in the United States, and served as justification for the reduction and/or abolition of many of these selective social programs under the Reagan Administration.[11]

This pessimism about the possibilities of reform, and the associated lack of faith in a public policy founded on rational discourse, is not just found in the United States. It has also, if in a lesser degree, permeated Swedish politics and intellectual debate during the 1980s. An example of this may be seen in the "Study of Democracy and Power in Sweden" – more commonly known as the Power Study – a social scientific mega-project initiated by the Social Democratic government in 1985. The commission's final report, which it submitted in 1990, is largely marked by a pessimistic undertone as regards the prospects for directing social development by democratic means. It states that

> realizing the principle of the state as a producer of services necessitates a large bureaucracy, which becomes ever harder to oversee and to direct. Power over the public sector, which according to the theory should rest with elected representatives, comes in large measure to be exercised de facto by officials and experts. The power of the system increases, but power over the system diminishes.[12]

The report also summarizes the results of a study based on extensive interviews with Swedish citizens. This study reveals that, in areas within which much touted reforms have been carried out – schooling and health care, for example – large groups of users experience powerlessness in the

---

[10] For a critique of Murray's use of statistics, see Jencks (1992) and Katz (1989), pp. 153f. Cf. also Salonen (1993), p. 49f.

[11] There are several good studies of these events in United States politics, among them Katz (1989) and Dionne (1991). When asked by the press to explain the riots in Los Angeles in the spring of 1992, then-President George Bush answered that the cause lay in the welfare programs instituted during the 1960s. Quoted in Saskia Sassen, "To them that have not," *Times Literary Supplement* (05–22–92), p. 11.

[12] SOU (1990: 44), p. 28; Olsen (1990), pp. 127ff.: "Is it at all possible to control the course of social development, or to give it direction?" Brunsson & Olsen (1990) may be mentioned among the works written under the aegis of the Power Study which express pessimism about the prospects of reform.

face of the large-scale bureaucratic systems which have been created.[13] To quote one of the commission's members: "The institutions of the welfare state have become heavy, sluggish, and unable to satisfy reasonable expectations and demands on the part of citizens."[14]

The report's pessimistic conclusions about the effects of rationally planned reforms are based, in certain central parts, on a current in organization theory that, ever since Herbert Simon's famous book from 1955, *Administrative Behavior,* has questioned the possibility of making rational decisions, especially in large organizations.[15] In this field, study has been piled upon study, each in succession demonstrating the impossibility of managing organizations in accordance with models of fully rational decision-making.[16] In later years this pessimism has been carried to the point that scholars have doubted the possibility of even a limited form of rationality in this area. A typical quote from the genre is as follows:

> Organizations can also reflect inconsistent norms by systematically creating inconsistencies between words, decisions, and actions, i.e., they can produce hypocrisy. They can talk, then, in accordance with one group of norms, decide in accordance with another, and act according to a third.[17]

I am the last to doubt that organizations can function irrationally, that hypocrisy is common, and that much of what takes place should be described as "talk." My questions, however, are two: How far does this suffice as a *general* description of what organizations do? And how well are such economic models suited to describing the political sphere? Another author in this school describes how the Standing Committee on Industry and Commerce in the Swedish Parliament has shown itself unable, in a number of cases, to conduct economic policy in a rational manner. That is, the committee has mainly reacted to events, rather than directing them. This has introduced an element of irrationality into the making of policy.[18] In an insightful review of this book, Schmidt makes the following point:

> The only thing which undeniably would refute the author's ideas would be . . . if economic policy were conducted by Nobel Prize winner Herbert Simon's caricatured "Economic Man," who always knows exactly what he wants and can do, and what the result will be if he acts in the one way or the other. I doubt it is meaningful to search for this unlikely creature in

---

[13] SOU (1990: 44).   [14] Olsen (1990), p. 131.   [15] Simon (1955).
[16] As examples may be mentioned Jacobsson (1989) and Brunsson (1989).
[17] Brunsson (1990), p. 35.   [18] Jacobsson (1989).

the corridors of Parliament or the Ministry of Industry – or anywhere else.[19]

As a matter of fact, Schmidt points out that the data contained in this very study can be interpreted in a manner reflecting much more favorably on the possibilities of rational policy-making. That is, he finds evidence in Jacobsson's study for the claim that officials in the Ministry of Industry have acted much more actively to guide industrial policy along clear and well-defined lines than Jacobsson admits. That they have not always succeeded does not reflect any deficient rationality on their part, but rather the fact that politics is an activity involving *coping with opposed interests*. The Power Study's pessimism about the prospects for the rational conduct of policy has, accordingly, no obvious basis even in the empirical research conducted under its aegis.

Another critique of the possibility of governance comes out of neoclassical economics. The question raised in the following. Given that both are rational utility maximizers, how can elected officials (the principals) get the public authorities (the agents) faithfully to pursue the principals' policies. The problem stated is that (a) the agents have critical information about the policy process that principals do not have and (b) the agents are not likely to reveal such (critical) information to their principals if they know that the principals are likely to use this information against the interests of the agents (e.g., to streamline the organization). In designing policies and institutions (and thereby the incentives that according to neoclassical economics guide the behavior of the agents) the principals are likely to have incomplete information and thus make faulty decisions. This could, in game-theoretical terms, be described as the classical pathological "social trap". Such a situation can only be overcome if the principals can get the agents to trust them not to use the critical information against the interest of the agents. The problem is that in a democracy it is often the case that principals are supposed to do just this: to serve the interest of the electorate for efficiency against the (supposed) interest of the administration for organizational "slack".[20]

The pathology of the social sciences?

To a great extent, implementation research is misery research, a pathology of the social sciences, if you will. It has yielded a never-ceasing stream of studies of wasted resources, unforeseen side-effects, unclear political objectives, inappropriate organizational forms, and uncomprehending or generally malevolent bureaucrats. "Ours is an era of

---

[19] Schmidt (1991), p. 124.   [20] Cf. G. Miller (1992).

considerable pessimism and concern about government" – so goes the first sentence in a standard work on the subject.[21] "Even the most robust policy – one that is well designed to survive the implementation process – will tend to go awry. The classic symptoms of underperformance, delay and escalating costs are bound to appear," is another typical statement from the first generation of implementation researchers.[22]

However, no less than three different problems lie hidden herein. The first is that implementation researchers show a predilection for focusing on public programs that result (as these researchers know beforehand) in failure.[23] Now this is not particularly strange, nor is it under all circumstances methodologically objectionable. When, as in this case, it is a question of establishing a new field of research, illustrative studies of this sort – which aim first and foremost at verifying a new theory – are both necessary and legitimate. The objective has been to demonstrate the importance, for understanding the outcomes of the political system, of analyzing the implementation process. In such a case as this, therefore, focusing on known policy failures is altogether legitimate. This focus on the "heroic defeats" of public policy may be compared with the interest, which economists evidenced once upon a time, in the study of market failures.

This concentration on unsuccessful public measures is more problematic for our purposes, however. For the aim of our exploration of the possibilities and limits of public policy is to discern patterns of a general nature. It clearly would be fatal if the methodological distortion occasioned by the concentration on problem areas led us to view problems of implementation as insurmountable. Such an approach may be equated with drawing conclusions of a general nature about the problems and possibilities of private enterprise in a market economy based solely on the study of crisis branches or bankrupt companies.[24] Nor have students of military strategy based their conclusions solely on the analysis of defeats.[25] As Richard Elmore writes in an insightful article: "Analysis of

[21] Mazmanian & Sabatier (1983).
[22] Bardach, quoted in Winter (1990), p. 23.
[23] Goggin (1986) and Kettl (1993b), p. 414. This seems to apply as well to the above-mentioned "irrationalist school" within organization theory. For a critique of the Power Study's pessimism regarding social reform, see Olsson (1991).
[24] For such a careful and one-sided enumeration of all that can be imagined to go wrong, see Niklasson (1992), pp. 144–152. Other studies have expressed much greater optimism about the possibility of implementing even problematic programs. Examples are Levin & Ferman (1985), Cerych & Sabatier (1986), and Mazmanian & Sabatier (1981).
[25] These are clearly the most interesting to read, however. See, e.g., Palm (1981), Regan (1987), and Cohen & Gooch (1990).

social policy has come to consist of explaining why things never work as intended; a high level of knowledge about social policy has come to be equated with a fluent cynicism."[26] We can doubtless learn important lessons from studying failed programs and irrational organizations. The problem with a single-minded focus of this type, however, is that it only shows us what does not work, instead of what does. Clearly, it is methodologically unacceptable, on the basis of such limited knowledge, to draw conclusions of a general nature, and still more to give recommendations to policy practitioners on such a basis.

The selection of programs to investigate presents us with a second and closely related difficulty. Even when implementation researchers have not decided from the start to study policy failures, they have typically settled on policy areas in which (a) success requires collaboration between several different political levels, (b) the aim is to influence social areas characterized by a high degree of variability, (c) the field personnel must be granted a considerable freedom of action, (d) the expected changes are of a dramatic order, and (e) the technology for achieving the expected changes is unclear or even nonexistent.[27] Implementation researchers have thus exhibited a desire to investigate just such programs as they understand beforehand have a good chance of failing.[28] Also this has imparted a cynical and increasingly conservative character to the genre.

Thirdly, implementation research has taken an excessively mechanistic and rationalistic view of the process of implementation. Within few, if indeed any, administratively complicated areas is the rate of success 100 percent, if success is measured by the accomplishment of original decisions and plans. The normal course of events is quite different: altered conditions necessitate adaptation, and experiences gained require the changing of plans. The handy notion that implementation should be analyzed "against the background of a static set of circumstances upon which programs can be imposed . . . fundamentally misconstrues the realities of implementation."[29]

The political system and the public sector are by no means alone in being obliged to accept that objectives can be multi-faceted and hedged with restrictions, and that original intentions cannot always be realized

[26] Elmore (1983), p. 213; cf. Therborn (1991).
[27] The classical example is Pressman & Wildavsky (1973). See also Elmore (1983).
[28] The comparative ambition has been limited, moreover. Very few studies have been done comparing programs which are similar in the difficulty of their implementation and dissimilar in the success of their results. For some exceptions, see Cerych & Sabatier (1986), Immergut (1993), Janoski (1990), and Rothstein (1996).
[29] Wittrock & de Leon (1985), p. 48.

fully. As Aaron Wildavsky has argued, most policy problems are seldom solved; they are only worked on.[30] This state of affairs, less than ideal though it be, should not always be taken as an argument for a conservative and pessimistic attitude towards public policy.[31] On the contrary, organizations capable of adapting to altered conditions, and leaders able to reformulate objectives in the light of experiences gained, are usually to be preferred to more rigid structures and less flexible leaders.[32] Indeed, the more insightful political decision-makers sometimes try to build such a capacity for change into the organizations they create.[33] In short, things do not always turn out they way we imagine, but they can turn out well even so. I do not by this mean to contest that many public programs must, upon closer inspection, be judged as failures; my purpose is simply to argue that the assessment of success and failure must be based on a broader view than that expressed in the mechanical comparison of original goals with achieved results.[34] Implementation research has often neglected the importance of structures capable of learning over time, of programs which must adapt to changes in the environment, of plans that must be changed, and of the sometimes great value even of results that fall short of 100 percent plan fulfillment.[35]

Furthermore, implementation researchers have often studied programs that have been operative only a short while, and so have tended to underestimate the possible long-term effects and to neglect the possibility that mistakes can be corrected.[36] For public policy involves coping with a changeable reality in accordance with certain general guidelines, not surgically designing an automatic process in which known inputs yield known outputs.[37]

Implementation research is found in two major methodological variants – "top down" and "bottom up." The former takes the democratically established goals of a program as the starting point of analysis, and seeks thereafter to analyze the significance of the implementation process – to see whether, and if so how, the political intentions and program goals are realized. The opposite – "bottom up" – perspective focuses on

[30] Wildavsky (1979)
[31] March & Olsen (1989), p. 58.
[32] Cf. Wildavsky (1979).
[33] Rothstein (1996).
[34] For a critique of the simple goal model in evaluation research, see Vedung (1991), ch. 3 and Fischer (1995).
[35] Palumbo (1987), p. 95.
[36] Goggin, Bowman, Lester & O'Toole (1990).
[37] For a critique of this mechanical view of politics and society, see Petersson (1989), chapters 2 and 3.

the doings of the field organization charged with implementing the program, and seeks to analyze the results without worrying overmuch about whether the program's democratically established goals have any importance for its operations.[38]

Debating which of these two methods is the better is largely a waste of time. Normative and theoretical disputes cannot be settled by discussing the choice of research method. From a theoretical standpoint, the "bottom up" approach has the advantage of being better able to take account of the uncertainty and need for organizational adaptation mentioned above. From a normative perspective, however, this approach is highly problematic, for researchers pursuing this line of inquiry often take what the existing administration *can* do – or, alternatively, what lies in its interests to do – as the point of departure for what it *should* do. The empirical analysis is thereby converted, on account of a methodological choice, into a normative point of departure, without the normative analysis ever being made explicit.[39] Certainly, the existing field organization within a given policy area has legitimate interests and knowledge, for which due consideration should be shown, but to make the local bureaucracy (or network of bureaucracies) into the sole bearer of policy legitimacy seems most unreasonable.[40]

Analyzing the implementation of public policy

Faced with the above-mentioned problems, implementation research has taken two major paths. The one, which stresses the difficulty of reaching generalizations, represents a development toward a line directed toward organizational consulting. Pragmatism is here set on a pedestal; researchers in this current devote their efforts to the formulation of sturdy and situationally suitable – if often trivial, in my view – advice for public policy practitioners. The other, current in implementation research, continues to strive for systematization and generalization on a more abstract level.[41] The latter approach is clearly the more fruitful if our

---

[38] For a discussion and attempt at synthesis, see Sannerstedt (1996) and Matland (1995).

[39] For a more detailed critique of this approach, see Linder & Peters (1990).

[40] The most serious deficiency of this analytical approach is "its failure to start from an explicit theory of the factors affecting its subject of interest. Because it relies heavily on the perceptions and activities of participants, it is their prisoner – and therefore is unlikely to analyze the factors *indirectly* affecting their behavior or even the factors directing affecting such behavior which the participants do not recognize," Sabatier (1986), p. 35; cf. Matland (1995).

[41] Lundquist (1986).

purpose is to investigate the conditions of successful policy implementation (successful in the sense of realizing the greater number of the intentions of the responsible politicians). What, then, does this research tell us? Here again we run up against problems. To begin with, it is not so easy to grasp which variables in this literature are the critical ones. One who has tried, Laurence O'Toole, writes:

> Researchers do not agree on the outlines of a theory of implementation, nor even on the variables crucial to implementation success. Researchers, for the most part implicitly, also disagree on what should constitute implementation success.[42]

The problems here are many. For one thing, the numerous case studies of individual programs have not been integrated into any sort of unitary theory.[43] Moreover, the strong orientation towards empirical studies – the charting of what happens (i.e., what goes wrong) when a program is instituted – has plainly been achieved at the price of theoretical elegance. Implementation research cannot compete with the mathematical precision of microeconomics or the formal elegance of game theory. As one of the pioneers in this field argues, this is because "the implementation questions are so complex and subtle that one hardly knows where to begin."[44] If decision-makers are waiting for a definitive answer to the question of how to implement public policy, they will have to wait longer still. The focus on producing an empirically solid product sets definite limits, and requires an intellectual discipline from which one is spared if one confines the search to the purer realm of economic models. That we cannot, on the basis of implementation research, offer cocksure answers to the question of "what the state can do" is not surprising, and it should not inspire in us an unduly pessimistic view of our enterprise. For the same applies within most other social scientific fields in which the object is *empirically* grounded knowledge of how people and resources should be organized in order to achieve desired results (especially when these people and resources must operate in a dynamic reality).[45]

---

[42] O'Toole, (1986); cf. Ingram (1990), p. 462: "the field of implementation has not yet achieved conceptual clarity."

[43] Palumbo (1987), Kelman (1984).   [44] Williams (1976), p. 536.

[45] One may compare here another complicated activity which states are in the habit of undertaking, namely military operations. A contemporary analyst has written as follows about the views of the hitherto unsurpassed German theorist of war, Carl von Clausewitz: "Clausewitz believed that although much could be learned from the systematic study of war, it would always be a highly unpredictable affair shaped by friction, uncertainty, and chance as well as by non-rational psychological, moral, and creative forces . . . The most elementary fact about war is that it cannot be governed by immutable laws." Handel (1989), p. 3.

A typical example is the management of commercial enterprises (i.e., the object of study in business economics); another is military strategy. Nothing can be found within either of these areas – which have been studied much more extensively than policy implementation has – which resembles certain knowledge of how to achieve good results (i.e., how to make profits or win wars).[46] As soon as we leave the world of purely theoretical models, the difficulties of generalizing increase enormously.[47] What distinguishes empirically oriented research from what we may term model research is *not* the desire to produce theoretical generalizations. The difference lies rather in the fact that the empirically oriented researcher cannot content himself with the analysis of such empirical evidence as he knows beforehand will verify his chosen model.[48] The object is instead to search for such empirical facts as will expose his model to the severest test, that is, empirical evidence for which the theory *must* account if it is to be of any worth.

What implementation research has yielded at best, in other words, is a set of empirical generalizations. Researchers have been able to observe that certain empirical phenomena are associated with successful implementation, but they do not really know why. Concretely, this has found expression in long check lists, that is, enumerations of factors which appear to be critical for successful implementation. I shall look more closely here at one such typical list, in which David Mazmanian and Paul Sabatier summarize their recommendations for how to design a public program so as to maximize its chances of being implemented successfully. The program should:

1 be clearly formulated and have a specified goal;
2 be based on an accurate theory of cause and effect;
3 give those charged with implementing it sufficient legal means for carrying it out;
4 be structured in such a manner that the target group can be expected to behave as intended;
5 be placed in the hands of a skillful and motivated organizational leadership;

---

[46] Williams (1989), p. 252; cf. van Creveld (1985), p. 261; and Handel (1989), pp. 3ff.
[47] Research on the implementation of public policy by means of massive public efforts has much to learn, in my view, from research on military strategy. How does one induce large, necessarily hierarchically organized units – which must operate in an exceedingly dynamic environment – to perform as desired?
[48] Pedersen (1977). Pedersen avers that this approach has been typical of Marxist-inspired research. For my part I believe this bad habit is more widespread, not least within traditional neoclassical economics.

6   have the support of organizations representing the target group;
7   enjoy the support of critical politicians and officials;
8   not conflict with other public programs;
9   not be carried out if the socio-economic preconditions are unfavorable;
10 be endowed with sufficient resources;
11 be entrusted to public organizations with a sympathetic attitude towards the program;
12 not be so formulated as to conflict with the courts.[49]

It is not clear what we should make of this and other similar check lists, in which implementation research abounds.[50] The above list says nothing, for example, about which factors are more important than others, and under what conditions, or which types of programs are harder to implement than others, and it does not say much about which organizational forms are suitable for which tasks.[51] Many of the factors seem so obvious as to be trivial. That programs which lack sufficient resources and support among politicians, officials, and target groups, which are blocked by other public programs, which lack a sufficient legal basis, and so on – that such programs will fail is scarcely a surprising notion.

Another question is in what degree these recommendations are absolute or relative. It has at times proved possible, for instance, to implement public programs in spite of strong opposition from the target group; other programs have proved practicable despite commanding insufficient resources, and so on. The problem, as I see it, is that implementation researchers usually have not raised their analysis to the level of more general categories. That is, they have not merely generalized on the basis of the empirical reality faced by policy practitioners (which of course must be done); they have also chosen to conduct their theoretical analysis on that level. Often, therefore, these researchers are unable to say anything of which policy practitioners are not already well aware.

Another critical question concerns the degree in which those involved in implementing public policy can influence the variables highlighted by

---

[49] Mazmanian & Sabatier (1983), pp. 41f. For a compilation of other similar check lists, see O'Toole (1986) who in his review of more than one hundred implementation studies found that together they refer to over three hundred key variables.

[50] The record-holder is probably Chase (1979), who lists no less than 44 different factors.

[51] Goggin, Bowman, Lester & O'Toole (1990).

implementation research. The more advanced attempts at generalizing about the difficulties of implementation emphasize the so-called "embeddedness" problem. This refers to the existence of complicated analytical hierarchies in public policy, so that what appears on one level to be a decisive factor in a program – for example, the knowledge and values of the field personnel – is embedded in larger social structures, and is therefore influenced by factors operating on deeper levels. According to this view, public policy is structured into various partially autonomous levels functioning as "limits within limits . . . the practices at the surface level follow a set of rules to that level and are limited by sets of rules at deeper levels."[52]

A crucial insight to be gleaned from this research is that many variables operative on the immediate policy level, which appear both critical and possible to influence, can be embedded in deeper structural conditions which limit what can be changed (within a reasonable length of time, at least, and with the use of limited resources). These deeper conditions may be of an ideological, social, geographical, organizational, or economic nature, and the prospects for changing them can vary substantially.

[52] Benson (1982), p. 149; cf. Lundquist (1987), ch. 2.

4

What can the state do? An analytical model

Viewed historically, there is no end to the things – for good and ill – that states have undertaken and succeeded in doing. States can obviously achieve (under favorable circumstances, at least) goals of the most varied kind. As mentioned earlier, implementation researchers have mainly produced long lists of factors associated with the successful implementation of public programs. In order to bring some clarity into this discussion, I shall make use of a simple analytical outline. The idea is to sort out the various factors on a general level. One reason for this approach is to facilitate an analysis of these issues in terms of principle (in a higher degree, at any rate, than has marked the production of those unsorted check lists). Another purpose of the outline is to assist in the formulation of a more general theory of policy implementation – of what, in other words, the state can and cannot do.

To begin with, we may distinguish among factors associated with implementation failure in the following manner: do the causes of failure lie (a) in the design of the program as such, or (b) in the stage of execution, that is, in the organization of the implementation process?[1] The basic idea is simple enough – that any program, however cleverly designed it may be, will fail if its implementation is entrusted to an organization unsuited to the purpose.

As Sören Winter points out, however, an unfortunate division of labor characterizes the field here:

---

[1] Mayntz (1975). This in itself correct but incomplete thesis is repeated in as good as every summary work within the genre. See, e.g., Ingram (1990).

71

Scholars specializing in policymaking and legislative processes have rarely shown an interest in what happens after the laws are passed, and scholars specializing in implementation and policy evaluation have typically restricted their interest to the implementation process.[2]

Policy analysts have traditionally considered it beyond their competence to question the objectives of public policy, and so have limited themselves to offering recommendations about the best methods of implementation. It is clear, however, that if we want to understand what the state can do, we must examine its capacity not only for rational implementation, but for rational decision-making as well.

To these two main areas of implementation research, therefore, I would like to add a third: the analysis of a policy's *political legitimacy*. It is scarcely possible to carry out a program successfully – however ingeniously designed it may be, and however well-organized its implementation – if it does not enjoy the confidence of the group towards which it is directed, or of the citizens at large. For example, many programs require the consent (or non-hostility, at least) of their target group in order to be implemented successfully.[3] Similarly, measures known to counteract or even to solve certain social problems may be considered too Draconian, integrity-violating, costly, unjust, or otherwise morally objectionable – and by so large a portion of the population – that they cannot be carried out, for the simple reason that the political support they enjoy is too slender.[4] The question of legitimacy is in this context highly related to the notion of trust in government institutions.[5]

These three areas – policy design, organization, and legitimacy – can each be divided, moreover, into questions of substance and of process. The former category has to do with the content of the program in question, the latter with its dynamic. Substantive problems concern such matters as how the goals of a program can be changed in response to the attempts of clients and officials to achieve (or obstruct, for that matter) its implementation. Problems of process concern such things as how different levels of the political system can be made to operate in concert, how centralized or decentralized a program should be, etc.[6]

All of these factors must be seen, moreover, in a dynamic perspective. What applied during period A need not apply during period B. A policy can only work under certain external conditions, and if these conditions change, the means requisite to achieving the objectives of the program change as well. Since the concrete form a program takes when it is

[2] Winter (1990), p. 24.   [3] Mazmanian & Sabatier (1983).
[4] Mayntz (1975).   [5] Luhmann (1979), p. 88.
[6] Palumbo & Calista (1990), pp. 12f.

	Substance	Process
Design	1.	2.
Organization	3.	4.
Legitimacy	5.	6.

Figure 4.1   Six major categories of factors affecting policy implementation

implemented reflects "the interaction of the program with its setting, we cannot anticipate the development of a simple or single retrospective theory of implementation."[7] External conditions (economic, social, political) naturally influence the prospects for implementing public measures. This point is trivial from the standpoint of theory, but it is highly significant in practice.[8]

Our model thus has six primary categories (see figure 4.1), which we shall examine in greater detail. Public policy can suffer, then, from shortcomings of many kinds. The purpose of our model is to categorize these failings. When the state cannot accomplish what it sets out to do, its incapacity may reflect deficiencies in policy design, organization, or legitimacy. Its failures in each of these areas, moreover, can be in either substance or process. In principle, there must be a "green light" in each of the six boxes for it to be possible to implement a program in accordance with the objectives motivating its creation. We shall examine each box below, in order more clearly to specify (with the aid of the existing research) what the state can and cannot do.

Knowing what you want: The substance of policy design (1)

The first major category concerns the manner in which a program is designed. I should first stress that this field is difficult to penetrate, both analytically and practically. Analytically, because the state of knowledge is unclear, above all when it comes to how to categorize different programs. Practically, because the various public measures involve many types of substantive knowledge, about which we, as students of implementation, may find it difficult to form a clear opinion. Even if fragments of knowledge exist about what causes, for example, youth criminality, pollution, unemployment, child abuse, drug dependency, inflation,

---

[7] Berman (1980), p. 207.   [8] O'Toole (1986), pp. 203f.

poverty, gender discrimination, etc., we know rather little about what measures can counteract or reduce these problems. Even if, in theory, solutions to such social problems might exist, it may for a variety of reasons (ethical, legal, political, economic) be impossible to apply them. Clearly, a program of fundamentally mistaken design cannot be implemented successfully, even if it is placed in the hands of a motivated, well-informed, and well-endowed organization.[9] (A program of mistaken design is one which, when executed faithfully according to plan, proves not to have the effects intended, or has such serious side-effects that it would be better to do nothing at all.)

It is said, among policy analysts, that a program's *causal theory*, or its *policy theory*, must be correct for its successful implementation to be possible.[10] Providing the unemployed, for example, with a type of training not demanded on the labor market would not seem to enhance their prospects for finding work, even if the training itself is of high quality.[11]

A program's design is clearly central to whether or not it achieves its purpose. Often, however, the discussion of this question takes a hyper-rationalist form, with researchers deploring the fact that the political process at times produces irrational results, such as unclear or contradictory (or even impossible) instructions to the public administration.[12] This problem reflects in part, however, the nature of the political process.[13] When powerful mass media focus on a certain problem, for instance, politicians may consider themselves forced to institute public remedies of some sort, even when there are no tested or even known solutions to the problem at hand. The result is "a tendency to throw intractable social problems at bureaucrats who become scapegoats when the problems are not solved."[14]

This may be why some programs exist whose value is purely symbolic, that is, programs in which most of those involved proceed on the assumption that the measures applied are not intended to have any other effect than showing that something is being done to remedy a widely felt

[9] Lundquist (1986), pp. 76f.
[10] Or as Winter (1990) writes, on p. 23: "irrespective of the commitment and resources of the agencies in charge of implementation, some policies are impossible to implement from the outset."
[11] Cf. Lundquist (1986), pp. 180f. We may also refer to this as the policy's validity.
[12] Nakamura & Smallwood (1980), pp. 34ff. This does not just apply to public organizations, however. Most organizations, actually, must work with conflicting objectives, cf. Ingraham (1987); Perrow (1986), p. 133; and March & Olsen (1986).
[13] And, I would add, in the nature of human action.
[14] Palumbo (1987), p. 95.

problem (although what is being done, and to what effect, may be less than clear).[15]

On the other hand, there are situations in which very strong moral reasons dictate that we take public measures, notwithstanding our insufficient knowledge of the relation between efforts and outcomes. Indeed, we may not even know what the outcomes are. Symbolic policies do not just have a supply side; they also have a demand side.[16] The growth in demands for state action to relieve social problems has not been matched by an equivalent increase in state capacity.

As mentioned earlier, implementation researchers recommend that policies have clear and precise objectives, and that those framing them have prior knowledge of the relation between efforts expended and results achieved. These scholars call for a "sound theory identifying the principal factors and causal linkages."[17] Nakamura and Smallwood, for example, maintain that:

> Both the goals of a policy and the means to achieve those goals must be stated in terms that are precise enough so that implementers know what they are supposed to do.[18]

This, however, is in many cases a completely unrealistic picture of what public policy is about. It assumes, moreover, a fundamentally misguided view of the relation between knowledge and political action. For it is often the case that the state must take measures even when certain knowledge is not to be had, either about the effects different measures will have, or about the conditions prevailing when the measures are applied. One classical area of state activity – military defense – may serve to illustrate this point. In this area, the empirical research speaks plainly for once (to put it mildly). A great many countries have invested in military programs which, in respect of both technology and strategy, have proved to be misguided. Furthermore, these programs have not been based on an accurate theory of the relation between resources invested and results achieved.[19] This is because, in military campaigns as in many

---

[15] Winter (1990), p. 25; cf. Lowi (1984).

[16] For a fascinating analysis of the "War on Poverty" as symbolic politics, see Zarefsky (1986).

[17] Mazmanian & Sabatier (1983), p. 41; cf. Hasenfeld & Brock (1991), p. 469f.; O'Toole (1986), p. 188; Ingram (1990), p. 466. Paul Sabatier has later agreed that "the emphasis . . . placed on 'clear and consistent policy objectives' was a mistake," Sabatier (1986), p. 29.

[18] Nakamura & Smallwood (1980), p. 33.

[19] The classical example is the behavior of the British Army on the Western front during the First World War. See, e.g., Cohen & Gooch (1990), pp. 12f.; and van Creveld (1985), pp. 166ff. As late as during the great August offensive of 1918,

other activities, it is always exceedingly difficult to predict the relation between efforts and outcomes. It is very hard to know, for instance, when the inputs are sufficient either quantitatively or qualitatively. This, in turn, is because one cannot determine the conditions under which the inputs come into use. The accelerating development of technology is just one of the factors contributing to uncertainty in this area, and to the consequent need for flexibility.[20] Another is the uncertainty characterizing the scenarios on which defense planning is based. As Regan put it, "the greatest problem which faces the military planners is to gain information from their political masters about the kind of war for which they should be preparing."[21]

Nevertheless, there are very few who would seriously wish to argue that the uncertain state of knowledge about the relation between efforts and results means we should not maintain a military defense, or that we should not try to organize it as rationally as possible in the light of the best available knowledge. In this sort of public undertaking, as in so many others, it is rather a question of framing public policy so that it can accommodate uncertainty and the need for flexible implementation. It is naive to think we can always decide our actions on the basis of prior and certain knowledge of what will work.[22] The only thing of which we can be wholly certain is that, if a military defense were organized according to the rationalistic principles of implementation research, it would either (a) not exist at all, or (b) be completely useless in the event of war, since it would lack the flexibility and capacity for handling uncertainty needed for success in military operations.[23]

This point – about the importance of appreciating the limits of our knowledge – can be applied to many areas of public policy.[24] We do not know with any certainty which measures will do the trick in prison

---

massive cavalry units made it impossible to bring tanks and artillery up to the front. The mental prison created by the belief in the possibility of "the great" cavalry breakthrough could only be broken by the one leading general who was *not* a professional soldier from the beginning, and who accordingly had not been completely indoctrinated in the traditional thinking of the general staff: the commander of the Australian forces, Sir John Monash. See Pedersen (1985) and Regan (1987), pp. 78ff., on the talent of hierarchical organizations for holding fast to traditional habits of thought.

[20] Handel (1989), pp. 51ff.; and Regan (1987), pp. 77f.

[21] Regan (1987), p. 78.   [22] March & Olsen (1989), pp. 57f.

[23] On p. 26, Cohen & Gooch (1990) point to three attributes of especial importance for the ability of military organizations to avoid the mishaps that can lead to catastrophe: the ability to adapt, to learn, and to foresee. Cf. Regan (1987), ch. 2.

[24] For an now classic work in organization theory which takes up this question, see March & Olsen (1986). See also Nakamura & Smallwood (1980), pp. 34ff.

policy, curative and social policy, health care, environmental policy, education, the combating of unemployment, or (to take a timely example) monetary policy.[25] And in such instances as our knowledge is reasonably reliable, it applies only in certain situations. The state of knowledge, moreover, is highly changeable: "In many fields . . . the pace of change is so rapid that a major theoretical work can become obsolete within a generation or a decade, and textbooks must be updated or replaced every few years."[26]

The notion common among implementation researchers – that public programs must be based, if they are to have any prospects of success, on an indubitable causal theory – is at best naive, and at worst downright dangerous.[27] This idea reflects, one might say, the Fordist assembly-line society (or the Soviet epoch of five-year plans), in which those highest up in the hierarchy always know what needs to be done and how, and the role of those executing the tasks is simply to follow the precise instructions laid down from on high. In the post-Fordist, post-Soviet information and knowledge society, however, this idea is completely obsolete. The rate of change in most areas is so rapid, and the need to adjust operations to a variable reality so great, that the prospects for possessing certain knowledge at the central level of what has to be done, and of passing this down to the local level in time, are extremely small.[28]

Can we find a reasonable basis, then, for classifying the various types of public program according to their difficulty of implementation? The answer is in part that given above: the greater the uncertainty that must be handled in the stage of execution, the greater the difficulty of implementation. A first distinction to be made concerns the nature of the operative conditions into which a given policy seeks to intervene. Such conditions can range from the altogether dynamic to the completely static. A moving object is harder to hit than a sitting duck. Striking the first target requires much greater adaptability. Put differently, the ques-

---

[25] On the uncertainty characterizing measures applied within health care, see Maynard (1993).

[26] Handel (1989), p. 53. This was also the problem that brought about the downfall of the centrally planned economy, see Nove (1983). Marxists with a predilection for central management of the economy would have done well, then, to look more closely at implementation research, cf. Rothstein (1992b).

[27] As organs for the implementation of public policy, military organizations are especially interesting in this context. They must, on the one hand, be hierarchically organized; on the other, they must operate under extremely dynamic conditions, and must cope with very rapid technological change. Among the works inspiring this section, besides von Clausewitz (1836/1984), are Handel (1989), Aron (1983), and Howard (1983).

[28] Lidström (1991), p. 11.

tion is whether public policy must be adjusted to the unique circumstances of each case, or whether more general and standardized measures will do the trick.

The second dimension has to do with the degree to which a policy is intended to influence social conditions, that is, how directly or indirectly the state wishes to intervene.[29] It is one thing to establish a system of rules setting the framework within which individuals or organizations in civil society can act as they will. Examples may be seen in civil law and marriage legislation. Such areas are characterized by reflexive legal "systems which are both self-regulating and independent."[30] This is distinct from formal law (which states what private actors may and may not do) and material legal rules (which specify what individuals can demand of the state, and what the state can demand of them).[31] Civil law does not regulate which goods and services shall be exchanged, and marriage legislation does not contain much in the way of specifications as to who shall marry whom, or of what shall take place upon the union's consummation. In such matters the state does not meddle (within very broad limits); however, certain precise rules for the framing of contracts apply.[32] Some instruments of overarching economic management, such as taxation and general benefits, belong in this category as well. Let us refer, for the sake of simplicity, to policies of this type as *regulatory*.

It is another matter when the state, through its own organizations, tries to influence citizens' behavior (especially when the purpose is to do so in a thoroughgoing fashion). This applies to so-called "human processing" activities of all kinds, that is, those taking place in schools, social agencies, prisons, alcoholic-treatment centers, labor exchanges, and so on. We may call such policies *interventionist*. In figure 4.2, I have cross-tabulated these dimensions, and classified different types of public policy accordingly.[33] Which types of program are the hardest to implement, then, and which are the easiest? Here we can draw an inverse benefit from the proclivity of implementation researchers towards misery research, that is, their inclination to search out the most problematic cases. There appears to be rather wide agreement that the most complicated programs to implement are those that might be described as *dynamically interventionist*, while it is much easier to carry out programs aimed at regulating static conditions.[34] Examples of the former include

---

[29] On pp. 148f., Lundquist (1986) distinguishes four dimensions: (a) targeted/non-targeted, (b) direct/indirect, (c) specific/general, and (d) precise/imprecise.
[30] Hydén (1988), p. 145.   [31] Ibid.   [32] Esping (1994), p. 372.
[33] This section builds in large part on Ripley & Franklin (1982), who in turn are inspired by Lowi (1972).
[34] Seidman (1983).

Operative conditions

	Static	Dynamic
Regulatory	Universal child allowances Flat-rate basic pensions	Civil law
Interventionist	Means-tested housing allowances	Curative social care Active labour market policy

Type of measure

Figure 4.2   Dimensions of public policy

labor-market policies for increasing employment among those with low qualifications, housing policies for providing the homeless or socially maladjusted with housing, educational policies seeking to ensure that advancement within the educational system is more equally distributed between socio-economic groups, and social policies that apply directly curative measures.[35] Three features are common to programs of this type: (a) they seek in various ways to influence citizens' behavior in a dynamic process, (b) the state of knowledge about what works is uncertain, and (c) the variations out in the field are great.[36]

Adapting public measures to shifts of a general but temporary nature (e.g., swings in the business cycle) presents difficulties for two reasons. To begin with, it is no simple matter to build an effective system of management into the public administration. Getting public organizations to adjust their operations to shifting circumstances *in the right way* is notoriously complicated.[37] In contrast to companies operating in an ideal market, for instance, the typical public-administrative organ does not immediately feel the impact of a diminishing demand for its product, for that demand is usually politically determined. In addition, there is often a certain value – not least from a constitutionalist standpoint – in the fact that the public administration is a relatively stable organization at a

[35] Elmore (1978). One can also reach this conclusion simply by studying what kinds of programs implementation researchers have concentrated on. Cf. O'Toole (1986) and Matland (1995).

[36] Wolman (1980), p. 437.

[37] See Rothstein (1996), ch. 3, and literature cited therein.

certain distance from the legislating power.[38] To take a classic case: courts should not, for a variety of reasons, be subject to political influence. They must be able, that is, to withstand the wishes of parliamentary majorities – especially when rapid social or political changes are in progress – to impose immediate changes in the pattern of juridical judgment.

Thirdly, the parliamentary system of decision-making is, owing to its inherent logic, rather sluggish in sending signals to the public administration. In normal cases, for instance, the legislative assembly makes decisions of principle for each policy area once a year. Changes may occur a great deal more rapidly than that in a given policy sector. And thousands of decisions – each one covering an individual case – may have to be made. This point is cogently expressed in a now classic formulation of Charles Lindblom: the state has "strong thumbs, no fingers."[39]

The problem of adapting the operations of public programs to individual cases brings us to one of the few fairly well-researched questions within implementation research, namely the problem of "street-level bureaucracy." According to a prominent theory about this phenomenon, the character of measures taken within dynamically interventionist areas is decided, in actual fact, by the operative field personnel. This is because it is impossible, on account of the factors of uncertainty mentioned above, for central political organs to prescribe in detail all of the disparate measures which must be taken in each of the various cases to be handled. Accordingly, the operative staff who work face-to-face with the clients – teachers, health staff, social workers, police, etc. – must be granted a relatively wide freedom of action, for it is they who must choose exactly which measures to apply in the individual case.[40] They must, that is, be granted the right to judge, independently, and on their own responsibility, which measures are appropriate in a given situation. It is the sum of their actions which constitutes the public program. As to whether these actions reflect the objectives laid down by the democratically constituted organs – this must be regarded as an open question.[41]

Accordingly, many decisions of very great import for individual citizens are made by local public organs and individual officials.[42] What we might call a *black hole of democracy* appears here, that is, it can be difficult (well-nigh impossible, in fact) to hold the administrators and officials who decide about the welfare of citizens in any way responsible for their actions.[43] The elected politicians thus have but limited influence

---

[38] Cf. Algotsson (1993), ch. 1.   [39] Lindblom (1977), p. 65.
[40] Adler & Asquith (1981).   [41] The seminal work is Lipsky (1980).
[42] Cf. Elster (1992).
[43] For an overview of these problems of management, see Lindensjö 1987. Cf. also Åström (1988).

over the actual substance of public policy – or, expressed more directly, over what the state in these cases actually does with the citizens. For the operative personnel must be granted the prerogative of assessing the constantly changing situations *in their context*, and of taking measures in accordance with this assessment. This places heavy demands on (a) the organization of the program in question, and (b) the legitimacy of the measures taken.

In contrast to a static regulatory policy, dynamic interventionism is problematic, in view of the institutional forms on which democracy has been built. It is relatively easy, for example, to change the sums mailed out by the universal flat-rate pension scheme; all that is needed by and large are some new instructions to the central computer at the National Social Insurance Board. It is a great deal harder to change the attitudes and behavior of field staff like teachers, social workers, and police officers.[44] Even in cases where this is possible, we need to know whether the policy change will have the desired effect among the members of the target group, and if so how. The length of the chain of command – from central politicians to top officials to mid-level administrators to field staff and then finally down to the citizens – makes the whole affair exceedingly complex.[45]

I shall illustrate this with a typical case of what I have termed static regulation, namely universal child allowances. The problem with this and similar benefits is that, on one level, they meet the needs of citizens rather badly. Simply put, the poor get too little and the rich get too much. In ballistic terms, one could say this is like aiming at the widest possible target – trying, that is, to hit everyone equally. It would be better, from the standpoint of needs, to adjust child allowances continually to the shifting and varying economic circumstances of families. One could, in theory, calibrate the system so finely that each family is visited every month by a social worker, who reviews the household's economic situation together with the family, and thereafter writes out a check for the appropriate sum. Such a finely calibrated system, the purpose of which is to target benefits with maximum precision, is certainly possible.[46] The price of achieving such precision, however, would be very high. Firstly, because it would require a great number of social workers; secondly, because encroachments into citizens' private lives would become severe; and thirdly, because real power in such a system would gather into the hands of officials (for the concrete decisions taken in each individual case would depend on their judgments).

---

[44] Zald (1981).   [45] Lundquist (1986); cf. Lindensjö (1987).
[46] It depends on how the implementation process is organized.

It would of course be satisfying simply to conclude that states should not busy themselves with policies of a dynamically interventionist type, for it would seem they lack the capacity to carry out such policies successfully. This recommendation cannot be generally applied, however; reality is not so simple and well-ordered. To begin with, many studies show that states do, in actual fact, have the capacity to implement policies of a dynamically interventionist kind. States can very well – under certain circumstances, at least – carry out this type of task. Below we shall see the conditions under which this can be done.[47] In addition, however, it is simply impossible politically to let things be. If, for example, we want society to take measures against the gross maltreatment of children, to ensure care and employment to the handicapped, to offer rehabilitation to those struck by industrial injury, to conduct an active labor-market policy, or to employ a police force for the maintenance of order, then it is quite simply impossible to do without public programs of this sort. The lesson to be learned is rather that, if measures of this type are to work, policy-makers must understand that they place stiff demands on the organization of the public administration and on the legitimacy of the measures applied.[48]

Being clear: The process of policy design (2)

One factor implementation researchers often stress in connection with public programs has to do with the impact of political conflicts over their design. The establishment of welfare programs can sometimes be a conflictual process. The difficulties involved are many. One such problem is that, in order to surmount the political conflicts mentioned, politicians often enter into compromises – which can have the effect of rendering the programs' overall objectives unclear. The different political groups try, in such compromises, to get their own favored formulations written into the text of the law. The outcome is sometimes a text whose substance cannot be penetrated by the most subtle content analysis. The result is that

> The implementation of the compromise policy has to satisfy all the conflicting interests, and they in turn are expected to fulfill the commitments they made in the process of bargaining which led to the statement of the policy. But this means translating ambiguous words and symbols into unambiguous, or at least less ambiguous, reality. In addition to operational requirements for greater precision, those directly affected by a policy may want the rules about its applications set out in a detailed

---

[47] The classical study in this area is Kaufman (1960).
[48] Lundquist (1986), p. 188.

language in order to limit the discretion of staff at the working level who may have quite different values . . . It seems almost inevitable that some of those concerned will end up disappointed or discontented.[49]

The political language in such settings has its own inherent logic, which is manifested in a generalized use of terms with a positive ring but an ambiguous meaning.[50] The need or desire to reach consensus can thus lead to the result that program objectives are expressed in terms which are not just unclear, but even contradictory.

The vagueness often characterizing those sections of legal texts devoted to explaining policy objectives is thus no accident. For the political process has some aspects which encourage this vagueness.[51] By contrast, a system of management by precise rules is marked by greater clarity: political decisions are directly linked to a duty on the state's part to undertake specific measures (such as, say, increasing pensions by a certain sum). The link between decisions of this type and the preconditions for their implementation (i.e., their financing) is plain. This, we may assume, helps to discipline the process of public decision-making. By contrast, political decisions over policy goals have the opposite character; they are not tied, that is, to any immediate duty on the part of the state to do certain specific things. Legislators tend therefore to write exceedingly ambitious aims into the text of the law – at times, in fact, on so high a level of abstraction that it is well-nigh impossible to evaluate them.[52] It is, so to speak, free of charge for politicians to be generous to a fault when it comes to the general goals of public policy, as long as such goals remain general in nature.

Needless to say, the point of the above reasoning is not to recommend abstinence from political compromise. Compromise is both unavoidable and necessary in parliamentary politics; to complain about it, as many implementation researchers do, is more than permissibly naive. We are faced here, rather, with a generally neglected connection to the matters discussed above.

For programs which are dynamically interventionist in nature, and which involve precise targeting therefore, must necessarily be framed in an imprecise manner. This paradox – that precise implementation requires imprecise instructions – is a consequence of how parliamentary organs work. It inheres, one might say, in the logic of legislation. Precise

---

[49] Lewis (1984), p. 211.

[50] As Lewis writes: "There is a prudent wish to avoid precise statements which would carry the risk that a policy could be incontrovertibly judged a failure," ibid., p. 208.

[51] Cf. Ahlbäck (1995).   [52] Cf. Åström (1988), pp. 81ff.

implementation requires, that is, that the field personnel can adjust the
operative measures to the nature of the concrete situation. The latter is
complex and changeable, and there is no way of foreseeing all the
variables of which the field staff must take account when making their
decisions, or of specifying them in the legislation. If those framing the law
try to do so nevertheless, the result is a piece of legislation so complicated
as to be impossible to understand or to apply. Achieving precise targeting
therefore requires that we settle for the abstract aims laid down in so-
called framework laws.[53] This is not a novel insight, of course. Aristotle
himself observed that written laws cannot be applied precisely in every
situation, since the legislators, "being unable to define for all cases . . . are
obliged to make universal statements, which are not applicable to all but
only to most cases."[54]

Here is yet another interesting paradox. Management by rules can be
seen as a result of demands that political power be exercised in keeping
with constitutional norms. The exercise of power must, according to the
principles of constitutionalism, be subjected to codified legal rules which
make it possible for citizens to foresee the effects of their dealings with
the state. This can, however – in the case of dynamic interventionism
most especially – lead to rules of such complexity and impenetrability
that the result is in fact exactly the opposite, that is, uncertainty over
which rules apply and which do not.[55]

An example of this may be seen in the fate of the unique Swedish
arrangement for rationing alcoholic beverages – known as the liquor
ration-book system – which was in force from the 1910s until 1954.[56] The
idea behind the system of liquor ration-books was by no means to set a
uniform maximum ration for every well-behaved Swedish adult; the aim
was rather to sell to each individual citizen the precise amount of the
intoxicating substance that he could be expected to handle in a socially
acceptable fashion. The need for precise targeting was therefore very
great. The provisions issued by Parliament about who would be allowed
to purchase how much alcohol, on the other hand, were extremely vague.
The law stated simply that "all selling of wines and spirits shall be so
ordered as to bring about the minimum possible damage." The system
presupposed that the operative rules for achieving this objective would be
worked out in the stage of implementation; not surprisingly, then, the
system grew into an enormously complicated affair. The result, in the

---

[53] I have described this in Rothstein (1992a), especially in ch. 3 and on pp.
150–153, 168, 190–192, and 281–283.
[54] Quoted in Brand (1988), p. 46.
[55] See Algotsson (1993), pp. 17ff, cf. Goodin 1982.
[56] This section builds on Rothstein (1992a), ch. 7.

view of critics, was a policy marked by unpredictability, arbitrariness, and disregard for such central legal norms as the primacy of individual rights and the principle that the law is to be no respector of persons. Authority in this system was highly decentralized, which meant concretely that the directors of the local liquor monopolies exercised autocratic power. A Byzantine system of rules was developed, including many questionable details which local authorities often exploited. To such criticism, however, a commission appointed in 1934 to investigate the system replied that:

> A fairly complete codification of the grounds for refusing the right of purchase would thus have made for a very heavy legal text. Nor would it achieve the desired result to incorporate such detailed rules into the directive. It would, undoubtedly, be impossible to specify all circumstances and viewpoints to be considered in the examination, and the directive's enumeration of these would therefore need to be complemented with a rule of a more general – and therefore in some measure less determinate – character. The purpose of such a solution – to state in the directive itself all cases in which the measures in question are to be taken – would therefore not be achieved.[57]

Sure enough, the liquor ration-book system broke down in the early 1950s, in part because the demands it posed for precise implementation could not be met. It just was not possible to gather enough information about individuals as to make an informed judgment possible about how much liquor they were capable of consuming in a responsible manner.[58] My point here is that the need for precise targeting in the stage of implementation leads necessarily to the consequence that the law must be framed in an imprecise and general manner. This leads to (a) diminished clarity about the program's operative goals, and (b) an increased risk that political conflicts surrounding the program will issue in compromise formulations of program objectives which are so unclear or contradictory that they cannot be reconstructed on logical grounds, that is, cannot be converted into functioning operative recommendations for action on the part of the field staff. The logic of this paradoxical situation is that the will to be precise in targeting in the process of implementation will lead to extreme decentralization and the use of framework laws, which in its turn will result in a lack of clarity about the central goals of the program.

---

[57] SOU (1934: 39), p. 149.
[58] Studies showed that among those taken into custody for public drunkenness was a large group who had been granted the maximum allotment, and an equally large group which had been shut out altogether, i.e., those who had succeeded in coming by alcohol despite being granted no rations at all.

By contrast, political compromises in which broad targeting is accepted from the outset facilitate precision, and afford therefore no problems of implementation on this point.[59] Examples include the size of the general child allowance, or the amount of alcohol all citizens are entitled to buy. These can be specified precisely (in crowns and centiliters, respectively). This yields, then, another argument for accepting wherever possible broad targeting in the design of public programs. It is also an argument against the idea of *political perfectionism,* an idea that has permeated many Swedish policies ever since the days of the liquor ration-books, and on up to the current Law on Social Services. The conclusion here as earlier is that strong arguments favor an *anti-perfectionist* public policy – that it is better, in other words, to be vaguely right than precisely wrong. The conclusion we came to in chapter 2 about what the state should do finds strong support on this point.

A further problem is that political systems embrace many different levels – local, regional, and central (and, perhaps I should add, suprana-tional) – and that a program's successful implementation often requires that measures be taken on several of these. If sharp political antagonisms exist, and if the implementation of a program requires that action be taken on different levels, then difficulties may arise, for the political majorities on the various levels may differ.[60] Such problems clearly increase in severity, moreover, the greater the need is for precise targeting, since the higher the degree of uncertainty, the more authorities on the local level must be allowed a wide freedom of action. Officials on the local level might then use this freedom of action in such a way as to impart another character to a given policy than that which had been intended. Or they might even block the policy.[61] This is in itself no argument against decentralization, but rather against allowing political responsi-bility and power over implementation to be lodged on different levels. For problems easily arise when the central level takes political *responsi-bility* for carrying out a program, but delegates *power* over its implemen-tation to local political organs.

Since implementation research has been conducted to a great extent in countries with federal systems of government (such as the United States and the former West Germany), this problem has received a great deal of attention. That the courts, moreover, play an important role in political decisions over public programs in these countries (the United States especially) complicates the picture further. In any case, we can say as a general matter that a distribution of power in which political responsi-

---

[59] Cf. Goodin 1982.   [60] Sharpe (1986).   [61] Ibid., p. 176.

bility and power drift apart from one another does not promote successful implementation.[62]

If one regards welfare policy as linked to national citizenship, it is natural to take the view that public policy should not allow great variations in the treatment accorded to citizens just because they reside in different regions. The state may decentralize the implementation of welfare programs to regional or local authorities, but surely the reason for this is to facilitate the adjustment of such programs to local conditions, and to achieve broader political participation. The point cannot be that citizens' rights to "equal concern and respect" and equal "basic capabilities" should vary according to where in the country they reside.

On the art of organizing (3)

In the study of organizations, two quite different schools may be found. The one, based on neoclassical economics, views the firm as a system of incentives. The critical task, according this theory, is for the "principal" to create an economic structure that rewards self-interested "agents" who fulfill the goals of the organization. In other words, it is the incentive structure that is the most important factor in steering the organization. The other school, which consists of behavioral scientists, instead sees the organizations as a common culture held together by strong social norms about motivation, work and professional ethics. Accordingly, the task of management is therefore to inspire individuals to share the goals of the organization, and to cooperate of their own accord to attain them.[63]

These two schools have not, up to now, had anything to say to each other. The "hard" economists, with their mathematical models, have regarded the "soft" behavioral scientists – whose studies are often based on participant observation or archive materials – as anachronistic "storytellers." Amusing and anecdotal perhaps, but hardly scientific. Behavioral scientists, on the other hand, have viewed the economic way of analyzing organizations as a meaningless search for law-like regularities in an unpredictable and changeable world, and have in some cases regarded neoclassical economics' underlying assumptions as a threat to the very normative values which make the organization (seen as a collective project) possible at all.

In his book *Managerial Dilemmas*, Gary Miller has sought to build a

---

[62] See Wolman (1980) and Palumbo (1987).
[63] Compare the discussion of "the logic of exchange" versus "the logic of appropriateness" in March & Olsen (1989).

bridge between these two worlds.[64] His point of departure and analysis are certainly in neoclassical economics, yet he succeeds in demonstrating that designing the "right" structure of incentives is a fundamentally hopeless enterprise. This is because of a number of "impossibility theorems" – taken from rationalistic economic theory itself – which demonstrate that no incentive structure can be designed that is capable of inducing actors within a company to cooperate and to work efficiently in the company's best interests. The reason is, simply put, that in order to design the "right" incentives, the "principals" need information about the work process from the "agents". However, if the "agents", according to the theory, are self-interested utility maximizers, they will never reveal this type of critical information because they have good reasons to believe that the "principals" will use it against them. Following the standard logic of game theory, there is simply no reason for rational, self-interested individuals to act cooperatively in the pursuit of common objectives, for the goods produced by such cooperation are collective in nature. With the wrong type of information about agents' genuine preferences, the "principals" are likely to design the wrong type of institutions, thereby creating pathological dilemmas of collective action. In such a situation it will always be worthwhile for a sufficient number of self-interested actors to see only to their own objectives rather than the organization's, and to reduce efficiency thereby.[65]

According to Miller, the great risk for opportunistic behavior and non-cooperation within organizations imparts an altogether fundamental role to management – that of creating trust among employees and between departments. Morally based personal leadership and cooperation-oriented organizational culture are crucial factors for overcoming the problem of collective action in companies competing on the market as well as in government organizations. A strategy based entirely on economic incentives is doomed to failure, according to Miller; indeed, he goes so far as to claim that those companies which succeed in creating a climate of cooperation between employees and management will always enjoy a comparative advantage over those which fail so to do. Miller thus starts out in "hard" economic theory, and proceeds from there right into the domain of "soft" behavioral science. One could say that he takes a

---

[64] G. Miller (1992), cf. Wolf (1993) and Kreps (1990).

[65] The neoclassical position is not strengthened by the claim that cooperative action can be explained by the previous existence of cultural, social, or political bonds. Such bonds, it is thought, would increase each actor's confidence that others will cooperate. The formation of such a norm is, according to Robert Bates, "subject to the very incentive problem it is supposed to solve" (Bates 1988: 395, cf. Scharpf 1990: 477ff).

very long (and very interesting) detour on the way towards discovering the economic importance of norms and professional ethics. The message to the "principals" is very clear, they should seek to induce "agents" to disregard their own short-term self-interest, and to take responsibility for the entire organization As Miller himself points out, such conclusions will seem nonsensical to economists in the neoclassical tradition. Yet this is exactly where we end up if we begin from their starting point.

A great many of the recommendations offered by implementation researchers about how to organize the implementation process have to do with the significance of resources and motivated and capable staff, and with the importance of continuously evaluating the implementing organization. For there is naturally no end to what can go wrong, organizationally speaking, when carrying out complicated programs.

Above and beyond these rather obvious points, however, implementation researchers have discovered little else. They do not know which organizational structures are generally best for implementing public policy. Now this is not really so strange, for the simple reason that the suitability of a given organizational type depends intimately on the character of the task to be performed. Since public programs vary greatly in the degree of uncertainty they must handle, there is no single best type of organization and no single best type of incentive structure. The organizational needs involved in handing out general insurance payments differ fundamentally from those involved in supplying preventive health care. This point is important and bears remembering, for a widespread notion has it that the public administration is a monolithic organization, and that uniform models suffice for analyzing it. Traditional theories in this field have generally emphasized the uniform structure of the public administration.[66]

Such an approach does not accord, however, with the findings of the empirical research. It is not so surprising, perhaps, that the nature of the system of management is dependent on the character of the tasks facing the administration and the degree of uncertainty to be handled. The research shows that fundamentally distinct organizational types exist within different parts of the public administration;[67] that the staff within different administrative branches hold fundamentally differing views of their task, and of the relation between politics and administration besides;[68] that fundamentally different organizational cultures may even be found within different units of the same administrative area;[69] and, finally, that similar countries applying one and the same strategy of

[66] See, e.g., Birgersson & Westerståhl (1985). [67] Rothstein (1996).
[68] Norell (1989). [69] Grosin (1992).

reform in a given administrative sector may end up with wholly dissimilar results.[70]

If we want to know which organizational form is best, then, we must consult the *IDO-theory* ("It Depends On").[71] Two main factors, in general, must be considered – the type of *task* the organization must carry out, and the type of technique it has to employ.[72] In either case, it is a question of how much *uncertainty, friction,* and *chance* the organization must cope with in the process of implementation.

I have no ambition here of being definitive (this area is enormously complex), yet I would like to elaborate on these factors with the aid of two simple distinctions. To begin with, the *tasks* facing the administration can be uniform or varied. To what extent, that is, do the measures need to be adjusted to individual cases? Put another way, does implementing the program require a high degree of situational adjustment, or can it be routinized?[73] In regard to the type of technique, on the other hand, the question is whether standardized action repertoires are available for dealing with the various situations that can arise, or whether the state of knowledge is instead more uncertain (so that the implementing organization must seek new knowledge and solutions in each new case).[74] I have cross-tabulated these dimensions in figure 4.3, and placed ideal-typical forms of organization in each of the resulting squares. *Bureaucratic* organizations[75] function tolerably well when the tasks are uniform and the technique can be standardized. Precise rules (and maybe even correct incentive structures) can thereby be used in managing the organization. Population registration, land surveying, and driver's license registration may serve as examples. The state is generally very good at this sort of infrastructural task. The political authorities, moreover, can direct activities of this kind quite effectively, since they apply standardized techniques and are enjoined with the performance of relatively simple tasks.

In areas in which many different kinds of cases must be dealt with, and

---

[70] Lindbom (1995).

[71] Within organization theory, this goes under the name of "contingency theory." See the nearest textbook in business economics or organization theory – e.g. Aldrich (1979), p. 57.

[72] "in effective organizations, structure reflects technology," write Gortner, Mahler and Nicholson (1987), p. 113.

[73] Cf. Perrow (1986), p. 150.

[74] This section builds on Perrow (1986); cf. Demchak (1991), especially ch. 4.

[75] I do not use the term "bureaucracy" here in any derogatory sense. It is, rather, a neutral concept denoting a particular organizational form, the major ingredients of which are, on the one hand, hierarchy, and on the other, management on the basis of precise, explicit, and codified rules applied by neutral and impartial officials.

Tasks

		Uniform	Varied
Technique	*Standardized*	Bureaucratic organization	Professional organization
	Non-standardized	Cadre or management organization	Knowledge/ investigatory organization

Figure 4.3   Tasks and technique for each organizational form

in which it is therefore difficult to apply precise rules, specialized *professional* knowledge may be required. When the type of task to be performed is plain, qualified professionals are charged with choosing the most suitable technique. Health care is perhaps the best example of this kind of activity. From a managerial standpoint, professionalism entails both advantage and drawbacks.

When the tasks to be executed are fairly uniform but the choice of technique is difficult to judge, cadre or management organizations are the most fitting. In such areas, a type of organization is needed which is more sensitive to changes in technique than professional organizations generally are. Cadre organizations (also known, in organization theory, as clan organizations) are highly sensitive to changing wishes on the part of their leaders, and are able rapidly to change their measures accordingly. Besides being responsive to changing signals from the top, moreover, management organizations are skilled at adjusting their operations to changes in technique. They are, in other words, that type of public organization which most closely resembles private companies.

Finally, if the tasks are variable and the technique cannot be standardized, then organizations are needed which are both willing to search for new knowledge and able to adapt this knowledge to a complex reality. This demands a high degree of organizational *autonomy*. This does not mean such organizations are wholly independent – only that, when they carry out their public charges, they do so on their own responsibility, and in an uncertain terrain. In exchange, they agree to submit their efforts to retrospective evaluation. The last-mentioned hurdle is doubtless the most difficult.

If one were to extrapolate from such tendencies as are observable at present, the conclusion would be this: with the rapid development of knowledge and technology in many areas, organizations capable of learning new things and of adapting this knowledge to changing conditions – that is, those located in the lower right-hand box of the table above – assume increasing importance.[76] This applies to professional organizations as well, for the knowledge on which they are based is changing ever more rapidly (which makes it harder to standardize the techniques they employ). One critical question is whether it is possible to build a capacity for learning into administrative organizations, while remaining faithful at the same time to the idea that their activities should stand under democratic control. Is it possible, in fact, to manage a program effectively while lacking information either about the state of knowledge in the field or about the conditions under which this knowledge is applied? I shall return to this question in chapter 8.

It would take us too far afield to examine in detail the advantages and drawbacks of these various organizational forms for the conduct of different public activities, and in any case it is not necessary here.[77] The purpose is rather to illustrate the IDO-theory, that is, that there is not *one* best way of organizing public programs (and thus no single way of reforming them either). The lesson to be learned is that using an inappropriate organizational form often leads to failure in the stage of implementation.

Forms of organization are like tools – they are only suitable for the performance of certain definite tasks. Arguing that a decentralized form of organization is in all cases right and fitting makes as little sense as arguing that management by goals is always to be preferred to management by rules.[78] *It depends on* the nature of the task, and on the prospects for standardizing the technique applied. It is undeniably possible to employ a decentralized system of management by goals which, as an example, could be phrased as "the citizen is entitled to obtain a passport in such cases as his journey abroad can be seen as generally beneficial to society, or in other ways of advantage to his well-being." But it may not be altogether desirable. On the other hand, a centralized system of management by rules can be an enormous obstacle to implementing programs successfully in areas characterized by great uncertainty.[79]

---

[76] Cf. Petersson (1989), pp. 53ff.

[77] See Rothstein (1996), ch. 3. A useful book on organization theory employing a similar approach is Mintzberg (1979).

[78] For a critique of management by goals, see Rombach (1991).

[79] A classic example is the exceedingly strict and centralized planning used by the Fourth British Army Corps under Rawlinson's command in the Battle of the Somme in 1916. The subordinate units could not, as a consequence of this rigid planning, exploit the few strategically important openings at the front that presented themselves following the first wave of attack. The result was one of the greatest military catastrophes of modern times. Defeat was already guaranteed in the planning stage. See van Creveld (1985).

Organization as process (4)

What problems of organization are involved in the implementation process, then, and what do implementation researchers recommend should be done about them? Since the duties of the state are not uniform – and since its component agencies therefore cannot be uniform either – I must restrict my focus here to a series of problems to which implementation researchers have repeatedly called attention (but the generality of which one must nevertheless question).

The general problem stressed by implementation researchers may be referred to as *responsibility drift,* and it applies on both the organizational and individual levels. By responsibility drift is meant a situation in which *power and influence* over a decision (or non-decision), and the political-administrative *responsibility* for carrying it out, are allowed to drift apart.[80] In an ideal democracy, these things are collected in the hands of one individual or organization. It is obviously tempting, however, to try to exercise power without taking full responsibility, politically or administratively, for the result.[81] This is the problem I earlier termed *democracy's black hole,* that is, that decisions about citizens' welfare are made in a vacuum of responsibility.

To begin with the organizational level: the traditional idea that the implementation of public measures can be assigned to a single public organization, which can be held responsible if something goes wrong, seems to have rather little to do with reality. Rather, it is nearly always the case – particularly when it comes to dynamically interventionist programs – that a number of different organizations are involved in the implementation process at the same time. These organizations can, moreover, be public or private (or intermediate or mixed) in nature. Organizations may also differ in type and approach despite all being formally public; they can, for example, be juridical or administrative in character. In addition, implementation often involves common efforts by central, regional, and local levels of government, which can create complications, inasmuch as the means by which the political leadership is held responsible (i.e., general elections) takes place at different levels of the political system.[82] It is common, finally, that implementation requires collaboration between organizations (private, non-profit, public) in which ultimate power rests in the hands of very different kinds of actors. The authority relations here can be extremely complicated.[83]

---

[80] Scharpf (1988); cf. Young (1981) and Hill (1972), p. 62.
[81] Hanf & Scharpf (1978).   [82] Scharpf (1988).
[83] Lundquist (1986) discusses this in connection with the structure/actor problem,

Public programs do not usually involve, then, a two-dimensional relation between the state and the citizen, but rather a three-dimensional relation between the state, the producer, and the citizen. The producer may be a municipal organization, a private organization, a local arm of the state, a central civil service department, an interest organization, a foundation, or a combination of all of these. Public policy is in fact seldom carried out by the state, but rather by partially autonomous institutions. Formally, of course, the latter are enjoined to act according to goals and directives laid down by the former; they enjoy, however, a not insignificant freedom of action when it comes to the actual shaping of policy.[84] The significance of this, as Jon Elster puts it, is that:

> The life chances of the citizen in modern societies do not depend exclusively on market choices or governmental decisions. To an increasing extent, they also depend on allocations made by relatively autonomous institutions, beginning with admission or non-admission to nursing schools and ending with admission or non-admission to nursing homes.[85]

It is therefore appropriate, when it comes to this aspect of welfare policy, to define *the state* in a rather narrow sense, roughly equivalent to what are usually called the state authorities (the government and the central state agencies). What *the state can do* is thus often a question of how well it can coordinate or direct these relatively autonomous producing institutions, and regulate their dealings with the citizens.[86]

This also tells us that the simple distinction between market and state does not suffice for analyzing these problems. The traditional picture of a public program is one in which production (staff and organization), resources, and priorities are hierarchically determined by politicians and the public officials subordinate to them. The problem with this picture is that political leadership can be exercised here in many different ways, for example, solely by means of regulation, or by directing economic resources to private producers.[87] Policy is often implemented by more or less autonomous institutions which are dependent on state direction, and on various forms of extra-state influence as well (market mechanisms,

---

i.e., the question of how structural conditions on different levels affect each other and the various actors as well.

[84] Elster (1992), p. 4. Lundquist (1986) distinguishes three levels here: (a) how politicians direct top officials, (b) how the latter manage their agencies, and (c) how these agencies try to control citizens. He terms these administrative management, organizational management, and societal management, respectively.

[85] Elster (1992), p. 2.   [86] Cf. Petersson (1989), ch. 8.

[87] Salomon (1989), ch. 1.

professional norms, local power centers, etc.).[88] This applies whether the institution in question is formally to be reckoned as public or private.

By analyzing the implementation process from below, a genre within implementation research has succeeded in mapping out "implementation structures" of great complexity. This method (known as the snowball technique) takes its starting point in a given social problem – unemployment, environmental degradation, criminality, etc. – and traces the associated public measures simply by asking which public organizations are in any way involved. These implementation structures consist of a range of organizations or parts of organizations connected to each other in networks. Such networks may be altogether different in different parts of the country, despite their common role in executing policies which formally are the same. (For it has often been the case that the conditions of responsibility and participation which are formally prescribed have rather little to do with the actual form the implementation process takes.[89])

A drawback of this multifarious organizational network, when it comes to implementing policy, is that organizations (whether public or private) have their own political interests, standardized action repertoires, and ideological ambitions. The problems of coordination are therefore immense. Clarifying which organization is responsible for what (and when) is notoriously difficult. In their review of thirty-seven contributions to the field, Hasenfeld and Brock conclude that "the most striking observation is the heavy emphasis on interorganizational networks."[90] The triangular relation between the state, the producer, and the citizen is complicated indeed, and the last-mentioned may find it nearly impossible to establish who is responsible for what. In addition, the negotiations and decisions needed to induce the participating organizations to work in concert can be difficult, protracted, and at times even irrational.[91] In calling our attention to these problems of coordination, implementation research has made a significant contribution to our understanding of public policy.[92]

It might be added, however, that these implementation networks are not appropriately described as a misfortune, as something unwanted and unsought. Demands for decentralization have, after all, carried great

---

[88] See Ostrom (1992), pp. 14f., for examples of how a mixture of public and private regulation have made it possible for local groups of users of natural resources (subsoil water, fishing waters, etc.) to solve their problems of internal coordination.
[89] See, e.g., Hjern & Porter (1981) and O'Toole (1983).
[90] Hasenfeld & Brock (1991), p. 460.   [91] Cf. March & Olsen (1986).
[92] Winter (1990), p. 27; cf. Hasenfeld & Brock (1991).

political weight. Such decentralization can lead, however, to a situation in which local authorities acquire influence without having to take responsibility, or the reverse – they must shoulder responsibility without enjoying corresponding influence.[93] In the hope of improving policy effectiveness, moreover, politicians may wish to increase the number of organizations with influence over the implementation process. Instead of efficiency, however, the result can be just the opposite: organizational conflict and policy paralysis.[94] In its benevolent wish to let a hundred flowers bloom, the state can easily tie itself in knots. Implementation researchers usually conclude, therefore, that decision-makers should render the process of implementation, and the distribution of responsibility, as simple and transparent as possible.[95]

These rationalist words of wisdom are easy to say but hard to apply, for the simple reason that many programs require the participation, on different levels, of a range of organizations of varying character. Many social problems are so complex that their solution or mitigation necessitates using a range of resources and a variety of types of expertise, which – on account of the logic of the modern division of labor – are often collected in different organizations. However complicated such programs are, in any case, they need not necessarily fail.[96] For the state has the capacity to implement programs necessitating a high degree of coordination, even if success in this area may require extraordinary efforts. That is, the state can structure the implementation process so that local problems of coordination are minimized or at any rate rendered manageable.

This can be done in various ways. One way, discussed earlier, is to apply anti-perfectionist policies rather than complicated, perfectionist ones (to accept broad targeting, in other words). Another is to allow large regional variations in implementation networks, while retaining central control of certain critical managerial instruments. Decentralization can require centralization, paradoxically enough – in order to avoid responsibility drift.[97] Power and responsibility should be united on each of the various levels, for their separation leads to particularly unfortunate results.[98] A third method is to structure the incentives facing the implementing institutions in such a manner as to make it rational for them to act, *vis-à-vis* the citizenry, in the fashion desired by the state.

One problem concerns how to handle the discretionary power over

---

[93] Cf. Petersson (1987a), pp. 17ff.
[94] Wolman (1980), p. 448; and Scharpf (1988).
[95] Ham & Hill (1984), p. 99.   [96] Cf. O'Toole (1986), p. 201.
[97] Bardach (1977); cf. O'Toole (1983).   [98] Williams (1982), pp. 1–17.

implementation which local officials must sometimes be granted. Traditional methods of holding such power in check include such formal systems of evaluation and control as audits and inspections, procedures for appealing decisions, reports to the parliamentary ombudsman, and so on. Such control systems are clearly extremely important. They involve striking a delicate balance between the professional interests of the public staff and the efforts of citizens to hold the implementing organs responsible. In a great many cases, however, these control systems are scarcely serviceable, for the norms and rules required for such formal control systems cannot be formulated with sufficient precision.[99] This especially applies in such areas as education and care, where the public staff meet the citizens directly.[100]

On the one hand, formal rules are needed for regulating such programs, for it is a question of democratically established activities, and not just anything will do. In the absence of such rules, moreover, citizens are abandoned to the arbitrary power of the staff. On the other hand, rules which are too strict and detailed can function as a hindrance; they may, for example, undermine the care and professionalism we want to see in these programs.[101] Such regulations can also make it difficult to adjust the operations of the program to the varying needs and wishes of the clients, and may hinder creativity and development as well.[102]

One disadvantage of precise rules is that they are always *double-edged*. They can be used, on the one hand, to force officials to take a certain action (on pain of otherwise being found in breach of duty). On the other hand, such rules can also play into the hands of officials who can plead that, on account of what *the rules* say, they are not required in a particular case to do what is undeniably reasonable, rational, and in accordance with legislative intent.

Put another way, precise rules are double-edged because, in specifying what the public staff are required to do, they also specify what they are *not* required to do. One could add that such rules are open to abuse by other persons as well; they may open up opportunities, for instance, for citizens to exploit them in a manner other than that intended. The whole affair may be described as an endless contention between those seeking to exploit loopholes in the rules and those trying to close them.[103] This is a classic dilemma of public policy, and no obvious or simple solutions present themselves.[104]

---

[99] Cf. Elster (1992), pp. 167ff.   [100] See Lipsky (1980), ch. 1.
[101] Adler & Asquith (1981), p. 11; cf. Jon Elster (1992), pp. 169ff.
[102] See, e.g., Titmuss (1971).   [103] Elster (1992), p. 171.
[104] Cf. Lundquist (1992), ch. 2.

In a contributing article to a public report on the conditions of the handicapped, I suggested that the widespread criticism of management by rules in the public sector could be accommodated more easily if we distinguish between *internal* and *external* rules. As far as internal administration is concerned, I argued, precise rules should be replaced (to the maximum possible extent) by general goals. External rules, on the other hand – those regulating the relation of public organs to the citizens – should be strengthened instead: "the more precise these are, the more citizens are empowered in relation to the state, i.e., the more their rights are enhanced."[105]

There are two further things, moreover, that the state can do in order to deal with these problems. The one has to do with the ethics of public officials, the other with citizens' freedom of choice. Let us begin with the former. Professional groups with a developed ethical code play an important role in the implementation of many public programs.[106] As noted earlier, public officials in many areas must be allowed a considerable freedom of action in the stage of implementation; it is critical, therefore, that they be made aware of the ethical responsibilities this freedom of action entails. The primary way this can be done is through programs of ethical education.[107] Many professional groups have recognized these problems, and devised codes of ethics accordingly. In the training programs of many professions, moreover, ethical questions have assumed a more prominent place, and the investigation of such issues is now a vital research field.[108]

Trying to solve the problem in this way – by stressing the ethical dimension of officials' decisions – may seem a rather toothless method. I believe, however, that its possible role in the prevention of abuses has been badly underestimated. Its impact depends, of course, on the manner in which the ethical issues are posed, and (critically) on the extent to which officials can count on having to take responsibility for their actions publicly.

We may recall here the principle of "equal concern and respect" as interpreted in chapter 2. This principle can be applied, of course, both to overarching decisions about the distribution of values in society, and to the micro-decisions of individual officials. It can function, for example, as a general principle informing the actions of officials in particular

---

[105] SOU (1991:46), p. 104. Compare the British example of "citizens charters", cf. Tritter (1994).
[106] Cf. Arvidsson (1991), pp. 249f.
[107] An oft-mentioned example is the ethics program at the John F. Kennedy School of Government at Harvard.
[108] See Lundquist (1988) for a review of relevant problems and literature.

encounters with citizens.[109] Responsibility can be enforced, moreover, by special bodies resembling courts, to which citizens can turn when they consider officials to have been derelict in the performance of their duties. The need to justify their decisions publicly should be enough to induce officials to examine, more than otherwise, those aspects of their decisions which might be ethically problematic. We can reasonably hope that, when the doings of officials are the object of public discourse, they will practice their profession with greater care. The advantage of this norm lies in (a) its simplicity and clarity, and (b) its implication that those charged with implementation cannot easily take shelter in rules which for outsiders are hard to understand.

Another possibility is to give citizens the opportunity of "voting with their feet," that is, of choosing other service alternatives. Such a choice need not be just between public and private (or semi-private) producers; it can as well be among public alternatives. Chapter 8 of this book takes up the question of the political and economic consequences of privatizing public services. My point here has to do with the role of citizen choice in mitigating the problems of discretionary action and responsibility drift mentioned above – what I have called "democracy's black hole."

The idea behind the freedom of choice strategy is simple: what politicians cannot manage from above can be opened to the influence of citizens from below. If the users of a public service think the staff employs its discretionary power in ways that are not fitting, they can certainly make their voice heard through such formal or informal channels as are available. If citizens have access to various alternatives, however, they can simply drop such producers as they find deficient in favor of those they prefer. By organizing the process of implementation according to these market-like principles, moreover, central decision-makers ensure themselves access to a steady stream of information about which producers succeed and which fail in meeting the wishes of citizens.

Public policy's substantive legitimacy (5)

During a stay at Cornell University in the autumn of 1990, I was invited to hold a lecture on the Swedish welfare model for a group of American students. It proved, I am afraid, a rather monotonous droning-on about such mystical entities (for an American college student) as supplementary

---

[109] As a matter of fact, many of Dworkin's philosophical ideas seem to be derived from his attempts to solve a genuine problem of implementation: how judges should decide when neither legislation nor precedent offers clear guidance. See R. Dworkin (1977), chapters 1 and 3.

pensions and parental insurance, vacation legislation and study support, child allowances and labor-market policy. In the discussion that followed, a student put the following request to me: could I say a word or two about the Swedish taxes? When I informed the student (whose name unfortunately I never wrote down) of the tragic truth – at this time the Swedish tax level was 57 percent, seen in relation to GNP, or about twice the American level – he looked at me in astonishment and burst out: "But how is it possible to exist in such a society?" Somewhat at a loss over the question, I tried to explain that there was in fact a certain logic in paying high taxes if one receives something valuable in return. Yes, the student grasped this certainly, but I had misunderstood the question. It was not "value for the money" that was his problem; he accepted that the Swedish welfare state probably succeeded in producing all the things of which I had told. No, the problem was: how were such citizens constituted that could entrust *"the government"* with almost two-thirds of what they earned – how was this possible? Either there was something special about the Swedish citizens or something special about the Swedish state. For under no circumstances, the student averred, would the citizens of the United States entrust *the government* with all that money. It just was not possible that Swedes did so voluntarily. To this I had no other answer, however, than that we had not (yet) seen anything resembling a tax revolt in Sweden.

The question was a telling one, however, inasmuch as it addressed an issue largely neglected by implementation researchers – that of state legitimacy and popular trust in political institutions. It is quite possible for citizens to demand all the things offered by a general welfare state like the Swedish one, yet reject the notion that it should be the responsibility of *the state* to provide them. Whether or not citizens view the political system as meriting their trust is thus critically important for *what the state can do*.[110] Public programs which, on paper, are as rational and well thought-through as can be, may meet with general rejection if citizens regard the state (as in "welfare state") as a wasteful, corrupt, or generally mismanaged organization.[111] Without citizens' trust in the institutions responsible for implementing public policies, implementation is likely to fail.

One of the most prominent conservative analysts of social policy in the United States, professor Nathan Glazer of Harvard University, takes up this question in his book *The Limits of Social Policy*. In an insightful analysis, he points out the drawbacks of the selective welfare policy pursued in the United States, and finds that the universal model is much

---

[110] Cf. Tarrow (1996).   [111] Cf. Skocpol (1995).

to be preferred, and that instituting it would remedy many of the problems he considers. He writes, for example, that "we could have begun, and we still can and should, to attach to low-income jobs the same kind of fringe-benefits – health insurance, social security, vacations with pay – that now make higher-paying jobs attractive."[112] Nevertheless, he argues against introducing a universal welfare policy in the United States, for some of the following reasons.

Taxes would be much higher, for one thing, and the general benefits offered to the citizen (in compensation for those high taxes) "may be fouled up by the computer, or lost in the mail, or filched from his mailbox." For another, "the government is not going to make a fine distinction between what it collects in taxes for general government functions and what it collects for transfers." There is no reason to believe, according to Glazer, that "an impregnable line will divide what government does with the vast additional amount it has taxed away for universal transfers and the rest of the money it has taxed away for government functions." Thirdly, the American citizen can be counted on to lodge a number of certainly irrational yet ideologically weighty objections, such as: "it's *my* money . . . Why should the government take it, even if it promises, cross its heart, to give it all back?" Glazer notes, moreover, that "However far we are from a Swedish level of taxation, people feel taxation severely and don't want to pay more, even if it is explained that the 'more' goes to give them services."[113]

How should we interpret this? It is evident that Glazer doubts the American government's ability to handle computers. He is also suspicious of the US Post Office, indeed to the extent that he considers it incapable of sending a check to the right address.[114] He is skeptical, finally, that politicians will keep their fingers out of the huge cookie jar of social-insurance monies created in a general system.

I have no reason to think that Glazer's genuine suspicion of the capacities of the American state is unfounded.[115] My point here is simply

---

[112] Glazer (1988), pp. 13f. Elsewhere in the book he writes: "Universal social programs have virtues. They can help create a common society and a common nation," p. 95.

[113] Glazer (1988), pp. 89f. and p. 93.

[114] Here, however, Glazer ignores his better judgment. One of the few successful social programs in the United States is Social Security – which somewhat resembles the supplementary pension system in Sweden – which is marked by its success in doing precisely this (sending a check to the right person at the right time). This social program was also, be it noted, one of the few that the Reagan administration did not succeed in cutting. See further Dionne (1991), pp. 285ff and Pierson (1996).

[115] On this point, paradoxically enough, he receives strong support from Theda

that Glazer's argument illustrates very well the critical importance of state legitimacy. For the degree of legitimacy a given state enjoys is decisive for what it can and cannot do. Theda Skocpol also uses this argument in an explanation of the failure of the Clinton health plan in 1994, arguing that the fear of "bureaucracy" in general and "means tests or cumbersome application procedures" made middle-class Americans turn away from the idea of universal health care.[116]

In respect to the question of state legitimacy, all positions on the ideological scale are well-represented nowadays. Classical Marxists who consider the state the executive committee of the capitalist class, an instrument for oppressing and exploiting wage-workers. Anarchist and libertarian views of the state as a plundering beast of prey controlled by a despotic bureaucratic elite. Social democratic notions of the state as a people's home to which we can confidently entrust the solution of our social problems. Social liberal ideas of the state as a gigantic social insurance agency. Social conservative theories of the state as an educator of the people. The public-choice perspective working from the assumption that the state is dominated by rent-seeking self-interested politicians and bureaucrats. Social-anthropological ideas of the state as a cultural order. Feminist theories of the state as an instrument of patriarchal oppression. Legalistic ideas of the state as a neutral order in which citizens can be dealt justice in independent courts. Theories of the state as first and foremost a military machine. Fascist ideas of the state as an organic union of blood and soil. Theories about the state as a corporatist arrangement dealing with functional interests. Ideas portraying the state as a threat to civil society, on account of its intervention in an ever larger portion of the public sphere. And so on.

It is not my intention here to argue that any one of these conceptions of *the state* is more correct than the others. For all of these states have undoubtedly existed, at some time and in some place. If one searches throughout history, one can easily find evidence supporting almost any theory of the state's innermost nature. So many different kinds of state are there for the choosing – it is Christmas Day for the model

Skocpol, who has often argued in her writings that the relative underdevelopment of social policy in the United States (as compared to Western Europe) can be explained precisely by the inadequate capacities of the American state when it comes to administering such things. See Skocpol & Finegold (1982) and Skocpol (1991) and (1995). What makes this paradoxical is that Skocpol is one of those forcefully arguing that the United States should try to solve its social problems by establishing public programs of a universalist type. See Skocpol (1991).

[116] Skocpol (1991).

verificationists. Every such empirical illustration, however, can be immediately opposed by another. Searching for the true nature of the state is ideologically serviceable but theoretically meaningless.[117]

I am doubtful that analyses of a general type can help us much in this matter, for they obscure more than they reveal about what the state *really* is. The idea that we can characterize, on the basis of a single formula, all collective, geographically fixed orders of decision-making (i.e., "states"), across all space and time – this idea is nonsense, in my view.[118] The nature of state formations varies. In some situations, no doubt, the machinery of the state can fall under the domination of a social class, a race, a tribe, a clan, a religious current, a claque of gangsters, a party, a social elite, or (most common) a gender. During other historical periods, by contrast, different social, ethnic, and ideological forces may balance each other's influence over the state (or parts of the state, for that matter).

My point here is that state capacity is more than a matter of program design, causal theories, or organs of implementation. It is also a question of what views citizens hold about the nature of the actually existing state. From a game-theoretical perspective the strategic question for the citizens is if the state as a unit of collective action can be trusted or not. As Glazer's work makes clear, state legitimacy in the area of social policy can differ greatly between two developed and democratic Western nations. It bears noting that Glazer is fully aware of this, inasmuch as he claims that certain European countries have been able to construct welfare states more comprehensive and generous than the American one because (a) the legitimacy of the state in these countries has historically

---

[117] An example may be seen in the ideas of Hans Kelsen, the German legal theorist. He portrays the state as identical with the legal order. This notion must either be false (for states have existed in which no legal order applies) or analytically empty (i.e., correct in the trivial sense that all states represent some kind of order). There is one way, however, that one can argue that Kelsen is right, even while retaining a concept of legality with some substance: one can claim that the Soviet Union of Stalin and the Germany of Hitler were not states, for no legality was to be found within their bounds. This definitional maneuver may be a solution of sorts to the theoretical problem indicated above; its drawbacks, however, are too obvious to need pointing out. In the words of Norberto Bobbio, Kelsen's definition of the state "deprives the notion of a rights-based state of all descriptive force." Bobbio (1990), p. 13; cf. Kelsen (1945 and 1992).

[118] A common idea, derived from Max Weber, is that the state is distinguished from other organizations in being empowered to use force legitimately. This is however incorrect, inasmuch as, in most known societies, force can also be exercised legitimately within the family.

been greater, and (b) their societies are ethnically and religiously more homogeneous.[119]

According to most theories of Western democracy, state power can be legitimized by such democratic processes as free and fair elections, combined with the usual battery of rights and freedoms. These theories have in common that they address the input side of the political system, that is, they examine the means by which citizens can influence government decisions. As mentioned above, however, it is often far from simple to implement policies that have been chosen in good democratic order. For no government is capable of framing rules so exhaustive as to cover every contingency. And no parliament, be it ever so direct an expression of the popular will, can ensure that citizens will view the decisions of all public bodies as reflective of a legitimate democratic process. Further measures are required if the power exercised in the stage of implementation is to appear legitimate in the eyes of the citizens.

Three aspects of state legitimacy may be distinguished. These concern the extent to which citizens:

(a) tolerate the intervention of the state;
(b) accept state decisions aimed at influencing the behavior of individuals or of groups;
(c) cooperate with the state to achieve the goals it has set.[120]

One important lesson is that public policy legitimacy can vary. It can vary between different states, and between different policies within the same state as well. Moreover, it can be either specific or general: it may attach to particular programs and institutions, or to the entire political system.

It would be a simple matter here to compose a long list of proposals for enhancing the legitimacy of the public administration, for example, measures against corruption, the abuse of power, administrative incompetence, etc. I shall refrain from so doing, however, since most of these measures are fairly obvious (in conception if not in application). My purpose is rather to shed light on a general problem which, as I adumbrated above, has largely been ignored by implementation researchers. I should note as well that I assume the legitimacy of the state to be in part historically given, and in part open to modification by political

---

[119] Glazer (1988), pp. 16f. In the next chapter, I will show why I think Glazer is wrong on the last of these counts. Suffice here to note that two European countries are strongly divided along ethnic and religious lines, yet are relatively comprehensive welfare states notwithstanding. These are Belgium and the Netherlands.

[120] Mayntz (1975), p. 263. Mayntz's work builds in large part on Luhman (1969).

decision. I assume further that this legitimacy and trust in political institutions is hard to build up but easy to erode.

The outstanding figure of bureaucratic theory, Max Weber, stressed the importance of analyzing the state as a *form of administration*:

> For the state to endure, then, the persons living under its rule must submit to the authority to which the wielders of power lay claim. When and why do they do this? On what bases of internalized legitimacy, and on what outward instruments, do the rulers ground their authority?[121]

Weber's analytical focus was, in the first instance, on the *legitimacy* of the established order. How could the governing class most effectively uphold popular respect for its right to rule? The answer lay in ensuring that the governed – the citizens – regarded the administrative exercise of power as *legitimate*.[122] In contrast to most other social theorists, Weber viewed political legitimacy as depending not just on the political system's input side, that is, on whether or not citizens democratically determine policy by voting and democratic representation. For Weber, the output side – the implementation of policy by bureaucrats – was at least as important, for it was this side of the state with which citizens came into direct contact, and on which they were dependent. Weber thought, for example, that the state's legitimacy was more dependent on tax-collectors' relations with citizens than on whether or not suffrage was universal.[123] Weber's view – that the output side is especially critical for state legitimacy – is probably still more apposite in the era of the modern welfare state than during his own time.

The problem can also be of a general nature. The approach to managing the public sector that has recently been introduced in many Western countries may serve as an illustration. The new method may be described as management by objectives, as distinct from the traditional method of management by rules.[124]

One could portray this transition in two ways, as far as its impact on the legitimacy of public policy is concerned. The more pessimistic picture is as follows. Instead of prescribing exactly what the implementing agencies are to do, the state authorities content themselves with formulating the general goals of policy. Those charged with implementation are then instructed to bend their efforts in the indicated direction. But we should note that these general objectives are not of such a nature as to

---

[121] Max Weber (1919/1977), p. 14.   [122] Friedman (1981), pp. 6–9.
[123] Beetham (1985), pp. 265ff.
[124] Cf. Lindbom (1995), Olsen and Peters (1996), Osborne and Gaebler (1993), ch. 4, and Esping (1994).

enable citizens to place legally binding demands on the state. As noted above, this allows politicians to write exceedingly ambitious goals into the text of the law, and then to hand over the whole matter to the operative administrative body (with the law functioning as a mere indicator of the preferred direction of travel). From the standpoint of the individual citizen, it is unclear in the highest degree what these statements of goals are worth, for they largely lack legal value. The state is not, one might say, bound to deliver what it says it will. If the discrepancy between policy goals and practical measures grows too large, we may expect the legitimacy of public policy to fall. Furthermore, management by goals increases citizens' dependence on the discretionary power of local officials, and thus contributes – by rendering citizens largely bereft of rights in their tussles with the administration – to undermining the legitimacy of public policy. According to this first picture, then, the introduction of management by goals and of framework laws brings declining legitimacy in its wake.[125]

The more optimistic account is as follows. The state authorities have embraced the new managerial method because they understand public measures must often be applied under conditions of great uncertainty and rapid change. By restricting themselves to formulating overarching goals, central policy-makers enable the operative organization to handle this uncertainty. Instead of dictating what to do (which they do not know), they encourage the implementing organization to be flexible in the face of change, that is, to gather more knowledge and to be creative and foresightful. Management by goals thus enhances the capacity of state agencies to meet the needs of citizens, and the legitimacy of public policy is thereby increased.

Which of these pictures is accurate? I would say this varies, depending on how legitimacy as a process is handled. There are areas in which framework laws appear to have low legitimacy.[126] Is there any policy area governed by a typical framework law which has high legitimacy? Indeed there is. One such area is health care, which enjoys a high and stable legitimacy among citizens, as is clear from the interview-studies conducted as part of the "Society, Opinion, Mass Media" project at Gothenburg University.[127] The Swedish health-care system is governed, even so, by a pure framework law: the Law on Health Care and Medical

---

[125] Cf. Esping (1994), pp. 392ff.

[126] An example may be seen in the infected question of taking children into custody. See Hollander (1985) and T. Lundström (1993). For a legal analysis of framework laws, see Hydén (1984) and Esping (1994).

[127] According to an investigation of this subject by Elliot (1992), the health-care system enjoyed the highest public esteem among eleven social institutions by a

Services, from 1982. The Riksdag did not prescribe in this law what kind of treatment citizens have the right to receive for what illness. Such things are rather determined by, among other things, the priorities of the various county councils (which run the public health service in Sweden).

Health care is a classic learning field – new techniques are constantly coming into use and being adapted to new conditions, that is, there is a functioning contact between knowledge generation and clinical application.[128] What is it, then, that accounts for the high degree of legitimacy? I can suggest four tentative answers here. The first is the widespread respect for the expertise of doctors, the second the medical profession's established code of ethics. The third is that an independent court of appeal exists – the Health and Medical Disciplinary Board – which is independent of the health-care producers. If citizens think they have been treated unfairly, they can always turn to this board and argue that, in their particular case, the health-care system has not properly pursued the goals it is charged with. The board then tests their case against a general norm – whether or not the applied measures rest on "science or tested experience."[129] A fourth possible explanation is that a degree of freedom of choice exists in this area nowadays. Citizens can "vote with their feet," that is, they can drop those care-givers not meeting their demands for expertise, reception, accessibility, etc.

This example demonstrates that state capacity can be high even where (a) policy-makers lack knowledge of the relevant technique, (b) the implementing organization must work under conditions of great uncertainty, and (c) a large "black hole" in the democratic process therefore appears. For the "black hole" is largely filled in again, by means of the four elements mentioned above. As this example shows, implementation researchers (and exponents of the "irrationalist" current in organization theory) overstate their case badly. Their pessimism concerning *what the state can do* is, as a general matter, unfounded.

considerable margin. The others, in descending order, were radio/TV, the police, the elementary schools, the daily press, the armed forces, large companies, the Riksdag, the trade unions, the government, and finally, the banks.

[128] See Carlsson, Garpenby & Bonair (1991). For an analysis of how this has functioned in Sweden in regard to the working environment and the labor market (which face the same problems of management as does health care), see Rothstein (1996) and Lundberg (1982).

[129] For a sociological–legal analysis of the Health and Medical Disciplinary Board, see Carlsson & Isaksson (1989).

Legitimacy as a process (6)

What, then, can a democratic state do in order to ensure that its policies are implemented in a manner regarded as legitimate? As mentioned above, it helps little to argue that a policy was promulgated in good democratic order. I shall make use here of an outline on the relation between implementation and legitimacy.[130] In this outline, I distinguish six ideal-typical models, each with a different basis of legitimacy. A brief description of each model follows.

The legal-bureaucratic model

In this model, precise and uniform rules regulate the administration's dealings with the citizens. These rules exhibit a considerable staying power. State measures are regarded as legitimate because citizens can, on account of their knowledge of the rules, predict the outcome of their dealings with the state. If the rules are changed abruptly or often, the ability of citizens to calculate the impact of state measures is impaired. This model further assumes that the rules are applied by neutral, uncorrupt, and impartial bureaucrats. The Achilles' heel of this model lies in its rigidity, that is, it is difficult or impossible in many contexts to draft rules sufficiently precise for the model to work.

This model can be combined, paradoxically enough, with market (or market-like) processes, and with freedom of choice. Rules can be enacted, for instance, guaranteeing all citizens the right to choose (among physicians, schools, etc.). The result is increased legitimacy, for the right to choose ensures that citizens are not left to the mercies of service producers.

The professional model

In this model, the state transfers power over implementation to a specially authorized profession. The members of this profession are thought, by virtue of having completed a specific fixed training, to possess a certain expertise, and often a special code of ethics as well. They can therefore be entrusted, as practitioners of policy, to make decisions on their own responsibility. Their expertise must be founded in an established science, and it must be applicable in the concrete process of implementation. The relation between the professional group, the citizens, and the state is often complicated. To begin with, the state is dependent on the professional

---

[130] Rothstein (1992a) and (1996), especially ch. 3.

group's support and expertise in order to implement certain programs. This dependence entails limitations, moreover, on what measures the state can take within the professional group's field. The professional group, for its part, is often dependent on the state – for granting its members a monopoly over the practice of their profession, and for in other ways fostering citizens' faith in their expertise. The confidence in which citizens hold the knowledge and discernment of the professional group is decisive, moreover, for the degree in which the latter can be used to legitimize the concrete execution of policy.[131]

The corporatist model

The basic idea in this model is to make over the discretionary decisions involved in implementation to representatives of the group towards which the policy is directed. Inasmuch as these representatives are chosen in some organized democratic fashion, they are assumed to enjoy the confidence of the members of the target group. One reason for granting influence to these representatives is that, if they are denied such influence, they can employ the resources of their organization to block the implementation of the program in question. There have also been occasions, however, in which the state (in Sweden, at any rate) has seen fit to create organizations from above, in order to ensure that implementation decisions enjoy legitimacy, and can therefore be more easily carried out.[132]

The user-oriented model

This model involves granting influence over implementation to those citizens who, directly and personally, come into contact with a given public program (i.e., who use its services). Concretely, this means that the users (on their own or together with the field staff) make the critical implementation decisions. The advantage of this approach is that people are seldom critical of decisions they themselves have made, or at any rate had a hand in making. The problems of this model, on the other hand,

---

[131] The various professions differ here. Compare the confidence in which citizens hold physicians with that they express for social workers. This difference can of course reflect differing degrees of professionalism exhibited by these occupational groups, i.e., in their mastery of their respective areas of knowledge. The difference can also depend, however, on the greater applicability of current medical knowledge, as compared to the knowledge on which social work is based.

[132] Rothstein (1992a), chs. 11 and 16.

can be many: some arise in connection with the professional ambitions of the field staff, others reflect the strong conflicts of interest that can arise within one and the same group of users.

The politician-oriented model

In this model, the state tries to endow the process of implementation with legitimacy by directly involving elected politicians at the local level in the making of implementation decisions. Politicians are assumed to possess a certain civic discernment, such that their participation in decisions will generally be regarded as legitimate. Since they are democratically chosen, moreover, they can be seen as representative of the community. Cases in point from Swedish administrative practice are the participation of lay judges in the district courts and of municipal politicians in the social-insurance committees. In other political systems, furthermore, both judges and police commissioners are elected. The more directly such political representatives are elected, we may assume, the greater the legitimacy of the implementation process. One drawback of this model is the risk it entails of politicizing administrative decisions; another is the danger that only citizens who support the politicians in question will view them with confidence and trust.

The lottery-based model

The models mentioned above are all based on the supposition that legitimacy can be achieved if only those making the decisions have the right expertise, resources, and values. It is sometimes, however, impossible to find such persons, at any rate in sufficient numbers. This can be because there are too many decisions to be made, or because it costs too much to collect the necessary information about each individual case. Decisions must sometimes be made even when, purely technically, the state is unable to formulate any reasonable criteria whatsoever for making them. In order to avoid pure arbitrariness, therefore, states sometimes resort to lotteries. A lottery is, on the one hand, an arbitrary procedure for making decisions; on the other, everyone taking part has an equal chance. In this latter sense, then, a lottery is not arbitrary at all (as long as the random number generator is working as it should). A classic example of this model may be seen in the procedure employed – in countries with selective military service – for choosing who shall serve in the army.

These are the six different ways, then, in which the state can endow the process of implementation with legitimacy. These models are obviously analytical constructions (or so-called ideal-types). Many hybrid forms may be found, of course, in the actually existing administrative process (as seen in the example of health care above). The purpose of this presentation has been to isolate, as far as possible, the different methods available for filling in democracy's "black hole." These models' characteristics are summarized in table 4.1. All these different models have both positive and negative attributes. We may recall the IDO-theory here, that is, these models can only function in a legitimacy-creating fashion when their special features are suited to the task at hand. Professionals are only useful in areas where professional expertise applies. The legal-bureaucratic model is best suited to applying "broadly targeted" policies in social areas marked by fairly static conditions. The corporatist model will likely fail in cases where the target group has not formed an interest organization enjoying its confidence,[133] or where many organizations compete with each other. Another problem of the last-mentioned model has to do with the role interest organizations play in relation to the state. Where the strategy is to legitimize public policy by drawing in interest organizations and making them co-responsible for implementation, it is critical that such organizations succeed in a difficult balancing act: they must keep some distance *both* from the state *and* from their members. If the state regards them as unwilling to compromise on behalf of their members, or if their members regard them as devoted wholly to the interests of the state, then the corporatist model will not function properly. If legitimacy is to be achieved, interest organizations must function as a sort of transmission belt between the state and the target group.[134] If the interest organization(s) comes too close to either the target group or the state, the corporative strategy for legitimizing public policy will in all likelihood fail.

Conclusions

During their mere twenty years of scholarship, implementation researchers have made significant contributions to answering our question of what the state can do. In the main, however, we have drawn an inverse benefit from their work – for the opportunity it has afforded us to criticize these researchers' super-rationalist approach and their hypercritical attitude towards public policy. And where such researchers have pointed out policies that are especially difficult to carry out, we have been able to ascertain which types of policy seem to work well. We thus have

---

[133] Cf. Öberg (1994) and Bennich-Björkman (1991).
[134] For some empirical illustrations, see Rothstein (1992a), chs. 7, 17, and 18.

Table 4.1. Six different models for achieving legitimacy in the implementation process

Model type:	Bureaucratic	Professional	Corporatist	User-oriented	Politician-oriented	Lottery-based
Basis of legitimacy:	General rules	Scientific knowledge	Shared interests	Co-determination	Free and general elections	Equal chances
Organization:	Hierarchical	Collegial	Multipartite	Self-managerial	Dualistic	Nonexistent
Main actor:	Official	Professional	Organizational representative	User	Politician	Lottery overseer
Precondition:	Precise rules	Applicable knowledge	Monopolized interest	Active participation	Representativeness	Reliability
Positive effects:	Predictability	Scientific rationalism	Co-optation of opposition	Participation	Political responsibility	Statistical objectivity
Negative effects:	Inflexibility	Negative *esprit de corps*	Dominance of special interests	Differences in interest	Political manipulation	Unpredictability
Type of decision:	Interpretation of rules	Professional judgment	Negotiation	General meeting	Political judgment	Drawing of lots

little use for the "laundry lists" that implementation researchers have produced. Nor are there any *general* grounds for the cynicism which implementation researchers and "irrationalist" organization theorists have spread regarding the possibilities of public policy.

My first conclusion is that the state both can and must act even when it lacks certain knowledge about what works and what does not. The idea that an indubitable causal theory must first be available lacks an empirical basis, and theoretically it assumes an excessively rationalistic conception of politics (and indeed of human action generally). Successful policy implementation is often a question of so organizing the implementation process as to accommodate the need for flexibility and the uncertainty in the policy theory.

We can thus devise a simple formula for discovering what the democratic state can do. State capacity is a function of

1 the degree of uncertainty in the policy theory;
2 the extent to which an adaptive and learning organization capable of compensating for this uncertainty can be formed;
3 the extent to which legitimacy-creating measures can be applied in the implementation stage.

The general relation between these conditions may be described as follows: the greater the uncertainty in the policy theory, the stiffer the demands on organization and legitimacy (case 2 in figure 4.4). The opposite situation – case 1 in the figure – of course applies as well: the more certain the policy theory, the simpler the tasks of organization, and the more easily legitimacy can be achieved in the process of implementation.

Several choices are available, then, when it comes to policy design. By targeting policy broadly, for example – that is, by increasing the certainty of the policy theory by settling for a less perfectionist ambition – we can minimize the often costly and troublesome demands on organization and legitimacy. General child allowances and basic flat-rate pensions are typical examples of this. If, on the other hand, it is necessary to apply policies of a "dynamically interventionist" and thus more perfectionist character, then factors of organization and legitimacy assume greater weight.

This is no argument against designing public programs according to the best available knowledge. On the contrary. My argument is rather directed against the notion that certain knowledge about the causal relationships operative in society must be available before any measures can successfully applied, that is, that the center must always know beforehand what should be done. Even if there is, in an experimental

	Policy theory	Organization	Legitimacy
Case 1: Broad targeting (static regulatory)	+	–	–
Case 2: Dynamic interventionism	–	+	+

Figure 4.4   Preconditions for the successful implementation of public policy

sense, certain knowledge within many policy areas, a long and exceedingly difficult passage remains on the way towards rendering this knowledge "clinically" useful. This applies within the social-scientific field not least. An example may be seen in the econometric models which underlie much of the framing of economic policy – these cannot always be used, it seems, when it comes to the stage of practical (clinical) application. For instance, one cannot so easily predict, on the basis of these experimental models, how the large number of economic actors not controlled by the Ministry of Finance will react.

A second conclusion is that the state cannot do everything. The problems of organization and legitimacy are sometimes too great, as shown in the fate of the Swedish liquor-ration book system. It is here that the argument for an anti-perfectionist policy applies. The idea permeating the Swedish Law on Social Services, for example – that the state (in this case the municipality) has a total responsibility for citizens' well-being – this idea is patently absurd, for the simple reason that so many different kinds of ill-being exist, and that we know too little about which measures might be effective in mitigating many of these.[135] The state lacks the organizational capacity to intervene – with its legitimacy in repair – and to put such citizens' lives in order. That a social problem exists is not in itself an incontestable argument for establishing a public program. If the state of knowledge is uncertain, and if organizational forms cannot be found for dealing with this uncertainty, or if the problems of legitimacy cannot be solved to satisfaction, then there are good reasons to refrain.

A third conclusion is that general organizational recipes probably do more harm than good. The state can achieve a good many things if it is not confined in an organizational straitjacket. That type of organization

---

[135] My thanks to Lennart Nordfors, who has called my attention to this aspect of the Law on Social Services.

should be chosen which best suits the tasks to be performed and the technique that must be used. Fourthly, we may observe that in many cases implementation is not a two-way affair – that is, between just *the citizen* and *the state*. For a third party is involved – *the producer*. This last-mentioned is a partially autonomous institution acting on public instructions. It can, however, be either public or private, and in any case it enjoys a not inconsiderable freedom of action in carrying out its tasks. What the state can do depends much on how it structures the relation between the partially autonomous *producer* and *the citizen*.

5

Just institutions matter

A just system must generate its own support. This means that it must be arranged so as to bring about in its members the corresponding sense of justice, an effective desire to act in accordance with its rules for reasons of justice. Thus the requirement of stability and the criterion of discouraging desires that conflict with the principles of justice put further constraints on institutions. They must be not only just but framed so as to encourage the virtue of justice in those who take part in them.[1]

This quotation from John Rawls may serve to illustrate the major question of this chapter, namely: what is the relation between the institutions making up the political system (most especially those charged with implementing social policy) and the norms of justice prevailing in society? And how can such institutions be shaped so as "to encourage the virtue of justice in those who take part in them"?

The story of *The Pale Rider*

The course of events portrayed in *The Pale Rider* (a western made by Clint Eastwood in the mid-1980s) may serve to illustrate the point of departure for this chapter. The events in question (freely interpreted after three viewings) proceed as follows. A small settlement of gold miners is harassed by the powerful and wealthy owner of a mining company. This is because they have staked a claim to some land downstream which the mine-owner covets (in order to expand his operations). At first, the

---

[1] Rawls (1971), p. 261.

mine-owner tries violence against the miners' property – periodically, his henchmen ride into the settlement and destroy buildings, release animals, kill dogs belonging to the children, etc. This strategy of harassment fails to produce the desired result, however; instead of being frightened away, the gold miners are welded together, and their opposition to the mine-owner hardens.

The evil mine-owner then switches tactics – from the stick to the carrot. He offers each member of the mining colony a considerable sum of money, in exchange for his share of the mining concession. The destitute miners have been less than successful in their efforts, so they are badly tempted to take the offer. It lies quite simply in their well-considered self-interest to exploit the situation economically. They also know that, should they refuse the offer, they can expect to meet with further (and quite possibly deadly) violence. So it may seem natural that the miners accept the offer. The problem, however, is that they must agree collectively on their response, as the offer only stands on condition that every miner sell his stake (for the affair is otherwise worthless to the mine-owner). This means the miners must reach a common decision – they cannot accept or reject the tempting offer on an individual basis. Every miner must, accordingly, take part in a public discussion about how the group should proceed, and openly defend his standpoint before his fellows.

As the debate by the camp fire proceeds, two things become clear. The first is that most of the miners view the offer as highly favorable, economically speaking, and consider that they have good reason – from the standpoint of their rational self-interest – to accept it. The second is that none of them wants to accept it. No miner wishes to sell his stake – some out of fear of being thought a coward inclined to sell out his mates, others out of a disinclination to bow to the will of a bullying mine-owner, be he ever so mighty. To take the offer just would not be right. Certainly, the miners judge their prospects of withstanding the likely reprisals as dim, but rather than leave their friends in the lurch, or betray their ideal of freedom, they undertake to endure this chance. They choose to stay and to fight (and of course are saved in the end by Eastwood's courage and skillful use of firearms, but that is another story).

The point I want to illustrate with the help of *The Pale Rider* is the following: democracy is not solely, or even primarily, a question of counting votes and mechanically aggregating preferences. The democratic process is also a *discursive* politics. Its institutions – the parliamentary assembly and the open debate – force participants to defend their positions publicly.[2] Those taking part must therefore justify their actions in moral terms. Moral argumentation assumes a special importance. Democracy thus acquires a special moral logic, which differs in part from the logic of other institutions (such as the market). To return to the example above: it was not a change in the miners' preferences or incentive structure that dissuaded them from each taking the offer and being off. It was, rather, the specific form of the *institutional* order within which they had to make their decision. This institution was special, because (a) each individual was forced to adopt a public standpoint, (b) each was forced to justify his position through argument in a face-to-face situation, and (c) the decision had to be a collective one, because the problem was a common one, that is, the property was collectively owned. This meant the decision concerned whether *all* would remain or *all* would go. Although the mine-owner's offer – considered from the standpoint of individual utility maximization – was an advantageous one, the miners simply thought it unjust that, on account of their material self-interest, they should pull up stakes and abandon the concession.[3] The institutional setting, moreover, convinced everyone that they could trust that all the others would stay, that is, that none of them would risk becoming a "sucker". Their decision – to remain and to resist – arose therefore from the *institutional form* of the decision-making forum, which encouraged the participants to see to the public good instead of their own narrow self-interest. Put differently, action guided by social norms such as solidarity and trust assumed a heightened importance.

However, we need not depart for the promised land of Hollywood films in order to illustrate the significance of political institutions for

[2] Dryzek (1990), Elster (1986). The idea that participation in the democratic process alters the preferences of citizens (from self-interested to common welfare-oriented) is not exactly new, cf. Mill (1861/1972), p. 217. A modern theorist of note in this area is Jürgen Habermas, whose *Moral Consciousness and Communicative Action* (1990) I made a brave but, I must confess, wholly unsuccessful attempt to understand on just this point. How is one to understand his *metanorm*, which, he explains, is the sole valid process for justifying other (action-oriented) norms? How does it arise? Can it vary over time and space? Etc.

[3] The connoisseur of westerns will doubtless cite a contrary example here, namely the classic *High Noon,* in which the town's citizens spurn the efforts of the sheriff to organize a common defense against a gang of bandits (a classical problem of collective action). A closer analysis of *High Noon* reveals, however, that the reason the citizens spurn the sheriff is that they re-define the problem: they choose to view the threat as directed not at the community as a whole but rather at just the sheriff. For the leader of the bandits has some unfinished business with the sheriff in connection with a (if I remember correctly) sensationally beautiful woman, and so is out for personal vengeance; the citizens, accordingly, conclude that the matter does not concern them as a collectivity.

social norms such as these. In her important book, *Governing the Commons*, Elinor Ostrom has studied a large number of cases involving how – in widely varying contexts – people have managed the common resources on which they depend. The resources in question are of a particular type – examples include fresh water supplies, grazing lands, and fishing zones – which possess three key characteristics. First, individual actors face strong incentives to exploit them to the full; secondly, they do not admit of regulation in their use, since they are generally available; and thirdly, they are limited, so if users exploit them to the full they are exhausted soon enough (which of course injures the interests of all who have need of them). In such areas, then, the unregulated pursuit of self-interest yields a worse outcome for all involved than would have resulted had the affected parties chosen to collaborate and to regulate consumption in some fashion. This is the central problem of collective action.

Let us look at one of Ostrom's many examples – water consumption in southern California during the 1940s and 1950s. Analyzing how the water-dependent farmers of that region transformed their mutual dealings from a resource-wasting war of all against all to the establishment of a *voluntary*, self-governing institution for the common regulation of limited water supplies, she writes:

> In each basin, a voluntary association was established to provide a forum for face-to-face discussions about joint problems and potential strategies . . . The provision of a forum for discussion transformed the structure of the situation from one in which decisions were made independently without knowing what others were doing to a situation in which individuals discussed their options with one another.[4]

As Ostrom demonstrates with her many well-documented examples, the design of the decision-making situation itself plays a decisive role in altering individuals' conception of their self-interest, and their actions thereby. They still possess, in respect to their short-term self-interest, a motive for acting non-solidaristically. However, when they are placed in a situation which forces them openly to argue for their chosen course, the importance of social norms becomes decisive, and the result is various kinds of collective and solidaristic solutions.[5] This does not mean that the actors in question are transformed from egoists into the purest of

---

[4] Ostrom (1992), p. 138.
[5] Cf. Hermansson (1990), p. 175: "in a market-like, non-cooperative decision-making situation, there is no reason to consider the consequences for anyone but oneself; a collective decision-making situation, by contrast, gives cause to consider the consequences *both* for oneself *and* for others."

altruists, but rather that they *re-define* their self-interest so as to bring it into line with the collective interest (of avoiding drainage to the common resource, as in the example above). This is an important empirical result because it contradicts one of the basic theorems in the economic approach to politics, namely that "the representative . . . acts on the basis of the same over-all value scale when he participates in market activity and in political activity."[6] On the other hand it is in accordance with a general result from experimental studies, which is that if the institutional structure is such that a possibility to communicate exists, this greatly increases agents' cooperative and solidaristic behavior.[7] Otherwise expressed: individuals' actions are neither uniform nor fated by an unchanging "human nature." The logic of action varies, rather, according to the *institutional* forms within which individuals must act. For instance, their behavior is not the same under conditions of anonymity (as in the market or a voting booth) as when it must take place within the view of, and in discussion with, others (as in a parliament or other representative assembly).[8]

The social scientific search for a one true "human nature" (such as e.g., "homo economicus") from which simple and therefore elegant general models may be deduced, is therefore fundamentally a futile enterprise. Our analysis thus far points instead to the following: under certain institutional conditions, a strict economic rationality may prevail, while under others, social norms may achieve a critical importance. The task of social science is therefore to discover how this relation between political institutions and the logic of individual action actually functions.

John Rawls' theory of the hypothetical original position has often been interpreted in a one-sided manner: various critics have assumed that it deals with how rational – in the sense of utility-maximizing – individuals would choose if placed in a situation in which they know nothing of their future resources or position in society.[9] Rawls has changed his views on this central point, however. His theory does not build on any "economic man" rationality.[10] In his latest book, Rawls demonstrates how, if one

---

[6] Buchanan & Tullock (1962), p. 20.

[7] Frolich & Oppenheimer (1992), Dawes, Orbell, & Simmons (1977), Frank, Gilovich, & Regan (1993).

[8] See further Sunstein (1991) and Elster (1986), as well as Myrdal (1970), p. 36, who called attention to this early on.

[9] See, for example, S.-O. Hansson (1989), Kymlicka (1989), pp. 65f., and Lewin (1991), pp. 162f.

[10] Rawls (1993): "Justice as fairness rejects this idea. It does not try to derive the reasonable from the rational," ibid., p. 52. "To see justice as fairness as trying to derive the reasonable from the rational misinterprets the original position," ibid., p. 52.

wishes to understand his theory, one must distinguish between two different logics of action – "the rational" and "the reasonable" – and that it is the latter which is thought to guide persons in the original position. It should be added that Rawls himself contributed to this misunderstanding (which he admits) about how to interpret his theory, with an unfortunate formulation in A *Theory of Justice:*

> it was a mistake . . . (and a very misleading one) to describe a theory of justice as part of a theory of rational choice. What I should have said is that the conception of justice as fairness uses an account of rational choice subject to reasonable conditions to characterize the deliberations of the parties as representatives of free and equal persons.[11]

The reasonable may be distinguished from the rational, according to Rawls, in the following ways. To begin with, "persons are reasonable . . . when, among equals say, they are ready to propose principles and standards as fair terms of cooperation and to abide by them willingly, given the assurance that others will likewise do so."[12] Rawls does not derive reasonable action from any economic rationality; rather, he sees the reasonable and the rational as equivalent in status, in the sense that both are fundamental and independent categories capable of guiding human action. It is not the case, then, that Rawls denies the existence of "economic man." He simply points out that another type of non-altruistic behavior exists as well: "reason."[13]

Moreover, the rational individual lacks an important quality possessed by his reasonable counterpart: "the particular form of moral sensibility that underlies the desire to engage in fair cooperation as such, and to do so on terms that others as equals might reasonably be expected to endorse . . . Rational agents approach being psychopathic when their interests are solely in benefits to themselves."[14] The essential difference, then, is that "the reasonable is public in a way the rational is not." What can be defended before others at the camp fire is therefore different from what is acceptable in an anonymous contractual situation. This means, according to Rawls, that:

> we enter as equals the public world of others and stand ready to propose, or to accept, as the case may be, fair terms of cooperation with them.

---

[11] Rawls (1985), note 20.

[12] Rawls (1993), p. 49. Rawls' own example from daily speech is the following: "We say: 'Their proposal was perfectly rational, given their strong bargaining position, but it was nevertheless highly unreasonable, even outrageous,'" ibid., p. 48.

[13] Rawls credits Scanlon (1982) for this distinction between the rational and the reasonable.

[14] Rawls (1993), p. 51.

These terms, set out as principles, specify the reasons we are to share and publicly recognize before one another as grounding our social relations.[15]

It is impossible therefore to analyze the original position – which plays so central a role in Rawls' theory – solely on the basis of game theory, because the original position is not a situation in which actors set their course with no communication beyond analyzing the strategic choices of their "opponents" after the fact.[16] Rawls' conclusions cannot be criticized, as for example Lewin has done, as proceeding from deficient or mistaken assumptions about participants' calculation of risk, because Rawls' theory treats with the institutional shaping of the democratic discourse, which means that his assumptions about participants' risk aversion assume quite another weight than in Lewin's rationalistic analysis.[17]

Instead of an anonymous strategic game situation, then, the original position is intended to be a *discursive* institution, in which representatives of different currents of opinion meet in order to try, through discussion, deliberation, and negotiation, to find the common principles of social and political order that should prevail in society. This presupposes that they can assume an impartial standpoint, and that their views in respect of ideological, religious, and other such questions diverge.[18] The decisional situation in Rawls' original position thus has nothing in common with the anonymity of the market, but rather resembles the type of collective and open institutions which were decisive for the outcome in *The Pale Rider.*[19] The similarity to the decision-making forum described

---

[15] Ibid., pp. 53f.

[16] It is possible theoretically, but the strategies would be too complex. As Ordeshook (1986), pp. 303f. has stressed: "Even a brief introspection into the nuances of human interaction reveals the great number of strategies that communication permits: threats, the timing of actions, lying, and severing communication itself. Each possibility communicates something about intentions, each affects perceptions and beliefs, and we can interpret each as a move in a monstrously complex game three." One can only say: "Good luck!"

[17] Lewin (1990), pp. 161f. Another example is Howe & Roemer (1981). It seems quite possible, on the other hand, that the "common spirit" to which Lewin (1970) refers, in his model of interactive democracy, is related to Rawls' idea of "reason."

[18] Rawls (1993), pp. 135ff. Soltan (1987) has developed this idea.

[19] Jörgen Hermansson has sought, following Elster, to distinguish economic from political rationality in a manner resembling, I believe, Rawls' distinction between "the rational" and "the reasonable." Hermansson (1990), pp. 353f. He calls, moreover, for a specification of the concept of political rationality. Such a specification becomes possible, in my view, upon examining the institutional character of the decision-making situation, that is, whether or not it makes discursive communication possible.

by Elinor Ostrom (see above) is also striking. It has been demonstrated, furthermore – in an investigation comparing the attitudes and behavior of citizens in the United Kingdom and the United States – that the opportunity to discuss politics is positively correlated with the desire to contribute to the common good.[20]

How should we understand "reasonable" action, then, which is neither the same as narrow self-interest nor can be likened to altruism?[21] The concept I shall use here is that of *political rationality*, which should be understood as something distinct from *economic* rationality. Political, because what is intended is an institutionalized and (in contrast to the market) *public discursive process*. Rationality, because it a question of arriving, after deliberation and debate, at a sort of constitutional solution making it possible for groups and individuals to reach common solutions to collective problems, even while showing due consideration for each other's differences. Democracy's actually existing institutions – parliament and the free debate most especially – are not arrangements for the mere aggregation of already existing preferences. The founders of democratic institutions have, rather, "always built in arenas for deliberation and for the discovery of a public good."[22]

The limited value of the theory of self-interest

As shown in chapter 1, contemporary Western welfare states differ greatly in size and scope. In what way can this be explained by economic models built on the idea of the self-interested utility-maximizing individual? This model of political behavior has enjoyed an almost dominant position in political science from the 1970s onwards. Recently, however, this economic approach to politics has been exposed to ever stiffer criticism.[23] Evidence has accumulated that political behavior cannot be explained on the basis of economic theories presenting self-interest as the driving force. Among such evidence may be mentioned the so-called voting paradox, that is, the puzzle that citizens choose to vote in elections in such great numbers, despite the fact that no sensible reasons founded in their self-interest can be adduced for their so doing. To cite one of the leading exponents of this school, Morris Fiorina: the voting paradox "ate rational choice theory."[24] Jane Mansbridge has summarized the state of the research as follows:

---

[20] Johnston, Conover, Crewe, & Searing (1990).
[21] Eriksen (1993), p. 153.   [22] Mansbridge (1990), p. 9.
[23] Green & Shapiro (1994).   [24] Quoted in Mansbridge (1990), pp. 14f.

we see a minirevolt in almost all empirical branches of the profession of
political science against the self-interest model of the way a democratic
policy actually works . . . the claim that self-interest alone motivates
political behavior must be either vacuous, if self-interest can encompass
any motive, or false, if self-interest means any behavior that consciously
intends only self as beneficiary.[25]

Another example is Dunleavy's ambitious review of the genre, which
concludes with the following statement: "Much of the recent discussion
of economic explanations in political science has not been helpful."[26] The
hypothesis that the actions of bureaucrats, voters, and politicians can be
explained on the basis of their self-interest lacks empirical substantiation,
as Lewin and Dunleavy among others have shown.[27] Nor do findings in
experimental psychology confirm the theory of self-interest:

In departments of psychology, management, and economics, hundreds of
recent experiments with prisoners' dilemma and other games that reward
self-interested behavior at the expense of the group indicate a stubborn
refusal on the part of a significant fraction (usually 25 percent to 35
percent) to take rational self-interested action, even under conditions of
complete anonymity with no possibility of group punishment.[28]

More recent analyses have also demonstrated the impossibility of explaining, on the basis of such a purely individualistic, self-interested
perspective, why people choose to serve the commonweal in any cases at
all. Since it is costly to act collectively, and since the results of collective
action fall as a rule to everyone (both to those who contribute to the
common effort and to those who do not), there is no reason for
individuals with a purely self-interested utility function to contribute to
defraying any of these costs.[29] Yet this is exactly what people often do, in
a multitude of situations – in companies, organizations, and states.

One way out of this dilemma has been to build altruistic behavior into

---

[25] Mansbridge (1990), pp. 19f.
[26] Dunleavy (1991), p. 258, cf. Green & Shapiro (1994).
[27] Lewin (1991), p. 126. Cf. Dunleavy (1991).
[28] Mansbridge (1990), p. 17. Most of these experiments were done on American
      college students. According to Frank, Gilovich, & Regan (1993), one group clearly
      diverged from the general pattern – students of economics. These proved much
      more self-interested than their fellows. The direction of the causal sequence
      which Frank, Gilovich, & Regan reports is of special interest in this discussion. It
      is the academic study of economics which leads to uncooperative behavior/
      preferences, rather than individuals with original preferences of this kind that
      seek out the study of economics.
[29] Lichbach (1994), Bicchieri (1993), Bianco & Bates (1990), Bendor & Mookherje
      (1987).

their models of rationality, that is, if A finds pleasure in B's consumption, then it is rational for A to bestow B with resources. As Mansbridge emphasizes, however, this maneuver empties the theory of rational action of all explanatory content, so that it becomes analytically meaningless.[30] Etzioni has formulated this point in the following manner: "From a methodological viewpoint, the all-inclusive expansion of the concept of utility violates the rules of sound conceptualization. Once a concept is defined so that it encompasses *all* the incidents that are members of a given category . . . it ceases to enhance one's ability to explain."[31] This approach may also be seen as an example of purely circular reasoning, in which anything an actor might undertake to do is held to be that which discloses his preferences regarding the object of the action. The dependent variable thus "explains" the independent variable, which is scarcely compatible with current rules of method.

There is, as Margaret Levi has stressed, "more compliance than selective incentives explain. More people refrain from jaywalking or littering, pay their taxes, or join the armed forces than the theory predicts."[32] The number of studies empirically and theoretically refuting the view of politics as driven only by rational self-interest has quite simply sharply increased. The market logic of explanation has to a surprisingly large extent shown itself inadequate when transferred to the political sphere.[33]

Faced with this empirical fact, a number of authors in this area have sought to contextualize their explanations. This has usually meant that they have tried to incorporate institutions into their models.[34] This leads their analysis, however, from a problematic situation into an even more difficult one, for it lodges the theoretical explanation in something other than the rational actor.[35] According to more recent developments in rational-choice theory, cooperation of the kind described above is virtually impossible to explain. Put simply, in a situation in which cooperation for a collective good requires the contribution of many rational and self-interested agents, it will always pay for the individual to

---

[30] Mansbridge (1990), p. 9. Cf. Sen (1977), p. 93.
[31] Etzioni (1988), p. 27. See also Lewin (1991), p. 134.
[32] Levi (1990), p. 408; cf. Lewin (1991), Laurin (1986).
[33] See Etzioni (1988), Cook & Levi (1990), Mansbridge (1990), Dunleavy (1991), Lewin (1991), Renwick Monroe (1991), and Zey (1992).
[34] See Sheplse (1989).
[35] Cf. Ordeshook (1986), pp. 1f.: "all explanations and descriptions of group action, if they are theoretically sound, ultimately must be understandable in terms of individual choice."

defect, i.e., not to collaborate.[36] Jonathan Bendor and Dilip Mokherjee conclude, on the basis of rational-choice theory itself, that the rational-actor model can explain why patterns of collective action persist, but it does "not explain how they arise." They state that "the emergence of cooperation is a hard problem – one that may require other methods of analysis." To explain why cooperation sometimes takes place and some-times does not, they opt for a couple of explanations rather alien to this type of theorizing: "idiosyncratic events, for example, an unlucky early defeat that creates widespread suspicion of shirking,"[37] or causes of another type arising from the specific historical circumstances at hand. Yet even were organized cooperation (for one or another irrational reason) to appear, it should – according to the rational-actor model – be highly unstable, on account of the constant temptation facing members of the organization to stop paying for its upkeep, even while continuing to draw benefits from its operation.[38]

Let me add that the rational-choice position is not strengthened by the claim that cooperative action can be explained by the previous existence of cultural, social, or political bonds or institutions. Such bonds or institutions, it is thought, would increase each actor's confidence that others will cooperate as well. The problem, as Michael Hechter has written, is that "institutions such as these represent the very Pareto-efficient equilibria that game theorists presumably are setting out to explain."[39] Establishing an institution in order to overcome a collective action problem itself presents a collective action problem.[40] For among rational self-interested actors, such institutions – and the selective incentives necessary for their creation – would never arise. Mark Lich-bach, who has analyzed a very large number of suggested solutions to the problem of collective action (CA), concludes that "the major difficulty is that each solution presupposes the existence of at least one of the other solutions" and that "all types of solutions simply push the explanation of CA one step further back."[41] In practice, this means referring to already existing institutions. Or to cite Hermansson's judicious words: "The rational-actor model can therefore never be generally applicable."[42]

The conclusion to be drawn from this critique is not, however, that the rational actor model should be abandoned. On the contrary, the most valuable insight from this approach is that most human agency is

[36] Tsebelis (1990) pp. 74ff. and Scharpf (1990), p. 476.
[37] Bendor & Mookherjee (1987), p. 146.
[38] Hechter (1987), pp. 10f.   [39] Hechter (1992), p. 47.
[40] Bicchieri (1993), Bates (1988), p. 395, cf. Scharpf (1990), p. 479.
[41] Lichbach (1994), p. 23.
[42] Hermansson (1990), p. 357, cf. Lichbach (1995).

strategic, in the sense that what we do (e.g., what type of welfare system we will support) depends on what we think that "the others" will do. Will they pay their share of the tax burden or not, will the government deliver what it has promised to deliver or not, etc. This "mental map" of who we think the others are and what they will do (i.e., if they will cooperate or not) is what in ordinary language is called social norms. This means that knowing that a person is "rational" and knowing his or her preferences (or utility function) may predict very little of that person's behavior if we do not also know what is in his or her "mental map" about what "the others" will do.[43] To take an extreme example, it may be fully rational to kill your neighbors today it you are convinced that they will otherwise kill you tomorrow, even if it is not in your utility function to kill people. But it may also be rational to ask them to work together with you to build a new playground for the kids in the neighborhood if you think (i.e., if there is a common social norm) that they will probably cooperate with you in such a project.

The political significance of social norms

We may reasonably conclude, then, that social norms and institutions clearly play an important role. Unfortunately, however, we know little more than this. Otherwise expressed: "if we can reject the hypothesis that self-interest guides most political activity in Western Democracies, we, as a field, are nowhere near being able adequately to test the alternative hypothesis that public interest is a major motivator."[44] We are able to understand and explain action according to self-interest, as long as we have information about the utility calculations of individuals and about the structure of the choice situation, but we know far less about what affects our social norms (such as the desire to act for "the common good").

Lewin has tried, following in the steps of David Hume, to solve this quandary by stressing the role of "social conventions." However, explaining a norm – such as public officials' loyalty to the elected politicians, to take Lewin's example – by calling it "a norm of action which they have agreed to follow" is less than persuasive, because in principle it amounts to a repetition of the data, much as saying that people do what they do because they want to do what they do. Nothing is thereby revealed, obviously, about the causal dimension – about how the convention and the norm can be explained. If, however, a logical *and* empirically valid distinction is made between social conventions on the one hand, and norms on the other, then Lewin's solution could prove

---

[43] Hardin (1996).   [44] Lau (1992), p. 1090.

workable.[45] Edna Ullman-Margalit has pointed out that the pioneers of game theory, von Neuman and Morgenstern, already realized (when they launched their model in the 1940s) that game theory cannot explain which point of equilibrium will prevail in cases – which in practice are very frequent – where several such points arise. They stressed the importance, for such cases, of, yes, established social norms – or in their terminology, "standards of behaviour."[46]

Ten years ago, furthermore, the Norwegian social scientist Jon Elster was among those arguing most strenuously for the methodological primacy of the analysis of individual self-interest, and for the applicability of formal game theory. Since trying to apply this approach empirically, however (on the Swedish system of wage negotiations!), he has become much more pessimistic about its value. In his introduction to his book about the Swedish system of wage negotiations, he writes that "it soon becomes clear that the complexity of these bargaining problems defies explicit modeling," that is, it cannot be captured in models based on the simple assumption that the utility calculations of rational actors are unitary."[47] In a number of more recent books and articles, moreover, he strongly emphasizes the importance of social norms ("the cement of society," in Elster's metaphor). Elster defines norms negatively: behavior governed by norms is the opposite of action according to rational self-interest. All non-consequentialist behavior[48] is norm-governed behavior, in other words. Norms become, in his analysis, a sort of a residual category in which we can dump everything that cannot be explained on the basis of the rational-actor model. Elster describes the problem in the following manner:

> why do specific norms exist in specific times and places? This is a question for the social sciences. Unfortunately, I have nothing to offer by way of an

[45] Lewin (1991), pp. 140f. It is not clear what Lewin means by "social conventions." I have interpreted this concept here, be it granted, in a rather stingy fashion; as Lewin assigns it a fundamental role, however, it seems reasonable to demand a more exhaustive analysis of its meaning.

[46] Ullman-Margalit (1977), pp. 15f. Why different countries end up at different points of equilibrium can only be explained historically. For an analysis of how rationalist theory and historical analysis can be combined, see, e.g., Ferejohn (1991), Lewin (1984), and Rothstein (1992c).

[47] Elster (1989). For a criticism of attempts to explain the appearance of norms purely on the basis of a game-theoretical approach, see Ullman-Margalit (1977), pp. 14–17.

[48] That is to say, action based on the conviction that deeds are right or wrong in themselves, rather than on account of the consequences they produce. The classical example is radical pacifism's absolute proscription against the taking of human life, regardless of context or consequences.

answer. I do not even know where to begin to look, or what general form an answer might take.[49]

Elster's comment is extremely disheartening, actually. If rational-choice theory is as unilluminating as he claims, and if norms are so important for explaining social and political behavior, then the predicament of the social sciences is serious indeed, for we have no answers as to how and why these norms arise, or even where we should start looking.[50] Nor is anything gained just by replacing the theory of the rational self-interested actor with its opposites – the irrational actor or the pure altruist – because such actors presumably follow norm systems which require explanation. As an intuitive matter, moreover, such actors are hard to visualize. The upshot seems to be to abandon the ambition to explain politics on the basis of the motives and strategies of individuals.

Norms vary, moreover, not just in significance but also in intensity between different social settings and institutions. If we wish to explain variations in human behavior (regarding, say, the willingness to act collectively or the appearance of a reasoned, open political discourse), and if we believe norms play a significant role in this connection, then we have no choice but to try to find a way – on the basis of a more sophisticated conception of rationality than that expressed in the simple principle of utility maximization – of explaining the variation in norm-governed behavior. I shall therefore again take up Rawls' distinction between "rationality" and "reason" (see above, pp. 120–123), and shall inquire into the institutional conditions under which the one logic of action will prevail over the other. But first, a short discussion of culture's role in the tale.

Can cultural theory help us?

In the brilliant British film from 1992, *The Crying Game*, the Irish Republican Army (IRA) kidnaps a soldier from the British Army. The IRA's purpose is to exchange their hostage for some IRA prisoners held by the British. The kidnapped soldier becomes on friendly terms with one of his captors, however, and little by little the two men begin to talk. The captured soldier is frightened, of course, and says he is convinced the whole affair will end badly for his part, while the IRA soldier/terrorist

---

[49] Jon Elster (1991), p. 120; cf. Elster (1989), p. 125: "I do not know why human beings have a propensity to construct and follow norms, nor how specific norms come into being and change."

[50] If this were true, there would be little else for social scientists to do but close up shop for good.

tries to console him, saying that despite everything there is a good chance he will not be killed; all that is needed is that everyone involved – including, most especially, the British Army – should act rationally in the situation that has arisen. The British soldier remains persuaded he will meet with a bad end, however, and relates the following story in support of this conviction.

A frog and a scorpion meet by the side of a river they both want to cross. The scorpion, who cannot swim, asks to be allowed to cross the river on the frog's back. The frog, aware as he is of the scorpion's venomous and treacherous nature, is exceedingly dubious about this idea, but the scorpion assures him there is nothing to worry about; after all, if he is so foolish as to sting the frog, they both will drown. The frog yields to the force of this rational argument, and so ventures out into the river with the scorpion perched upon his back. Halfway across the river, however, the frog feels to his horror the deadly sting. He cries out, just before dying: "Why have you done this?! Now we both will drown!" The scorpion replies: "I couldn't help doing it. It's in my nature."

The questions I mean to illustrate with this example are the following: are the norms that govern our actions structurally determined? Are they so deeply embedded in our history, biology, culture, etc., as to be beyond conscious human influence? Are we, owing to such factors as these, what Anthony Giddens has called "cultural dopes" and "structural dopes," or can we affect these things through conscious strategic action?[51] In other words, are the communitarian philosophers right after all?

The cultural theory which, in political science, has its foremost champion in Aaron Wildavsky offers a way out of the quandary created by the economistic models. Wildavsky's critique of Elster's (earlier) optimistic attempts to explain social processes from a purely rationalistic perspective is right on the mark:

> Elster rightly resists the temptation to explain all behavior by individual variations in opportunities; he recognizes that desires differ among individuals. But if this is so, then where is the nut or bolt that deals with why people want what they want, i.e., with the formation and alteration of preferences. A danger of rational choice explanations is that they make preferences into a *deux ex machina* that drops from the sky uncaused.[52]

To take preferences as given, as the economistic models do, is in Wildavsky's view to begin the analysis where it should end, and to

[51] Giddens (1979).
[52] Wildavsky (1991), p. 308. The phrase "nut or bolt" is derived from the title of a book written by Elster on the subject of social-scientific explanations – *The Nuts and Bolts of Social Science*.

exclude what is most interesting in social science – the question of why people want what they want.[53] Instead of being treated as a magic box, the explanation of why norms and preferences vary between individuals, groups, and indeed entire societies must become a central ambition of political science: "Not only getting what you want but deciding what you want are part and parcel of the interpersonal construction, modification, and destruction of institutions within which individuals figure out what they ought to prefer."[54]

Norms arise, according to Wildavsky, out of our various socio-cultural bonds. Preferences and norms – concerning the value of collective and solidaristic behavior, for instance – are formed by how we participate, voluntarily or otherwise, in social relations. They are, in other words, "socially constituted." Wildavsky divides cultures into four basic types – an idea he takes from the anthropologist Mary Douglas – according to whether (a) group cohesion is strong or weak, and (b) social control within the group allows much individual variation or only a little. By cross-tabulating these dimensions, Wildavsky arrives at four basic human norm-patterns: *hierarchy, fatalism, competition,* and *egalitarianism.* Depending on the category within which people fall, their norm-systems will vary in respect to collaboration and solidaristic action. Those stamped by a hierarchical culture think the individual should always sacrifice himself for the collectivity, without expecting anything in return beyond the right of belonging to the hierarchy. Fatalists, on the other hand, will not cooperate under any circumstances whatsoever, since they regard the assurances of others in regard to reciprocity to be altogether worthless – cooperation simply is not *in their nature.* Egalitarians, for their part, will not demand sacrifices of others who are not their equals, on the grounds that the latter have already suffered enough. Only the competition-oriented are basically open to choosing cooperation, as they are able to view cooperation as a contract in which their interests are served if commitments assumed earlier are discharged.[55]

[53] Economic analyses are often purely circular, in fact, as when they derive actors' preferences from their decisions, and then proceed to "explain" these decisions as the result of such preferences. Cf. Mayhew (1979).

[54] Wildavsky (1991), p. 305. Elster has not, as far as I have been able to see, tried to answer this criticism, but seems rather to have chosen to search for psychological explanations for political phenomena. This might be thought a logical terminal point for his virtually repressive crusade against structuralist approaches within social science. See Elster (1993).

[55] Wildavsky (1991), p. 312. This is a highly simplified account of Wildavsky's cultural theory. For a more comprehensive presentation, see (in addition to the above-mentioned works) Thompson, Ellis, & Wildavsky (1990). A programmatic summary may be found in Wildavsky (1987).

The difficulties with this sort of cultural theory are several, as far as explaining modern welfare policy is concerned. The first is that it does not take sufficient account of how the postmodern individual, if the expression be permitted, can participate in many greatly varying cultures simultaneously. As social development has proceeded, cleanly cohering, linear patterns of life have become ever less usual. Certainly, the high-level state official who has conservative values, votes bourgeois, is a Rotary member, and plays golf in his spare time continues to exist. But what shall we do with the ecologically oriented bank accountant who has exchanged his Volvo for a heavy black (easy-rider styled) Harley Davidson which he drives to work, plays an old Les Paul electric guitar in a grunge rock band at the weekends, is interested in anthroposophist philosophy, and spends at least one day a month at the parental cooperative day-care center "The Mini-Calculators"?[56] What I mean to suggest is that the variation in (post)modern Western societies is simply much greater than in the traditional tribal societies which have furnished the empirical basis on which anthropological theory has been built.

Another point of criticism is that it is difficult, on the aggregate level, to explain variations in social policy between countries by reference to the type of cultural differences that Wildavsky considers so crucial. Not least in the Anglo-Saxon literature can one find theories explaining the exceptional Swedish welfare system as the result of a particular Swedish cultural predilection for equality.[57] In a recent study, Stefan Svallfors has sought to test this claim by comparing (representative samples of) Swedes' and Britons' opinions and values concerning equality, justice, and welfare policy (in interviews done in 1991 and 1987, respectively). One of his conclusions is the following:

> at the level of citizens' opinions, little evidence could be found for Sweden as the homeland of social democratic hegemony and Britain as the bastion of Thatcherism . . . Instead it is more the similarities than the divergencies that are striking when we compare ordinary citizens' attitudes.[58]

Nor can Swedes' values be considered more leftist than those held by Britons; rather, surprisingly enough, they are somewhat further right on most of the dimensions Svallfors measures. In a later study including data on the views of German citizens, furthermore, Svallfors reaches the same finding: "there are no signs of any substantial 'leftist' traits in the general

---

[56] Among the many studies calling attention to this development may be mentioned Ingelhart (1990) and Pettersson (1992).

[57] See, e.g., Verba, Norman, & Kim (1987).

[58] Svallfors (1992b). For references to authors arguing that a cultural ideal of equality pervades Swedish society, see this paper.

Swedish population compared to the two other nations. The Swedes rather seem somewhat less 'leftist' than their German and British counterparts."[59] Those who argue, then, for the existence of a specific Swedish culture of equality, as compared to other Western industrial countries, find no confirmation for this thesis in Svallfors' investigation. This result is particularly interesting, I might add, in view of the fact that these three countries are so frequently classified as wholly different welfare models.[60]

There is, finally, something of a circularity at times in these cultural theories, especially when they are adduced to explain variations on such an aggregate level as that between countries. Not much is gained by saying that "a country has a limited social policy because the inhabitants of that country wanted a limited social policy."[61] This approach boils down to the claim that people act as they do because they want to act as they do, which is not much of a social scientific explanation, but rather a repetition of the data, particularly in the many cases in which preferences are deduced directly from the behavior they are supposed to explain.

A new argument on this topic has been put forward by Robert Putnam in his study of variations in regional democracy in Italy.[62] Putnam investigated why public institutions, that is, the democratic system, function so differently in Italy's different regions. With minor exceptions this is a north/south question. Putnam's study yields the surprising result that it is the density and weight of the local organizational network that is decisive. The more people have been organized in such bodies as choirs, bird-watching clubs, sports associations, etc., the better democracy works. Putnam's feat involves demonstrating that this factor is more significant than traditional socio-economic variables for explaining democracy's manner of operation. According to Putnam, participation in organizational life creates *social capital*, which enables interaction between citizens and between citizens and the political institutions to be built on *trust*, that is, people choose to cooperate with their fellow humans because they trust that the latter will cooperate too. In the various networks of associational life, a binding element arises in the form of norms facilitating cooperation. Expressed in economic terms, social capital reduces transaction costs in the economy, that is, costs associated with ensuring that contracts are kept. By taking part in a multitude of social networks and associations, individuals can build up social capital, which solves the problem of legitimacy. This is the good news from Putnam's

---

[59] Svallfors (1993a), p. 102.   [60] Cf. Esping-Anderson (1990).
[61] Orloff (1993), p. 57f. Cf. Mayhew (1979) for an absolutely brilliant discussion of this question.
[62] Putnam (1993).

pioneering research. The bad news is that this state of affairs cannot easily be brought into being. There is a string of historical determinism as Putnam traces the independent variable back to regional variation in Italy's political culture of the middle ages.[63]

The conclusion I would like to draw, then, is that while this cultural approach has, in a meritorious manner, placed the question of where values and norms come from at center, its own answer to this question is, at least in this context, less than fruitful. For this model is simply too one-dimensional. In this, if in little else, it resembles the self-interest model of individual utility maximization. Our search for the normative foundations of solidarity and welfare policy must therefore seek other ways.

Social norms and political institutions

Let us return to the story of the gold miners. The implicit solution to the problem we have posed is that the existence of social norms, such as the willingness to act in a collective and solidaristic manner, can be traced to existing political institutions. The gold miners had to reach a collective decision after having taken part in an open and (in the Rawlsian sense) *reasoning* debate. Without this institution that produced both the possibility for reason and secured interpersonal trust, the gold miners would undoubtedly – had they acted in their rational self-interest – have sold their share of the property. My major thesis, accordingly, is that Elster's pessimism about the prospects for finding rational explanations for the existence of social norms is quite groundless. Not only do we know that norms play an important role, but we also have an idea of where they come from, why they vary, and therefore how we can explain them. Social norms, I want to argue, *can be explained by the manner in which political institutions structure the decision-making situation faced by actors and influence trust.* This approach turns the prevalent way of seeing the relation between norms and institutions upside down.[64] It is *not* the case, according to this view, that "the just institutional form of social, political, and economic arrangements will in part depend upon the cultural norms shared by the members of a society."[65] The causal connection can also be the reverse.

The variation in norm-governed behavior, and the differences in norms between societies, can thus be traced to the design of political institutions. This idea has a politically interesting corollary, moreover, namely that a society's norms are not structurally given (by culture,

---

[63] Tarrow (1996).   [64] Cf. Soltan (1987).
[65] Weale (1990), p. 486, cf. Wilson (1993).

history, the World Spirit, etc.). If instead norms vary with the character of political institutions, then we as citizens have a critical role to play. We can, at least on some occasions, decide which norms shall prevail in the society we live in, *because we can choose how to design our political institutions.*[66] It has proved possible, for example (at least during certain special moments in Swedish political history), for centrally placed political actors to shape political institutions consciously, and in such a manner as to favor the generation of certain social norms (and interests).[67]

We must now take our leave of social scientific explanations based on one-way causal connections understood as the relation between Independent and Dependent variables. The institutionalist approach used here involves trying to grapple with two-way connections, with various dynamically operating causal chains. Opinions, interests, values, ideology, preferences, etc., all influence institutions and policies. But policies and institutions also influence opinions, etc. Depending on what normative standpoint you take, this is a question of historically developed paths in which the variables, be they dependent or independent, get into virtuous or vicious circles ending up in different but stable equilibria. Instead of just exploring how certain interests and norms give rise to certain institutions, or the reverse, we must try to explain how the *logic* of causation operates between these poles over time. In simplified form, the mental figure looks like this: institutions give rise to certain interests and norms, which in turn either reinforce or undermine the original institutions. We observe, in other words, a bi-directional causal logic between institutions and interests/norms.

Stefan Svallfors' comparative attitude surveys, referred to above (pp. 132–133), are of particular interest here. The question that naturally follows upon reading the results of his investigations is: why do countries, the populations of which seem to have very similar values as regards questions of justice and equality, nevertheless display wholly different welfare models, that is, such different institutional solutions to these problems? Svallfors himself concludes that, since the explanation is not to be found in differing moral conceptions held by the populations of the different countries, it should instead be sought "in the arena of public

---

[66] Cf. North (1990), p. 5: "Institutions are a creation of human beings, hence our theory must begin with the individual. At the same time, the constraints institutions impose on individual choices are pervasive. Integrating individual choices with the constraints institutions impose on choice sets is a major step toward unifying social science research."

[67] Tilton (1990), p. 34; Rothstein (1992a), chs. 6 and 16.

discourse."[68] The great differences in social policy are not the result of divergent values on the part of the different peoples; rather, they are "a matter of successful or failed political strategies."[69] According to Svallfors, then, the level of electoral support enjoyed by social policy crucially depends on which institutional model of welfare prevails, which in turn depends on the success or failure of various political strategies.

Inasmuch as one can show that institutions of this sort are consciously created by centrally placed political actors – with just their norm-creating effects in mind (and indeed this can be shown) – this leads to a more open (in the sense of non-deterministic) view of political history. The relation between strategic political action, political institutions, and the norms and values suffusing society becomes an empirical question, and thereby an open possibility for the future.

How, then, does this relation between institutions and behavior (guided by either norms or self-interest) work? I shall explore this question with the help of an approach developed by among others Amartya Sen, Howard Margolis, Margaret Levi, and Leif Lewin.[70] There is no reason, according to their view, to believe that individuals act on the basis of a single, basic utility function; it is, rather, more reasonable to assume that they have *dual utility functions*. As regards the question of whether persons should act solely on the basis of their self-interest, or should see instead to "the common good," Levi claims that:

> there is both a normative and an instrumental element in the decision to comply (or not) or to volunteer (or not). Certainly, there are segments of the citizenry whose utility function is unitary; they are purely income maximizers or purely moral. A large proportion, however, appear to have *dual utilities*. They wish to contribute to the social good, at least as long as they believe a social good is being produced. They also want to ensure that their individualistic interests are being satisfied as far as possible.[71]

Levi calls this "contingent consent," meaning that citizens will consent under certain conditions to collective (in this case government organized) action. The idea is that citizens try to balance their wish to act according to norms (like contributing to "the common good") with their rational self-interest. Otherwise put, they have a *dual utility function*.[72] They want to pursue their own interests, but they want at the same time to "do the right thing" (to borrow yet again from the promised land of Hollywood

---

[68] Svallfors (1992b), p. 24.   [69] Svallfors (1993a), p. 122.
[70] Sen (1977), Margolis (1984), Levi (1991), and Lewin (1991).
[71] Levi (1991), p. 133. My isalics. Cf. Levi (1997).
[72] Cf. with the above account of Rawls' view of "the rational" and "the reasonable" as complementary and fundamental categories of human action.

films). In a game-theoretical language, they do want to participate in solving the problem of collective action, but they also want to contribute even if it is not in their direct economic interest to do so. For moral reasons, their preferred strategy is to cooperate, but they do not want to be "suckers", that is, finding out that they were the only ones that chose to cooperate and "did the right thing." This presents the individual with two "nested games."[73] One is the game with all other citizens – will they cooperate or not. The other is the game with the government, can it be trusted to deliver what it has promised to deliver, or not. As stated above, this means that their actual behavior is not so much dependent on their ideology, interests, preferences, values or opinions. Instead, their choice to cooperate or not will depend on their "mental map" telling them what the others will do, that is, if other citizens can be trusted to cooperate and if the political institutions can be trusted to deliver whatever they are supposed to deliver.[74]

Unfortunately, we know too little about what types of political institution (besides the ideal market) give rise to what sort of behavior.[75] According to a common argument, it is primarily in small, local, and socially cohesive groups that the willingness to cooperate and act in concert is strong (as in *The Pale Rider*). A classical, closely studied example is that of small and cohesive groups of soldiers in war. When researchers in the United States during and after the Second World War began investigating what actually motivated soldiers at the front to go into battle, and risk their lives thereby, they discovered that it was the fear of appearing before one's fellows as a deserter, that is, as a morally deficient person, which was the most important motive.[76] Central orders, by contrast, mattered little. Rather than live with the knowledge that his fellows considered him a morally inferior person, the average soldier chose to risk his life in combat.[77] This assumed a belief in the ranks that "everyone" pitched in on an equal basis. An army fights, above all, on the *morale* of its soldiers, which in turn depends on a belief among the soldiers that certain basic requirements of *morality* are satisfied.

---

[73] Tsebelis (1990), cf. Moene & Wallerstein (1996).
[74] Misztal (1996), ch. 6 and Hardin (1996).
[75] Cf. Cook (1987).
[76] Keegan (1976), pp. 334ff. and literature cited therein. The story of the gold miners in *The Pale Rider* seems often to have been repeated in the real world, according to research in military psychology and history. Cf. also Howard (1985).
[77] This means, in game-theoretical terms, that what many actors want is to participate in a so-called insurance game. They will gladly contribute to "the common good" – even if materially they lose out thereby – as long as (a) they believe something good will result from these collective efforts, and (b) the great majority of other actors also choose to cooperate. See Hermansson (1990), p. 75.

However, the type of institutions under examination in this study – the various social policy programs – are not small, or local, or necessarily cohesive. On the contrary, they are national and often anonymous (as in the case of the social-insurance system). It is nonetheless an empirical fact that the welfare states of the Western world differ from each other, and not just quantitatively but also qualitatively. Put simply, some welfare states are more generous and comprehensive than others; or, otherwise expressed, the citizens of some countries are more inclined to solidaristic action than the citizens of some other countries. If this fact cannot be explained by "history" or "culture," or "self-interest," the question then becomes in what degree can it be explained as the result of behavior governed by norms – norms, that is, which are generated by institutions.

Interest in analyzing the significance of institutions has grown within the social sciences. Political institutions[78] are now thought to play an important part in explaining political behavior, because they determine who may take part, what resources may be used, and indeed what the rules are for decision-making. To cite George Tsebelis' felicitious formulation: "Selecting institutions is the sophisticated equivalent of selecting policies or selecting outcomes."[79]

What makes institutional analysis interesting is that, on the one hand, it emphasizes that political action must nearly always take place under certain definite rules limiting the choices of actors. Institutions are hard to change; they are tenacious structures affecting what it is possible and rational to do. At certain special historical moments, on the other hand, actors can create institutions – as, for example, after the fall of Soviet communism in Eastern Europe, when it suddenly became possible to write new constitutions. This means that what is rational, socially acceptable, or politically possible is *not* given once and for all by some true, unchanging human nature, but can be influenced through conscious, rational political choice.

As indicated above, I would like here to point to a third important role of political institutions – their norm-setting function. The idea is that institutions not only influence what political actors find to be a rational course of action, seen from the standpoint of their self-interest, but also what they consider to be morally defensible behavior. When one creates an institution by political means – for example, a social-insurance program, a tax system, or a parliamentary forum for decision-making –

---

[78] Defined as "formal arrangements for aggregating individuals and regulating their behavior through the use of explicit rules and decision processes enforced by an actor or set of actors formally recognized as possessing such power," Levi (1990), p. 405.

[79] Tsebelis (1990), p. 118.

one changes not only what future actors will regard as rational action. One changes *what they will regard as morally correct action as well.* The morality prevailing in a society is, in other words, a product of the institutions built by that society's citizens and their representatives. My hypothesis, then, is that social norms are not given by any such metaphysical entities as "the gender system," "class consciousness," or "the national character." They are instead a product of the institutional conditions which have been created de facto by political decision.[80] By this way of seeing things, it is not social norms of a particular type which give rise to specific institutions, but on the contrary, specific institutions that give rise to a particular collection of social norms. Political institutions are not here regarded as codified social conventions which have developed through evolution; the reverse is, rather, true – they produce social conventions. They are, as Robert Grafstein has lucidly put it, "social forces in their own right."[81]

To claim that institutions influence social norms is not new, of course. On the contrary, this has been a prominent view within that part of institutional theory flowing from organizational theory. A central tenet of this view is that institutions do more than just aggregate preferences; they also concern such things as "common cultures, collective identities, belonging, bonds, mutual affection, shared visions, symbols, history, mutual trust, and solidarity."[82] The problem with this sort of enumeration is that it leaves the questions "how" and "why" entirely unspecified. It is presumably correct that many institutions, perhaps most, have many or even all of these features, but it is also reasonable to suppose that some have them in a higher degree than others, and moreover that they exhibit a considerable variation in regard to the import and character of these features. If we assume that political institutions – a universalist welfare policy, for example – bear importance for the formation of social norms, then it is crucial to clarify the causal logic linking these norms with the institution.

Theories of social justice also touch on this set of problems. John

---

[80] There are surprisingly few studies on the origins of norms. In the recently published *Blackwell Encyclopaedia of Political Thought,* for instance, neither "norms" nor "social norms" are even to be found in the index. The problem with such studies as there are is that they typically take a functionalist approach, that is, they portray norms as arising because certain social situations – the famous prisoners' dilemma, for instance – require certain solutions (in the form of generally accepted norms). An example of this type of functionalist reasoning is Ullman-Margalit (1977), another is Hardin (1982). For an analysis of F. W. Hayek's thinking on this subject, see Lundström (1993).

[81] Grafstein (1992), p. 1.   [82] March & Olsen (1989), p. 126.

Rawls' famous original position is clearly nothing but a thought experiment about how reasoning political representatives, when placed in a particular sort of institution, might be thought to produce a norm system capable of being regarded as just.[83] The bad news, however, is that it is less than likely that we shall ever be able to place ourselves in any such original position. As with the events portrayed in *The Pale Rider*, the "veil of ignorance" is only fiction. The good news, as I shall show later on, is that actually existing institutions seem to vary on this point as well. If this is correct, we can analyze how the causal connection works, that is, what types of institution give rise to what norms. The critical problem is highlighted in the question Jane Mansbridge has posed, namely:

> Can we design institutions to encourage motivations that we believe on normative grounds are either good in themselves or will lead to good and just outcomes?[84]

How can this be brought about? What are the conditions for persuading citizens to give over their money (in taxes), their time (mandatory schooling, military service), and possibly themselves and their nearest and dearest (medical attention, education, and other forms of care) to the state? According to Levi, this consent is critical for the degree to which citizens will support a given policy. The theory of contingent consent entails the following: we imagine a situation in which citizens attach moral value to the object sought by collective measures. Such measures are hard to organize, however, since there are always difficulties with ensuring that all who benefit from common efforts also help to defray their costs, instead of acting as free riders. Achieving sufficient support for such measures presupposes that three conditions be fulfilled. These are that (1) citizens regard the program in itself as fair; (2) they believe their fellow citizens also contribute on a solidaristic basis;[85] and (3) they consider the program to be organized in keeping with

> procedural justice, and the object for evaluation is usually the government and its agents. Citizens who consider government to be fair in this sense generally feel they participated in the decision-making, perceive government decision-makers as relatively unbiased and neutral, perceive themselves as having been treated respectfully, and believe the outcome of the process to have been fair if not favourable.[86]

---

[83] See, e.g., Söderström (1977).   [84] Mansbridge (1990), p. 21.
[85] Levi (1993), cf. Levi (1991). Levi (1997) has a fourth condition, namely "bearable costs". My argument against including such a condition is that citizens would not value a policy as fair if it presented them with "unbearable costs."
[86] Levi (1993), p. 7; cf. Tyler (1990).

In order to appear legitimate, then, the state must first of all appeal to social norms emphasizing the value of collective political solutions and programs, and must show that these do not function in a manner that is discriminatory or otherwise unfair. Secondly, it must persuade the citizens that they can trust that other citizens will "comply, volunteer, or otherwise contribute in the specified ways." Thirdly, it must demonstrate that that the implementation of these measures "meets standards of fairness."[87] Those claiming that the state's exercise of power is illegitimate – in general or within a specific area – will argue, according to this theory, that conditions opposite to those listed obtain. They will try, for example, to persuade citizens to embrace "standards of fairness that government cannot implement."[88]

Clearly, the opinions citizens entertain about state legitimacy can vary between different policy areas. It is altogether reasonable, for example, to regard the existing agricultural policy as granting illegitimate advantages to a particular occupational group, and as leading to arbitrariness and economic irrationality besides, while at the same time considering social science research to be a critical public interest, and an undeniably legitimate recipient of state support therefore, especially since it is carried out by skillful and competent scholars who furnish the country with a first-rate return on its invested tax monies.

It is important to note that two of the above conditions are directly tied to how the institutions charged with implementing policy are organized, that is, they are concerned with what the state can do. How we design such institutions is therefore critical for the direction in which the dual utility function will go; or, in other words, for what norms will prevail in society; or put yet another way, for which view of what the state should do will prevail. I shall discuss these conditions in greater detail below.

As mentioned, the first condition has to do with the program's *general fairness*. Is the goal of the program just? For example, is the war in which citizens (in reality the young men among them) are asked to risk their lives a just one? Is the tax system which finances the collective undertakings designed in a fair manner? Is it fitting that the health-care system should encompass all citizens on an equal basis?

This condition has considerable implications for public policy and public discourse. For it means that public measures cannot be justified solely by reference to the judgments of professional experts or the results

[87] Levi (1993), p. 12. Levi's theory builds partly on Margolis (1984).
[88] Levi (1993), p. 11.

of narrow cost/benefit analyses. It can be difficult to fulfill this condition for selective programs, because such programs favor only specially delineated groups or interests. Those who design the program, that is, the leading political decision-makers, must be prepared to enter into a moral discourse, and to justify the program in terms of at least some kind of theory of justice and fairness. In other words, they must take part in a discussion about what the state should do. As Gutman and Thompson have argued, this means that "the forum in which we conduct our political discussion should be designed so as to encourage officials to justify their actions with moral reason."[89] We may call this the requirement of *substantive justice.*

The second condition has to do with whether citizens believe that their fellow citizens bear their fair share of the program's costs, that is, with the question of the *just distribution of burdens.* Citizens may certainly be of the opinion that the purposes of the programs in question are worthwhile (defense, welfare, etc.), and be prepared to support them therefore, but only on condition that other citizens pull their weight as well. Most of the goods the state produces have the general character of "steep goods" – that is, they can either be effected in full measure or not at all. The classical example from economic theory is that of a bridge: it is meaningless to build such a structure for 99 percent of the distance required, for in that case it is 100 percent useless. Or take the case of defense: to go out and defend the country on a solo basis is undoubtedly heroic but also quite pointless. Or take a third example: if the tax system is to function, the state must convince the citizens that all (or almost all) of the other citizens will also pay their duly allotted share. The willingness of an individual to contribute to "the common good" is dependent on his believing that others also take part in great numbers, and that no large groups draw wrongful advantage from the system.[90] In certain special situations, certainly, a collective rallying to the common need can be brought about solely by appealing to moral imperatives. More typically, however – especially in the case of larger collectivities – it must be effected through the construction of effective mechanisms of control, that is, by means of correctly designed institutions.

---

[89] Gutman & Thompson (1990), p. 141. From a rationalistic perspective as well, moreover, some scholars have begun emphasizing the importance of leaders able to endow the purposes of collective efforts with legitimacy. See Bianco & Bates (1990) and Bendor & Mookherje (1987).

[90] Cf. Rawls (1993), p. 53: "Insofar as we are reasonable, we are ready to work out the framework of the public social world, a framework it is reasonable to expect everyone to endorse and act on, *provided others can be relied on to do the same*" (my italics).

The third condition has to do with the program's implementation. Conditional consent requires that the program be carried out in a fair fashion, i.e., that it embody the virtue of *procedural justice*. For example, citizens may regard the war in which the nation is engaged as a just one (e.g., they may regard it as a defensive war), yet attempt to avoid induction nevertheless, on the grounds that the procedures for selecting which young men must fight are bitterly unfair. When it comes to the tax system, citizens might assuredly regard the principles of its design as fair, but seek even so to avoid paying their taxes, since they consider the system of tax collection – as it functions in practice – to be deeply unjust. And in the area of social insurance, it is altogether reasonable to take the view that such programs are badly needed, yet seek to thwart them all the same, because one believes benefit fraud is too common.

With the help of these three conditions for consent, then, I have tried to combine a normative theory about what the state *should* do with an empirical theory about what the state *can* do. A constructive theory about the bases of modern welfare policy can thus begin to take form. These otherwise distinct questions – "what is" and "what ought to be" – converge in the analysis of how political institutions (the organs of implementation especially) are designed. The object of the next chapter is to describe more concretely how this two-way connection works in the area of social policy. To conclude with the opening sentence of the quotation from Rawls which began this chapter: "A just system must generate its own support."

6

The political and moral logic of the universal welfare state

In the last chapter, I called attention to how human behavior is governed both by narrow self-interest and by the social norms emerging in an open, reasoning discourse. Put otherwise, human beings have dual utility functions and their behavior is strategic. What is the result of this in concrete politics? And what does it mean for the future of the universal welfare policy? The institutionalist approach I use here builds on the idea of a two-way relation between institutions and behavior.[1] This means we must explain both what social forces and factors lie behind the appearance and subsequent reproduction of a universal welfare policy, and what effects on these social forces the universal welfare policy as an institution gives rise to. If we recall here the idea of dual utility functions, moreover, two questions arise. Firstly, what types of institutions and social norms sustain a macro-institution like a universal welfare policy? Secondly, which norms and interests are strengthened, and which are weakened, by the manner in which this institution operates?

It would perhaps be advantageous, pedagogically speaking, to examine the political and normative logics each in themselves. As I stressed in the last chapter, however, the whole point of the idea of dual utility functions is that the political and moral logics are intimately connected to each other, and so must be treated in a single context. The willingness of citizens to assist in realizing the objectives of a universal welfare policy depends on their regarding both the substance and the process of the policy as correct. This depends in turn on how the political institutions charged with the making and implementation of collective decisions are designed.

[1] Or to use a different terminology, how the *dialectic* functions in this context.

Variations in social policy between countries

Seldom does the real world behave according to the predictions of social scientific models. If we go back in time, three decades say, we find that the proportion of gross national product spent by OECD countries on social programs did not vary especially much. Up until the early 1960s, Sweden was one welfare state among others, and its social policy was neither more comprehensive nor more generous that that in other comparable countries. Three decades later, however, the variation is much greater. Comparative developments in social policy have, one might say, followed the shape of a fan. Instead of convergence between similar countries, we have seen divergence. At the start of the 1990s, Sweden was distinctive in several ways. One was in the unusual breadth and comprehensiveness of its social policy.[2] The remarkable thing about this widening social policy divergence between countries is that it has occurred at the same time as these countries have experienced an increasing internationalization of their economies. Indeed, the overall political and social interdependence of these countries has increased during the last three decades. This ought to have led, one might reasonably conclude, to convergence in respect of social-policy ambitions, but evidently it has not.

The quantitative measurement of welfare policy variation mentioned above is obviously a very rough way of describing what distinguishes Western capitalist democracies from each other. Several attempts have been made, with varying degrees of success, to capture the qualitative differences between welfare models as well.[3] One usual distinction, mentioned earlier, is that between selective and universal welfare states. Some of the ways in which these two types differ are summarized in table 6.1.

As Diane Sainsbury has shown, the Swedish welfare state approaches the universal model, even if considerable departures from the pure form may be observed. One unavoidable feature of a universal welfare state, it should be noted, is a heavy tax burden. If benefits and services are to be made available to the entire population, and if they are to be of such a

---

[2] Esping-Andersen (1990); Stephens (1996).

[3] See, e.g., Esping-Andersen (1990), who identifies three different types: (a) the liberal welfare model, which coincides broadly with the selective model; (b) the social democratic model, which is largely the same as the general model; and (c) the Catholic-corporative model, which is a sort of middle category. Like the general welfare state, the last-mentioned type covers the entire population, but the programs are often divided up, so that different social groups make use of different services and social insurance programs.

Table 6.1. *Dimensions of variation between selective and universal welfare policy*

Dimension	Selective	Universal
Proportion of GNP devoted to social purposes	Small	Large
Benefit levels	Minimal	Adequate
Range of statutory benefits and services	Limited	Extensive
Proportion of population covered by benefits and services	Minority	Majority
Dominant type of program	Means-tested	Universal
Role of programs preventing need for assistance in first place	Nonexistent	Critical
Financing	Fees	Taxes
Significance of private organizations	Great	Small
Favored role of state direction	Minimal	Optimal

Source: From Sainsbury (1991), p. 4; cf. Korpi (1980), p. 303.

quality as to satisfy also the better-situated, then high taxes are quite simply indispensable. Naturally it is incomprehensible for a libertarian that a people could accept a tax burden of 57 percent of GNP. The obvious answer to this puzzle is that public acceptance of this state of affairs depends on the view being widely held that the results thereby obtained stand in reasonable proportion to the sacrifices incurred.[4]

This means that, if we are to understand the political logic behind the universal welfare state, we must think in the terms suggested by the classic Italian system of double bookkeeping. This system is based on the idea of a relation between costs and revenues, debts and assets. One should bear this approach in mind when considering Swedish social policy. The Swedish tax system is now, after the tax reform of 1990, only modestly progressive (and not just in fact but also in form).[5] Many scholars have maintained that, since benefits and services are distributed in roughly equal shares to everyone, and since the tax system is proportional on the whole, then no real redistribution between income

---

[4] Cf. Agell (1992), pp. 248f.
[5] Even before 1990, the tax system's real progressivity was not so great. See Steinmo (1993), pp. 1f.

Table 6.2. *The redistributive effect of the universal welfare state*

Group	Average income	Tax (40%)	Transfers	Income after taxes and transfers
A (20%)	1,000	400	240	840
B (20%)	800	320	240	720
C (20%)	600	240	240	600
D (20%)	400	160	240	480
E (20%)	200	80	240	360
Ratio between groups A and E	5/1	(= 1,200)	(1,200/5=240)	2.33/1

groups takes place.[6] Some economists have therefore claimed that the welfare system amounts largely to a costly bureaucratic roundabout.[7] Nothing could be further from the truth. This very common standpoint is, in fact, among the great follies of modern social science. Table 6.2 illustrates why. The redistributive logic of the model is as follows. In the first column, income earners are divided for the sake of simplicity into five groups of equal size, according to average income. We assume the average income of the group earning most is five times that of the group earning least. This difference, which we may call the inequality quotient, is 5/1. We further assume, *nota bene,* not a progressive but rather a strictly proportional system of income taxes. We set the tax rate at 40%, which corresponds roughly to that part of the public sector's presently 56.2% of GNP that is spent on social, educational, and other welfare policy. Finally, we assume that all public benefits and services are universal, which means that the individuals in each group receive *on average* the same sum in the form of cash benefits and/or subsidized public services. The result, as seen in the last column, is a dramatic reduction in inequality between group A and group E, from 5/1 down to 2.33/1. The level of inequality has thus been reduced by more than half in this model of how the universal welfare policy works. Note that this redistributive logic works in the same way if you take the groups' (or persons') income over a life-time as well as if you compare them at one

---

[6] The following builds on many discussions I have had with Peter Mayers, whose ideas and suggestions have been most valuable. Mayers was the one who first pointed out to me the redistributive effects in the model below.
[7] Tullock (1983).

single point in time. It is only if you can argue that over time the persons in groups A and B will switch with the persons in groups D and E that the redistributive effect decreases.

Nevertheless, it should again be stressed that the redistribution in the model is achieved with no progressivity in the tax system whatsoever, and with no targeting of benefits and services on (as the usual term goes) the truly needy. Such scholars as Amy Gutman, J. Donald Moon, Peter Baldwin, Brian Barry, Albert Weale, and Gordon Tullock, are thus mistaken when they claim that a universal welfare policy does not contribute in any significant degree to achieving social equality.[8] I believe their mistake results from their not recalling the simple fact that both incomes and expenditures must be counted when judging the net impact of all economic transactions. They have instead simply pored over the fact that "everyone receives the same," which obviously involves no redistribution. What they have missed is that different income groups part with different absolute sums, even if their tax rate is the same in percentage terms.[9]

The central message of Italian double bookkeeping – that where there is a credit entry there must also be a debit entry – has passed these authors by. When, as in this case, expenditures (taxes) are equal in proportional terms, while incomes (benefits, services) are equal in nominal terms, considerable redistribution takes place between those with high and those with low incomes. When Amy Gutman, for example, writes that a system of generally available social services is "the least likely to meet the material needs of the poor," she lacks both theoretical and empirical support for her conclusion.[10]

The stickler for detail can now point out that many benefits in the universal welfare state are not equal for all citizens, but rather are income-related, and that this limits their redistributive effect. In some cases, such as education, the middle class clearly recieves more.[11] This is true in theory but not in concrete policy. Even if one includes benefits of this type, the redistributive effect is considerable. The reason for this is that, in nearly all of the income-replacement programs typical of the universal welfare state, there is an income ceiling over which no further compensation is paid, but over which high-income citizens must continue paying charges nonetheless (in the form of wage taxes). The extent

---

[8] Gutman (1990), B. Barry (1990), Goodin (1988), Moon (1990), Tullock (1983).
[9] That some philosophers and historians make such a mistake is noteworthy, but that economists of the trade do so as well is striking indeed. See Lars Söderström (1988), p. 83.
[10] Gutman (1990), p. 11.
[11] Davidson (1989) and Goodin & LeGrand, and associates (1987).

of redistribution depends, in other words, not just "on accuracy of aim but also on the sums transferred," as Walter Korpi and Joakim Palme write.[12] Söderström's calculation of the redistributive effect of the Swedish social insurance system shows that, if one compares the 20 percent of households earning most with the 20 percent earning least, the inequality quotient falls, after taxes and transfers, from 3.75/1 to 2.43/1. It bears noting that Söderström's thesis – that the Swedish welfare state has largely favored the middle class and has had no redistributive effect – is fully contradicted by his own data, which show that the top (in the sense of economically strongest) 60 pecent of households are those which pay in more than they get back from the social insurance system.[13]

When, therefore, a philosopher like Brian Barry claims that this type of welfare state "has no inherent tendency to bring about . . . net transfers" between different social classes, he has no empirical basis whatsoever for his view.[14] Still stronger support for the thesis that the general welfare model is, as compared to its selective counterpart, a superior machine of redistribution may be found in empirical studies comparing income distribution in different countries.[15] Thanks to the data bank built up in the so-called Luxemburg Income Data Study, we now know a great deal more about these matters than earlier. As shown in table 6.3, the variation between countries in the area of income redistribution is rather great. One interesting conclusion to be drawn from table 6.3 is that a strong relation of the following type apparently obtains: the more universal the welfare system, the greater the redistributive effect. It is precisely the countries in the lower half of the last column which are usually classified as selective welfare states. This, it must be stressed, is a paradoxical and counter-intuitive result. One might reasonably expect that the countries

[12] Korpi & Palme (1993), p. 148; Weale (1990).
[13] Calculated from table 3A in Lars Söderström (1988), pp. 83 and 144. The data are from 1982 and include households the adults of which are between twenty and sixty-five years of age. If households whose members are over sixty-five are also included, the redistributive effect is strongly enhanced. According to information communicated orally to the author, neither consumption taxes nor employers' fees are included in the calculation of what the different groups pay in tax. If these are included as well, the redistributive effect in all likelihood becomes much greater. Lars Söderström's report has sometimes been taken as evidence that the Swedish type of welfare state largely redistributes between different periods in the individual's lifecycle, and not between income groups.
[14] B. Barry (1990), p. 505.
[15] See Korpi & Palme (1993). This is also stressed by Söderström (ed.) (1988), pp. 84f., who with a number of reservations nonetheless writes that: "higher public transfers contribute to a more equal distribution, even when account is taken of various types of repercussions."

Table 6.3. *Ranking based on Gini-coefficients[a] before and after taxes and transfers, and resulting net redistribution*

Gini-coefficients before taxes and transfers		Gini-coefficients after taxes and transfers		Net redistribution (percent)	
Norway	0.385	Sweden	0.197	Sweden	53
Canada	0.387	Norway	0.234	Norway	39
United Kingdom	0.393	Germany	0.252	Germany	38
Germany	0.407	United Kingdom	0.264	Netherlands	37
Switzerland	0.414	Australia	0.287	France	35
Australia	0.414	Canada	0.293	United Kingdom	33
Sweden	0.417	Netherlands	0.293	Australia	31
United States	0.425	France	0.307	United States	25
Netherlands	0.467	United States	0.317	Canada	24
France	0.471	Switzerland	0.336	Switzerland	19

[a] The Gini-coefficient is a standard statistical measure of inequality.
Source: Castles & Mitchell (1992), p. 22. See also Fritzell (1991), p. 148.

concentrating their assistance on "the truly needy" – where the state literally takes from the rich and gives to the poor – would be those achieving the greatest redistribution. Yet this is evidently not the case. It is rather the countries that take from "everyone" and give to "everyone" that exhibit the most marked redistribution. This is partly for the reason illustrated in the model above – that is, taxation is largely proportional, while most benefits are either flat or have a ceiling (i.e., they match incomes only up to a certain limit). The political factor is also important, however. Walter Korpi and Joakim Palme put the point this way: "If we take from the rich to give to the poor, the rich simply will not part with especially large sums."[16] Or to paraphrase what Lyndon B. Johnson said, soon after becoming President, in explanation of why he did not dismiss FBI chief J. Edgar Hoover: it is better to have the sharp elbows of the middle class on the inside of the system pressing it outwards, than the other way round.[17] The critical thing for whether or not the welfare state redistributes, contrary to what one might think, is that the system embraces not just the poor but also (and above all) the well-to-do.

[16] Korpi & Palme (1993), p. 148.
[17] From O'Higgins (1987), p. 14.

The political logic of the welfare state

How, then, can we explain this difference in scope and character between the welfare states of the Western world? As indicated in chapter 1, the research in this area is very extensive, and it reveals (not unexpectedly) that a range of factors is at work. There does, however, seem to be considerable empirical support for the so-called power-resource model, which stresses the importance of the mobilization of wage-earners in trade unions and social-democratic parties. The stronger trade unions are, and the greater the political influence of social-democratic parties, the more comprehensive and universal the welfare policy pursued.[18] The problem then remains of explaining why some capitalist democracies have stronger social-democratic parties and higher rates of trade-union organization than others. Is there a connection, perhaps, between the policies pursued and the strength of labor organizations? Have policies been enacted, that is, that favor the appearance of a strong social democracy and strong trade unions? The answer to this question is affirmative.[19] As is usual in the social sciences, the relation between these elements is not one-way, but two-way and dialectical.

Karl Marx's theory has played many tricks on the labor movement, one of them being the mistaken prediction that the development of the productive forces would lead, on the one hand, to the homogenization of the working class, and on the other, to this class becoming a numerical majority. It did not turn out that way, of course, and in the time since the Second World War, social-democratic parties in the West have had to wrestle with the fact that their traditional voting group has stagnated and thereafter diminished in size. It is instead the white-collar groups which have rapidly grown.

In the research on why different countries have different welfare arrangements, the relation between the type of programs social-democratic parties have established, and the electoral support they have enjoyed, has come into focus.[20] According to this theory, social-democratic parties must – if they are to attract a sufficient number of voters to achieve office – design welfare programs so as to favor not just the (diminishing) working class, but also that (increasing) part of the population working in various white-collar and service occupations (those termed in class analysis the middle strata or the middle class).

---

[18] Esping-Andersen (1990).
[19] This theory was first launched by Przeworski (1985). For an empirical illustration, see Rothstein (1992c) and Svensson (1994).
[20] For a more extensive discussion and analysis on this point, see Rothstein (1990).

This, however, has confronted social democratic electoral strategists with a difficult dilemma. They can, on the one hand, limit themselves to traditional working-class questions; this makes it difficult or impossible to win office, but it also reduces tensions within the labor movement and enables the party to retain a traditional working-class profile. Or they can try to broaden their electoral base by launching a welfare policy designed in such a manner as to attract not just workers but white-collar employees as well. This latter strategy has the advantage of making it possible to attract a sufficient number of voters to take power. However, it also entails the risk of creating tensions inside the party, and of being rejected as non-solidaristic by the party's traditional working-class voters, who might then abstain from voting or in other ways supporting the party.[21]

However, the severity of this dilemma varies between countries, according to the composition of the class structure and the organization of the labor movement. This, according to the theory, explains why social democratic parties have enjoyed varying degrees of success in different countries. This theory is interesting in that it does something relatively rare in social science, namely combine structural factors (class structure), institutional factors (working-class organization), and actor-level factors (choice of strategy in the form of social programs) in a dynamic process.[22]

I shall not attempt to test the tenability of this theory here. I take it, rather, to be a largely correct explanation of the two-way connection between the structure of the social democratic welfare state and its electoral support. For further evidence, I refer the reader to the literature cited. I would like rather to emphasize the point found in the research. The Swedish Social Democrats seem hold the world championship in handling this dilemma. They have succeeded in striking the best possible balance between blue-collar and white-collar interests; they have structured their various social programs in accordance with these *post facto* handbooks in reformist political strategy. They have, in general, succeeded in framing social policy in such a way as to gain the support not just of the party's traditional working-class supporters, but of white-collar employees and the middle class as well. This two-way process has been thought to function like a perpetual motion machine, in which the social-democratic-governed state has built up a universal welfare policy, which in turn has generated a continued increase in support for the party (despite the fact that its traditional electorate has diminished). In an alternative interpretation, this process has forced the parties to the right

---

[21] Przeworski (1985), Przeworski & Sprague (1986).
[22] Svensson (1994) shows how this has functioned in the Swedish case.

of the Social Democrats to accept or even embrace the ideology of the universal welfare state.[23] The first thesis, then, is that a universal welfare state can only exist if it enjoys support far up the social ladder. The "poor," the "underprivileged," the "working class," or any other such social group is simply too small to constitute a sufficient electoral base for a comprehensive universal welfare policy. And conversely, one can only reckon with support for this policy from white-collar groups and the middle class if it is so formulated as to serve their interests as well (however these are defined).

The critical political position occupied by the middle groups is also apparent if we take another look at table 6.2. Group C, the middle group, is central here for two reasons. The model shows, to begin with, that *for this group,* the universal welfare policy is largely an economic roundabout. That is, they pay exactly as much in taxes as they get back in the form of services and benefits. They neither gain nor lose economically.[24] This group could therefore be expected, on the assumption of rational utility maximization, to exhibit more uncertainty in their view of the universal welfare policy than any other group. Yet this group may – even considering the matter from a rationalistic standpoint – be won for a universal welfare policy, under two conditions.

The first condition is that the members of this group consider the value they get back to correspond tolerably well to the value they pay in. Be it granted, such a calculation may be exceedingly difficult for the individual to perform; still, let us assume that these persons perceive this connection, and possess a certain ability to calculate rationally. If they consider the public services to be of low quality, or inaccessible, or of otherwise unacceptable character, one may expect a diminished willingness on their part to support (i.e., pay for) the universal welfare policy. This means, in political terms, that they will withdraw their electoral support from parties pursuing such a policy. According to the theory of contingent consent, moreover, the same thing can happen if the universal welfare policy does not deliver what it promises, procedurally speaking, or if there is a widespread belief that the various systems are abused.

The other reason of a rationalist nature for this group to support a universal system, despite gaining nothing from it economically, has to do with its insurance character. For one not wholly sure of what the future

[23] Cf. Uddhammar (1993).

[24] Söderström (ed.) (1988) shows that the middle groups lose out as a result of the social insurance system. However, in view of the fact that they make more intensive use of the educational system, publicly financed culture, and municipal day-care than the low-income groups do, they probably end up roughly at a balance of plus minus nought.

has in store, there can be cause to support such a system, even if one will not gain by it in a statistical material sense. In the event of unforeseen economic difficulties occasioned by unemployment or illness, it is probably much more agreeable to be taken care of by a universal than by a selective welfare system. For the latter requires recipients to sell off all their assets before receiving any help, and it only offers such assistance as suffices to maintain a minimum level. To be forced, on account of temporary economic difficulties, to sell off large portions of one's assets may in fact be something which the middle class in particular finds extremely disagreeable. It can also make it harder to solve the situation or to return to working life.

The other reason for the centrality of this group is that, if rationalist assumptions about voting behavior as founded in self-interest are correct, it is the *electorally decisive* group. Groups D and E will obviously support the universal welfare policy, according to the rationalist viewpoint, since they gain from it materially. Similarly, groups A and B will oppose such a system, as they pay more in taxes than they get back. (They could support the policy anyway, of course, but for other reasons.) It is group C that determines the direction of policy, for its votes determine which side holds the majority. The middle group is therefore of absolutely critical political importance for the maintenance of a universal welfare policy. In part, this is because it is *economically* the most sensitive group for how the system works; in part, it is because it is *electorally* the decisive group. One could say, to simplify a little, that in those countries with a universal welfare policy a political alliance between groups C, D, and E has been successfully forged. In the countries pursuing a selective policy, by contrast, the majoritarian political constellation consists of groups A, B, and C. The simple mathematics of democracy tells us that three beats two.

Our model would lead us, then, to expect political alignments of this kind. And, in fact, this expectation is confirmed in the empirical research done on the Swedish welfare state's support base and design. Stefan Svallfors' study (which is based on interview data) of the support enjoyed by welfare policy in different social groups largely confirms the assumptions of our model: the higher up the social-class ladder, the thinner the support for the welfare state. It is, moreover, precisely the group in the middle that vacillates the most, ideologically speaking, and whose support for social policy is most conditional.[25] In respect of the welfare state's design, moreover, Torsten Svensson has shown that Social Democratic

[25] Svallfors (1989 and 1991).

strategists have regarded the support of middle groups as altogether critical, and have consciously designed their policies accordingly.[26]

However, this theory of why different countries pursue different welfare polices, and exhibit varying degrees of social-democratic strength, presents us with some problems. For one thing, if the Swedish Social Democrats have been so infernally skillful in building this cross-class support base for their welfare policy, then why, in the election of 1991, did they turn in their worst electoral performance since 1928? In both 1985 and 1988, the party had presented itself as the main guarantee for the preservation of the welfare state, and proposals from the bourgeois parties for (very modest) cutbacks gave the Social Democrats a great advantage in the election campaign.[27] Did the Swedish voters suddenly tire in 1991 of being cared for by the state "from the cradle to the grave?" Or did the Social Democratic strategists miscalculate in some way? Either something is basically wrong with our theory of the relation between the welfare state and its electoral support, or the party strategists did not study the handbooks closely enough this time.[28] I shall examine this question more closely in chapter 7, where I shall attempt to give a tentative explanation for this paradox.

Secondly, the theory under consideration proceeds on the premise – which earlier we examined and found wanting – that political behavior is founded in self-interest. It paints a harsh picture: policy is formulated so as to serve the self-interest of certain groups, and therefore attracts their electoral support. Voters smile, in other words, on policies that grant them economic advantage, and they do not allow matters of morality or the common interest to disturb their calculations.

One reason the universal welfare state cannot be explained solely on the basis of narrow rationalist assumptions is the following. In all of the Scandinavian countries, bourgeois parties have held the reins of power for relatively long periods during the past two decades. Notwithstanding this, one cannot in any of these countries during the periods of bourgeois governments discern a reduction in welfare expenditures or a change to a more selective social policy. If the universal welfare state has been the most significant factor behind the build-up of the parliamentary strength of the social democratic parties, why then have the bourgeois parties in Scandinavia not been more successful in breaking up this system and replacing it with a more selective one?[29] As Paul Pierson has shown, even

---

[26] Svensson (1994).   [27] Bergström (1991).
[28] I am aware, of course, that there were many reasons – over and above the design of welfare policy – for the Social Democratic defeat in 1991. Cf. Rothstein (1993a).
[29] Cf. Rothstein (1993a).

the Thatcher and Reagan governments got into problems with the "fairness issue" when trying to cut back welfare programs.[30]

One way to keep the analysis within the "rational self-interest" approach would be to argue that the middle and (to some extent) the upper classes support a universal system because they overestimate the risks of becoming unemployed, etc.[31] That would mean that even if it does not in economic terms pay back for them the self-interest model would still suffice to explain their behavior. My argument against this is that they would, being rational and risk adverse, then try to organize their social-insurance system and their need of social services separately on a class or professional-group base instead of taking on the costs for supporting the lower social classes that, in a capitalist society, pay less taxes and are likely to need more support.[32] There is thus strong reason to question whether self-interest is a sufficient explanation for political behavior (whether of politicians or of voters). The universal welfare state embodies a moral as well a political logic. What does the former look like?

The moral logic of the welfare state

I tried in the last chapter to show that social norms can be a function of institutions, as well as of the other way round. For instance, a norm that says state power is basically illegitimate weakens the ability of the state to function (to safeguard the common interest, for example), which in turn strengthens the norm of state illegitimacy, and so the cycle continues. Now then, if social norms have the importance we have ascribed to them, we must try to grasp the logic linking these norms with an institution like the universal welfare state.

I shall build here on the theory about consent, which I presented in more detail in chapter 5. This theory seeks to explain how the greater number of citizens can choose to support a universal over a selective social policy, despite it not lying in their direct material self-interest. I wish to emphasize again that arguments of a moral nature may be assumed to carry the greatest weight with those in the middle group above, because their calculation of utility in the face of the welfare system yields a balance of plus minus nought, at the same time as their electoral support is decisive for who gains a majority. I assume, then, that moral

---

[30] Pierson (1996), p. 102.
[31] About the theory of the risk society, see Beck (1992).
[32] This is an argument against the otherwise convincing attempt by Moene & Wallerstein (1996) to explain the difference between selective and universal welfare systems based on a model of self-interested voters.

reasoning can be assumed to be of especial importance for individual behavior when the rational calculation of utility yields an unclear result. If we are to understand this matter, then, our analysis must take account of both rational and moral behavior. Before undertaking this analysis, however, I would like to stress one point. The discussion below attempts to ascertain - *at the level of principle* - the moral logic underlying support for (and opposition to) various types of welfare policy. As mentioned above, the actually existing welfare system is founded, in all countries, on a mixture of principles. For instance, even if Swedish social policy may be characterized as largely universal in character, it exhibits many significant departures from this principle as well. The discussion below therefore treats not the moral logic underlying Swedish social policy as such, but rather some prominent features of this policy.

Substantive justice

As mentioned above, the first condition of contingent consent has to do with the question of *general fairness,* or otherwise expressed, the problem of *substantive justice.* That is, can one argue that the goals of a particular social-policy measure are just? We can find the answer to this question in the discussion of *what the state should do* in chapter 2: the state should treat all citizens with "equal concern and respect," and it should furnish them with "basic capabilities" so as to enable them to make autonomous choices. The first principle lies, we might say, at the heart of a universal welfare policy.[33] Indeed, the whole point of a universal welfare policy is not to discriminate between citizens, not to separate "the needy" and "the poor" from other citizens and to treat them differently. Social policy should seek instead to furnish citizens with *basic capabilities* according to the principle of *equal concern and respect,* thereby placing them on a more or less equal footing in respect to their ability to act as autonomous citizens.

In contrast to the situation under a selective system, the public discussion of welfare policy in a universal system cannot be conducted in the terms indicated by the question: "what shall we do about these deviant groups/individuals?" (Or as former US Vice-President Dan Quayle put it in a debate: "those people."[34])

In chapter 4, I called attention to the limits of public policy, and pointed out that the state cannot do everything. I stressed, furthermore, that such limits are particularly evident when it comes to implementing programs of a "dynamically interventionist" type. The idea of *basic*

---

[33] Titmuss (1967/1987).   [34] Quoted in Katz (1989), p. 236.

capabilities is in line with this. On the one hand, the state should supply all citizens with these *capabilities*; on the other, the state cannot have an all-embracing responsibility for citizens' well-being. Those *capabilities* not defined as basic are, in principle, the citizen's own headache.[35] The precise content of the notion of basic *capabilities* obviously varies, both over time and according to political ideology, and it cannot be definitively established on the basis of political philosophy. As a general matter, however, one can say that such *capabilities* are needed as enable citizens to take part as free and equal partners in the political discourse.[36] The critical thing is that we bear in mind what the debate over state responsibility should treat with, and that we formulate a principle for how these *capabilities* ought to be distributed.

My point is that, depending on the institutions we select for furnishing citizens with these basic *capabilities*, we create different types of moral logic in the social-policy discourse. In the case of a selective policy, the state separates out those citizens unable to provide such basic *capabilities* for themselves, and furnishes them with said *capabilities*. To do this, however, it must first determine whether or not they belong to the needy group, and if so, how much they need. The problem, as I shall show below, is that it is very hard to do these things without violating the principle that the state should treat all citizens with "equal concern and respect." The very act of separating out the needy almost always stamps them as socially inferior, as "others" with other types of social character-istics and needs, and results most often in stigmatization.[37] Michael Walzer argues that social policy of this sort is incompatible with the maintenance of recipients' self-respect. And persons lacking self-respect are scarcely able to act as autonomous citizens in the sense described in chapter 2.[38]

The public discussion of social policy in a selective system often becomes a question of what the well-adjusted majority should do about the less well-adjusted or, in varying degrees, socially marginalized minor-ity. The system's *general fairness* can thereby come under question by the majority, who might start asking (a) where the line between the needy and non-needy should be drawn, and (b) whether the needy themselves

---

[35] This does not exclude the possibility that a universal welfare state can take responsibility also for matters above and beyond the resources defined here as basic, but it need not then necessarily follow the principle of "equal concern and respect."

[36] Sen (1982), pp. 364ff.   [37] Salonen (1993), pp. 176–180.

[38] Walzer (1983), pp. 277f.; cf. Moon (1990), p. 35 and D. Miller (1978), p. 19. One can always, of course, consider this a reasonable price to pay for a lower overall tax level, as does Borg (1992).

are not to blame for their predicament (and so cannot legitimately claim assistance). We may refer to the first as the general and the second as the individual boundary-drawing problem. Contrary to the claims of such philosophers as Gerald Cohen and John Roemer,[39] there is often (as I showed in chapter 4) no practical possibility of solving these problems at the level of implementation. In the selective model, the discussion often comes to focus on "the undeserving poor."[40] In other words, an unending debate is set in motion about how and where to draw these two boundary lines. It is therefore hard to argue that selective programs are fair, for the simple reason that they are not universal. Public consent to the system is undermined, rather, because the social policy debate comes to turn not on what is *generally fair,* but on what is *specifically necessary* (for the deviating individuals needing the help of the state).[41] Moreover, since the majority can all the while question the way in which the two boundary lines are drawn (since this can almost never be done with sufficient precision), the moral logic of the discourse tends to undermine the legitimacy of the system. Most selective types of policies that are structured to integrate a specific group with the rest of society, seem to entail a paradox of the following kind: to motivate selective measures of whatever kind for a certain group, this group must first be singled out as *different* from ordinary citizens. But if the group is that different, how can they ever by any social policy initiative become like "ordinary citizens." If the selective policy has only marginal effects, the usual strategy for those advocating it is to argue that the group is even more different (and thus has even more special needs) than what had initially been presumed.

Under a universal system – in which the state furnishes all citizens with these basic *capabilities* – the moral logic is altogether different. For the distribution of basic *capabilities* is now designed in such a way that it cannot violate the principle of "equal concern and respect." Since the universal welfare policy embraces all citizens, the debate assumes quite another character: social policy is now thought to concern the entire community, and the question becomes what, *from a general standpoint,* is a fair manner in which to organize social measures. No discussion of the type above – concerning how and where to draw the two boundary lines – need ever take place, for the simple reason that no such lines need be

---

[39] See ch. 2.   [40] Katz (1989).

[41] Söderström (1994) proposes the introduction of a selective system. They write that: "The public commitment could be limited to some form of high-cost protection for those groups unable to obtain satisfactory solutions within the framework of the insurance and credit markets." Unfortunately, however, they do not discuss the problem of stigmatization.

drawn. Welfare policy does not, therefore, turn into a question of what should be done about "the poor" and "the maladjusted," but rather a question of what constitutes *general fairness* in respect to the relation between citizens and the state. The question becomes not "how shall we solve *their* problem?" but rather "how shall we solve *our common* problem (health care, education, pensions, etc.)?" As Hugh Heclo has put it, the best way to help the poor is not to talk about them, that is, not to set up programs targeted specially on them.[42] The delineation of certain citizens as "poor" entails portraying them as different in nature from other citizens, and therefore violates the principle of equal treatment. And in deciding *how much* such persons need, the state assumes a paternalistic role, which cannot be done while respecting the integrity of the individual at the same time.

Procedural justice

Condition number two concerns, as mentioned earlier, the implementation of policy. Can welfare policy be carried out in a fair manner? This is the question of procedural justice. In addition, the successful operation of a welfare system presupposes that citizens believe its proudly proclaimed aims are actually implemented in the intended manner. This is the question of *what the state can do.*

How does the choice of a universal or selective welfare policy affect the public's view of state capacity? To begin with the former: one should bear in mind that a typical universal welfare program – like flat-rate pensions or child allowances – is a great deal simpler, cheaper, and easier to implement than its selective counterpart. This is largely because there is no need, in a program of a universal type, for an administrative apparatus charged with carrying out the *two* types of eligibility tests which are a necessary concomitant of a selective program: for ascertaining (1) whether a given applicant is entitled to support, and (2) if so, to how much. In general programs, eligibility criteria can often be framed so simply (e.g., age) that the process can be automated. Social policy can thus be given the form of specified citizen rights, and the social duties of the state can be rigorously defined. Such an institutional arrangement respects the integrity of citizens more than any beautiful (but vague and non-binding) official declaration of social policy objectives could ever do.

As shown in chapters 3 and 4, selective programs present serious problems of implementation, for they allow administrators a wide field for discretionary action. There is often no solution to this problem

---

[42] Quoted in Skocpol (1991), p. 430.

(within the limits of such programs). The difficulty of finding usable criteria for selecting recipients can often become unmanageable. This creates a "black hole of democracy," in which citizens find themselves faced with an administration or system of rules which no one really understands, and in which no one can be held responsible. We may accordingly conclude that, from the perspective of legitimacy, universal (i.e., broadly targeted) programs are to be preferred to selective (narrowly targeted) programs. In other words, it is better to have a state that does a little well than a lot badly.

The difficulty of handling the discretionary power of administrators in selective programs has two important consequences. These consequences are often thought to be opposites, but in fact they are two sides of the same coin. They are the bureaucratic abuse of power, and fraud on the part of clients. Applicants in a selective system have a natural tendency to claim their situation is worse than it actually is, and to describe their prospects for solving their problems on their own as small to nonexistent. The administrators in such a system, for their part, tend to be suspicious of clients' claims. (They are often pushed in this direction by their superiors, moreover.) Empirical studies show, interestingly enough, that in countries with selective systems, the authorities devote great resources to checking up on clients and front-line officials, while this is a non-question in countries with universal systems, *even in their means-tested programs*.[43]

The question of procedural justice looms large in selective systems, which tends to undermine legitimacy. Even if cases of cheating, fraud, and the abuse of power are in fact relatively rare, we now must live with the logic of the mass media, which means that it is just such cases that will receive attention in the public discussion of social policy. This undermines public support for the welfare state. Moreover, the selective model leads, as even one of its champions – Robert Goodin – has been forced to admit, to "unavoidable," "insurmountable," and "insoluble" problems in respect of the arbitrary treatment of citizens seeking assistance.[44] The research on policy implementation has highlighted the difficulties of exercising democratic control over the fate of clients in the implementation stage. Suspicion of clients and the abuse of power are

---

[43] Weatherly (1991). In a conversation about an upcoming research report, Weatherly said that in countries with a selective social policy, control and supervision of clients is a significant question, and such tasks take up a large part of social workers' time and attention. By contrast, in countries with a largely general welfare policy, like Denmark and Sweden, this is to a great extent a non-question for social workers.

[44] Goodin (1988) pp. 219f.

built into the selective welfare model. The possibility of applying such a model in accordance with the principle of "equal concern and respect" does not exist in practice. It is impossible to combine means-testing with this principle, for means-testing itself entails a violation of citizens' integrity – either in the means-test itself, or in the verification checks which often follow.

In order to solve these "unavoidable," "insurmountable," and "insoluble" problems, then, Goodin offers an interesting solution. The bureaucratic arbitrariness and uncontrolled interference into the lives of clients, to which a selective social policy gives rise, can be moderated by instructing front-line officials to apply a certain method. When it is unclear whether or not a client's claim satisfies the requirements of the rules, administrators are to be generous, and are to give the applicant the benefit of the doubt.[45] I am convinced, however, that such a policy would severely undermine the legitimacy of the system. The mass media and the popular mythology would be full of stories about how clients with highly doubtful claims succeeded in reeling in benefits anyway, and the majority of citizens would conclude that the requirement of procedural justice is not fulfilled. The selective policy leads, then, to an "administrative nightmare,"[46] which in turn undermines the legitimacy even of this limited welfare model.

This can be explained, in game-analytical terms, as an effect of the so-called control game. It would be best both for the official and for the client if they could trust each other: the official would avoid having to check up on the client, and the client would be left in peace. But since the client (in Goodin's proposed system) can assume that the official will grant him the benefit of the doubt, he has a strong incentive to try to obtain benefits to which he is not entitled. And since the official can reasonably assume, after having experienced a number of such "games," that the chances are great that the client intends to cheat, he will consider it necessary to carry out control checks. The result is an eternal roundabout; the actors agree that it would be best to avoid having to administer control checks or to submit to them, but neither one can avoid this outcome. Expressed in game-analytical terms, the actors lack dominating strategies, and since there is therefore no point of equilibrium, the game lacks a solution.[47]

It also bears mentioning that needs-testing is administratively costly.

[45] Goodin (1988), pp. 220f.
[46] The expression is Hans L. Zetterberg's. See his article in *Dagens Nyheter*, 09-20-90, p. 2. Cf. Pierson (1996), p. 105.
[47] See further Hermansson (1990), pp. 118f.

On the basis of figures supplied by the Association of Local Authorities on the number of employees in various occupational categories, I have calculated that, between 1975 and 1984, the number of persons operatively taking care of children (so to speak) in the municipal day-care system increased by about 100 percent. Those involved (in various ways) in administering the system's queue increased, during the same period, by 270 percent. In view of the low esteem in which "administration" is held, according to the studies which have been done (see table 6.4), this would also seem to undermine the legitimacy of needs-tested public programs.

The just distribution of burdens

Condition number three in the theory of contingent consent has to do with whether or not all citizens bear their share of the costs of a given policy, that is, it concerns *the just distribution of burdens*. Citizens are portrayed here as players in a so-called insurance game: they are prepared to support the program in question – even if they cannot be sure they will themselves directly gain by it – as long as they can be convinced that all (or almost all) other citizens will also contribute to carrying it out. The willingness to contribute depends, that is, not just on the fulfillment of the requirements of procedural and substantive justice; it also assumes a credible organization of the collective efforts (so that such efforts are, in truth, *collective)*. The other side of the question, of course, is how to discourage the unsolidaristic use of the benefits the welfare policy brings. One can also express this in the following way: citizens who wish to contribute to the common good are only willing to do so if they do not believe others will take undue advantage of their solidarity. A minority will not behave solidaristically if the majority is unsolidaristic. It is heroic, but meaningless, to be the only one who defends the country. There is a certain threshold that must be crossed: citizens must be persuaded that others will also contribute before they are willing to pitch in themselves.

The universal model differs from the selective on this point as well. Typical for the latter is that assistance is granted only to those citizens who cannot in some other way provide for themselves or meet their "basic needs." This means as a rule that such citizens have no income, and therefore pay no tax. They constitute a category, then, which does not contribute economically.

In sum, to the extent that the welfare system is designed so that even net beneficiaries can play a role as partners who contribute, according to their ability, to the defraying of costs, the legitimacy of welfare policy will increase. It becomes a question of how citizens shall undertake to solve their common problems, rather than a question of what "we" shall do about "them."[48]

We observe here, then, two wholly distinct moral logics. The difficulty of implementing selective programs in such a way that their objectives are attained, and their processes considered fair, undermines public support for social policy in general. For example, the majority might be open to supporting social policy in principle, but constant reports of cheating, fraud, bureaucratic abuse of power, waste, inefficiency, and other irregularities lead to their taking the view that the policy's implementation is so deficient as to make the whole affair a waste of time and money. It is very hard to imagine, moreover, that a population with such a negative view of welfare policy would be receptive to proposals to give it a more universal form (for this would involve *expanding* social policy). Instead, a suspicion of state measures – to which Nathan Glazer, among others, gives clear expression – becomes the dominant attitude.[49] A state that fails to take care of "the poor" cannot of course be entrusted with the larger task of attending to the welfare of the entire population. Citizens are more willing, on the other hand, to agree to collective undertakings if they have confidence in the state as an institution.[50]

In a universal system, by contrast, this sort of discussion does not arise, because needs-testing is either unnecessary or can be done so simply that it can be automated.[51] The simplicity of universal programs, the clarity they facilitate in the matter of who bears political responsibility, and the possibility of organizing them on the basis of specified rights – these qualities enable such programs to fulfill (and to be seen to fulfill) the requirement of procedural justice. Sven Steinmo's comparative study of tax policy in the United States, Sweden, and the United Kingdom confirms this picture. Steinmo, who interviewed a large number of centrally placed actors in the three countries, maintains that these actors would make the same sort of choices were they faced with similar institutional settings. But of course they are not:

---

[48] Even Glazer (1988) argues, on p. 34, for this type of universalism: "it was foolish . . . to have a system in which the welfare poor received free medical care, while those who worked at low-paying jobs generally did not have medical insurance and lost their insurance when they lost their jobs. This alone made welfare more attractive than work."

[49] See ch. 4.   [50] Levi (1997); cf. Levi (1993).

[51] One must distinguish here, as I indicated earlier, between needs-testing undertaken in order to establish the client's ability to pay (which is in focus here), and needs-testing performed by professionals, as when a doctor in the public health care system seeks to establish what kind of medical attention is required. (The latter type of test is not at issue here.)

When asked, "If you could be guaranteed that increased government spending would be efficiently and effectively used to address society's problems, would you agree to an increase in your taxes?", the vast majority of people I interviewed, even the Americans, answered "Yes!" The respondents, especially the Americans, quickly add, however, that they do not believe that revenue from higher taxes would be used efficiently or effectively and therefore they would not approve tax increases.[52]

In interviews with trade-union leaders and Democratic Party representatives in the United States, moreover, Steinmo asked whether they would consider trying to introduce a value-added tax of a Swedish type, in order to raise revenue for the kind of social program which political groupings of this type in the United States generally advocate. The answer, according to Steinmo, was a unanimous "No." "In each case the respondent explained that given the way in which politics worked in the United States, they would not *trust the system* to use the increased tax borne by the poor to pay for programs that benefited the poor." Or as a high-level senatorial staff member answered: "This is not Sweden. How can we be sure that that extra money won't just be used to cut the taxes of the rich even more, or to buy more B-1 bombers?"[53] Steinmo explains the difference as reflecting "the faith in the legitimacy of the state's role in society" in the Swedish case.[54] Glazer's observations about the lack of faith in state legitimacy in the United States seem, then, to have some empirical basis.

In the popular Swedish debate, many good examples have been given of how individuals have tried to take undue advantage of an excessively generous system of income compensation.[55] Healthy persons have declared themselves ill, those able to work have pretended not to be, etc. The good intentions behind high compensation levels have sometimes come to naught in the stage of implementation: generosity has invited abuse (i.e., unsolidaristic behavior). Even if these examples are few (but they are telling), and even if the economic consequences of fraud and overuse maybe have not been so great in relation to total costs, such behavior damages, in a fundamental way, the values of solidarity which originally provided the foundations of the welfare state's legitimacy. Moreover, we must now live with the logic of the mass media, which means that individual cases of cheating are brought into public view and are highlighted. This leads easily to the prevalence of the view that fraud is the rule, not the exception. Unfortunately, if this view – that "everyone

---

[52] Steinmo (1993), p. 199.   [53] Ibid., pp. 199f. My italics.
[54] Ibid., p. 207.   [55] Isaksson (1992).

else" cheats – gets established by the mass media as a truth, this in itself leads to increased cheating (or, as it is also called, "concealing"). As Laurin has shown in his investigation of the extent and causes of tax fraud in Sweden, most people say they are willing to act solidaristically (i.e., to pay their taxes) on the condition that others do so as well. Laurin's study also indicates that the beliefs citizens hold about the morality of other citizens has a greater impact on their preparedness to try to withhold taxes than does their estimation of their prospects for so doing without being caught. The conception of which social norms prevail, in other words, seems to be more significant in this context than self-interest.[56]

One consequence that modern social science has brought is that citizens are asked now and again about their attitudes towards various matters. So also with welfare policy. How does the empirical evidence look, then, in relation to the theory of contingent consent? Can empirical support be found for the proposition that, if the institutions of social policy are structured according to the principles of this theory, they will create norms forming a basis for the reproduction of the policy? Some opinion surveys include questions of a general nature about what the Swedish people think about the public sector as a whole. Without specifying whether fighter planes or day-care centers are intended, they ask whether the respondent wishes to expand or reduce the public sector.[57] The problem with this approach is that it does not capture the dimension – which is of particular interest to us here – of how much support the various types of programs enjoy. Axel Hadenius and Stefan Svallfors have done investigations of the required sort, however. They have asked identical questions of representative samples of the Swedish population in 1981, 1986, and 1991. The results may be seen in table 6.4. At least two results of these studies are worthy of note. The first is the marked stability of public support for the major types of welfare policy. It appears that the right-wing wave which swept over the Western world (including Sweden) during the 1980s, and which had so striking an impact on the character of public debate, had no effect at all on the views of the population regarding social policy. Insofar as studies of this sort are able to measure such things, it is clear that all talk about the weak

---

[56] Laurin (1986). Laurin's data can also be interpreted, as he himself agrees, as indicating that the opposite causal sequence obtains, i.e., that the persons in question want for reasons of self-interest to withhold taxes, and seek to justify this by pleading that "everyone else cheats," even if they do not really know if this is so.

[57] See, e.g., Nilsson (1991), pp. 38f.

Table 6.4. *Attitudes towards public expenditure*

Year	1981	1986	1992
Health care	+42	+44	+48
Support for the elderly	+29	+33	+58
Support to families with children	+19	+35	+17
Housing allowances	−23	−23	−25
Social assistance	−5	−5	−13
Primary and secondary education	+20	+30	+49
Employment policy	+63	+46	+55
State and municipal administration	−54	−53	−68

Note: The material in this table comprises answers to following question: "Taxes are used for various purposes. Do you think the revenues spent on the purposes mentioned below should be increased, held the same, or reduced?" The figures in the table represent the percentage of those wishing to increase expenditure minus the percentage of those wishing to reduce it. *Source:* From Hadenius (1986), p. 85; Svallfors (1991 and 1992a).

basis of the Swedish welfare model in popular opinion lacks empirical support. The goals seem still to be held dear, at least by the population.

Another surprising result is the marked and stable difference in support for different types of programs. Support for the universal programs is unambiguouly strong and stable, while the opposite is true for the three selective programs. Two programs in particular are weakly supported – social assistance and housing allowances.[58] And both are clearly selective.

One way of interpreting this is according to the pure model of self-interest, that is, only those programs which benefit (at least potentially) a majority of the population are supported by a majority of the population. The support for different social programs, in this view, is directly related to whether or not one uses subsidized services or cash benefits. This would seem to explain the public support for child allowances, pensions, education, and health care tolerably well.

One point counting against such an interpretation, however, is the strong support for employment (i.e., active labor market) policy to be observed in these surveys. The risk of becoming unemployed, after all, is

---

[58] Another study shows that the increase in negative attitudes towards social policy detected in opinion surveys during the 1970s did *not* continue in the 1980s. The trend was rather in the opposite direction. See Nilsson (1991).

something one can on good grounds expect to be extremely unevenly distributed in the population. During this period, unemployment in Sweden has been below 3 percent which means that a majority of citizens will probably not need to make use either of unemployment compensation or of other, more active labor market measures. Employment policy thus clearly deviates from the expectations of the theory that self-interest is a sufficient explanation for variations in support for different welfare programs. It is evidently *not* always the case that the programs enjoying broad support are those benefiting a broad range of the population. Swedish employment policy enjoys very strong support, despite the fact that a majority of citizens do not benefit from it.

One reason for the broad support enjoyed by this policy is, presumably, that its founders attached great importance – when they were building up the administrative structures for its implementation – to the question of legitimacy. One critical method for achieving this was to give representatives of the groups towards which a policy was directed (e.g., trade unions and employers) a very strong influence over the implementation process. These groups have had strong interests (which have balanced each other, moreover) in supervising the procedures of policy implementation.[59]

There is reason to compare Sweden with the United States on this point. As Margaret Weir has noted, it is striking that no form of active labor-market policy has been successfully established in the United States, despite the fact that a strong work ethic pervades American society.[60] The attempt made beginning in the 1960s – CETA (Comprehensive Employment and Training Act) – was that social program which the Reagan administration found easiest to dismantle upon assuming office in 1981. This was because CETA was equated, in public opinion, with waste, bureacracy, and a focus on helping just certain socially distinct minority groups; it was, in short, a program exhibiting all the problematic features of selective policies. An American scholar puts it this way:

> The legitimacy of CETA was seriously eroded by the stream of "bad press" it was receiving – adverse publicity on waste, nepotism, patronage and corruption. Perhaps nothing contributed more to the loss of confidence and legitimacy in CETA and, ultimately, to its demise.[61]

Many other researchers have pointed to the deficiencies in CETA's implementation as the factor which undermined the program's political

---

[59] Cf. Rothstein (1996). For a comparison of Sweden and United Kingdom in regard to this policy's legitimacy, see King & Rothstein (1993).
[60] Weir (1992), ch. 1.
[61] Mucciaroni (1990), p. 176.

legitimacy, and made it possible for the Reagan administration to mobilize sufficient political support to abolish it.[62]

This also seems the most reasonable explanation for the low level of public support in Sweden for such programs as housing allowances and public assistance. Both are selective; but in addition, both are very difficult to implement in such a manner that the requirement of procedural justice is fulfilled. Fraud, waste, and bureaucratic abuse of power are particularly marked in such programs as these.[63] In contrast to the case with labor-market policy, no great efforts have been made to implement these programs in such a way as to reinforce legitimacy.[64]

In conclusion, it seems that the example of Swedish welfare policy provides empirical support for the theory of contingent consent. It is precisely the universal programs – which fulfill the conditions specified in this theory – that command widespread support in the population. At the same time, it is the two programs (public assistance and housing allowances) which appear most clearly to violate the principles of this theory that enjoy the least support. It is hard to argue on behalf of these programs by appeal to a conception of substantive justice. Moreover, these programs are difficult (not to say impossible) to implement in a procedurally fair manner. They make it easy, finally (at least in the case of public assistance), to argue that those receiving benefits do not contribute according to ability to defraying the costs of the program, that is, the benefits generally go to people who do not work and therefore do not pay income tax. In other words, citizens have reason to distrust both the government institutions and their fellow citizens. The strong support for needs-tested employment policy, on the other hand, can be interpreted as resulting from (a) the widespread view that justice demands that all be allowed to work; (b) the common belief that unemployment is not self-inflicted; (c) the relatively high level of confidence, historically speaking, in the organs of implementation;[65] and finally (d) the fact that those in relief jobs and labor-market training give something back, that is, contribute according to ability.

This indicates that even social programs with the following characteristics can achieve a broad legitimacy: (1) they benefit only a minority of the population; (2) they apply needs-testing; and (3) the relation between the resources they expend and the effects they achieve is often uncertain. This depends on how well the founders and administrators of the

---

[62] Weir (1992), pp. 125ff.; Janoski (1990), pp. 268ff.; and Donahue (1989), p. 181.
[63] Cf. Svallfors (1989), pp. 53f.
[64] For an examination of problems encountered in implementing the Swedish Law on Social Services, see Åström (1988), Sunesson (1985).
[65] Cf. King & Rothstein (1993) and Rothstein (1996).

program succeed in (1) arguing for the program's general goals in terms of justice; (2) finding (or founding) an organization capable of implementing it in accordance with procedures generally regarded as correct; and (3) designing an organization capable of handling the uncertainty and friction arising in the implementation process due to uncertainty in the policy theory (i.e., the causal link between inputs and outcomes in the program). This accords well with the conclusions drawn in chapter 4 about how uncertainty in policy theory can be compensated for in the stage of implementation, and that legitimacy can be achieved by other means than through the parliamentary process.

7

Putting history in order

The Swedish universal welfare state – promoting or violating autonomy?

The purposes animating the creation of the Swedish welfare model have been the object of considerable research.[1] The central question, for our purposes here, is whether the Swedish welfare state should be seen as, on the one hand, an attempt to increase the autonomy of citizens by furnishing them with certain basic capabilities they have been unable on their own to procure; or, on the other hand, as a centrally directed invasion of civil society by the state, that is, as a reduction of citizens to the status of subordinate clients deemed unable to manage their own affairs, and the corresponding assumption of responsibilities – once borne by a free citizenry – by an ever-more despotic and expert-directed state.[2] In other words, does Amartya Sen's theory of "basic capabilities" best describe the Swedish welfare model, or is Jürgen Habermas' apprehension of the state's continuous colonization of the private sphere – and the associated elimination of civil society – the more apposite description?

One of the more widely discussed contributions to this debate in recent years is that of the Swedish feminist historian Yvonne Hirdman. In a book written as part of the Swedish Investigation on Power and Democracy, a mega social-science project set up by the government and conducted 1985 to 1990, she has sought to describe and interpret the

---

[1] See, for example, Olsson (1993), Tilton (1990), and Rothstein (1985).
[2] The recent Swedish debate is summarized in Antman (1993).

ideological ambitions behind Social Democratic social policy – from the time of its founding during the 1930s up to the 1960s – from the perspective of the state's relation to the private sphere.[3] Hirdman's book also furnished the basis for those sections of the Power Investigation's final official report analyzing the history of Swedish social policy in a power-theoretical perspective.[4]

Hirdman's purpose is to reveal the ideology – in respect to the relation of citizens to the state – that guided some of the most prominent figures involved in the establishment of Social Democratic welfare policy. Alva and Gunnar Myrdal are the especial object of her attentions, on account of the prominence of their book *Kris i befolkningsfrågan* (*Crisis in the Population Question*) in the social-policy debate of the 1930s, and in view of Alva Myrdal's participation in various public commissions investigating this question up until the 1950s.

The picture that emerges in Hirdman's analysis largely confirms the thesis of a successive state invasion of the sphere of family and private life. This is symbolized by the title of the book, which refers to the desire of reformers to "put lives in order" – the lives in question being those of ordinary people. By means of a series of extremely well-chosen quotes, Hirdman succeeds in depicting the social-policy circles in which the Myrdals took a prominent part as inspired by a view of the relation between citizens and the state that must be termed both paternalistic and utopian (as expressed in the concept of social engineering). Through the direction of popular consumption choices, and popular lifestyles thereby, social policy would help to create a new, more rational kind of citizen – enlightened, well-adjusted, and socially committed. These reformers argued, for example, that it would be best to raise children in boarding schools; that household work is suitable only for feeble and indolent persons without ambition; that the raising of children should be regulated in detail according to scientific methods; and that the performance of such duties should be assigned in part to publicly appointed experts.[5] With the ideologically charged concept of "violation," then, Hirdman calls attention to the potential effects of such policies – the price, in other words, that benevolent intentions to "put lives in order" have for the autonomy of citizens.[6]

Hirdman has performed a valuable service in pointing out the strong

---

[3] Hirdman (1989). The project was organized and financed as a Government Commission but worked under traditional academic freedom.

[4] SOU (1990: 44), pp. 234f. Yvonne Hirdman was one of four members on this commission.

[5] Hirdman (1989), pp. 111–117, 122–124, cf. Tilton (1990), ch. 7.

[6] Hirdman (1989), pp. 17 and 227ff.

paternalism – perhaps materalism is the better word – characterizing the political views held by Alva Myrdal (and indeed her husband Gunnar as well). As an analysis of ideas, and as a document of the intellectual climate of the times, her book makes for extremely interesting reading.[7] For our purposes here, however, there are two critical problems with her analysis, as far as understanding the bases of Swedish social welfare policy are concerned. The first is that Hirdman does not distinguish clearly between two things: what was said and written in social-policy debates and commissions of inquiry, on the one hand; and what social policies were actually implemented, on the other. Politics consists of more than just ideas,[8] after all, and nowhere does Hirdman demonstrate a connection between the ideas she analyzes and the policies actually carried out. Instead, she takes this connection for granted: there "is a Social Democratic self-image according to which these reforms have been self-evident," as she claims in the introduction to her book. She writes also that "it is a question of the Social Democratic regulation – the putting into order – of the little life of society: the life of families, mothers, children."[9]

A second and related problem with Hirdman's argument, for our purposes here, is that she claims there was a "uniform view of man among the Swedish reformers," and an associated consensus as to the appropriate shape of social policy. There was, in other words, no prominent current within the Social Democratic leadership of the time opposed to such "violative" maternalist social policy, and favoring an alternative approach to such questions. As I shall show below, however, this claim is not borne out by the facts.[10]

Hirdman culls her evidence in large part from two types of sources: the texts issued by commissions of inquiry on the one hand, and personal archives on the other. Not a single government bill, by contrast, is quoted in her book. Nor has Hirdman made use of the reports issued by Riksdag committees, where policy is converted, so to speak, into applicable legal

---

[7] Or, as the author writes in the introduction to her book: she has chosen a subject "in keeping with the spirit of the times."

[8] And, I am tempted to add, political science is more than the analysis of ideas and language.

[9] Hirdman (1990), pp. 10 and 9.

[10] It is scarcely an exaggeration to state that Hirdman's book is that part of the Power Investigation which, aside from the final report, has attained the widest circulation in the Swedish public debate that followed on the commission's final report. It has, moreover, helped neatly to confirm all the prejudices of those who have seen Swedish welfare policy as a successive colonization of civil society by the state. See, e.g., Zaremba (1992), pp. 101–106.

provisions.[11] This choice of empirical evidence turns out to be fatal, for one receives the impression from her account that Myrdal-style maternalism came to predominate within the social policy actually laid down by the Riksdag. This was not the case, however; rather, the Myrdal line met with political defeat at the hands of those in the party who wore the breeches when it came to such questions – meaning, most especially, the Minister of Social Affairs, Gustav Möller.[12] For there was not, *pace* Hirdman, a single, uniform view of the relation between citizens and the state among the leading Social Democrats of the time. Two altogether different approaches, rather, vied with each other for dominance. Hirdman has well accounted for the one (which for the most part was never carried out); the other found its foremost champion in the person of Gustav Möller. The question, then, is whether the argument presented by Hirdman and the Power Investigation tallies with the policy actually carried out, and with the ideas animating that policy.

The Möller line within Swedish social democracy

What, then, were the components of this second approach to social policy, that were associated with Gustav Möller?[13] A first sign of divergent views as regards the use of the state to put the lives of citizens in order was evident as early as 1932, when, together with the architect Uno Åhren, Gunnar Myrdal called upon Möller as the latter commenced his second tenure as the Minister of Social Affairs. The subject of their meeting was housing policy. As Myrdal himself recalled, Möller regarded his visitors with great suspicion, and expressed no sympathy for their

---

[11] The bibliography cites fully thirty-four different public inquiries.

[12] Cf. Hermansson (1993), pp. 275ff.

[13] I limit my attentions here to the question of the welfare state and citizens' autonomy. For a more comprehensive analysis, see Nyström (1983), and Rothstein (1985). One research problem derives from the fact that Möller never wrote a large collection of continuous memoirs in the fashion of Tage Erlander or Ernst Wigforss. Nor did he collect his political ideas into one large work. In order to uncover his political thinking, therefore, one must resort to a number of different sources. Foremost among these are the texts of government bills, directives issued to commissions of inquiry, speeches in Riksdag debates, and a small number of journal articles. I have also relied on a couple of interviews I conducted with Professor Per Nyström, who served as Möller's under-secretary of state from 1945 to 1950. This situation in regard to sources is, in one respect, advantageous. That is, the desire for self-vindication – which so often renders autobiographies suspect as sources – does not pose a problem here. A more general overview of Möller as a politician many be found in Tilton (1990), ch. 5. In regard to Möller as a party and electoral strategist, see Svensson (1994).

ideas. Möller viewed them, according to Myrdal, as young idealists out of contact with political and social realities.[14]

Another example occurred during the Social Democratic party congress of 1936. A central question at that time was the so-called "population question." The prominence that Alva and Gunnar Myrdal's book (mentioned above) received was in large part due to the fact that this question until then had been a safe home turf of Conservative debaters and politicians, who worried about the dwindling of the Swedish population. The Myrdals' book took the question out of the hands of the social conservatives by framing the population question into a demand for greatly increased ambitions in social policy programs. In a debate at the Party Convention in 1936 on social policy and the population question, Möller stated that, for his part, he had no interest in the population question, save for the opportunity it presented for persuading the Conservatives and the Farmers' League of the need for various social policy measures.[15] Möller presumably realized, party strategist that he was, that the Social Democrats were forced in nearly all situations – both when introducing social policies, and later on when defending them from attack – to reach a compromise with one or more of the bourgeois parties.

Möller sought a social policy that would supply citizens with basic capabilities in a manner avoiding the stigmatization and violation of integrity characteristic of poor relief. He shunned the passivization and authoritarianism of Bismarckian-type social measures as well. He gave expression to these principles in his directives for one of the major social-policy commissions he appointed during the second half of the 1930s:

> A characteristic feature of poor relief is that assistance is rendered after an open-ended means test, in which the authorities' subjective assessment of the individual's need for aid is determinative, both as regards the character of the assistance granted and its extent. Certainly, the first paragraph of the law on poor relief enjoins the municipalities to furnish minors and the disabled with the necessities of life, but in practice the municipal authorities enjoy very much a free hand in implementing this mandatory poor relief . . . During recent decades, however, a new type of social assistance has emerged, which in the respects mentioned differs from poor

[14] Cited in Carlsson (1990), p. 56. They met with a more sympathetic hearing, by contrast, when they called upon Ernst Wigforss, the Minister of Finance.

[15] Hatje (1974), p. 202; cf. Carlsson (1990), p. 168, according to which Möller argued, in discussions with other Social Democratic Riksdag members, that it would be unwise of the party not to exploit the power of the population question on behalf of its social policy objectives. Carlsson writes further: "Möller exhibited a less-than-full embrace of pronatalist goals," p. 170.

relief altogether. In area after area, arrangements have been undertaken, by means of state measures, which secure to citizens a right to the assistance of society, under certain conditions stated clearly in statute or in law, and comparatively easily ascertained.[16]

Elsewhere in these directives may be found another of Möller's ambitions in the area of social policy, namely: avoiding "the dangers of excessive bureaucratization."[17] This was one of his most frequent political themes – how to expand social welfare without increasing the power of bureaucrats over citizens thereby.[18] It is scarcely an exaggeration to say that Möller's ideas in this area are similar to or even identical with Ronald Dworkin's view that the principle of "equal concern and respect," as presented in chapter 2, should govern the relation of public policy to citizens. One of Möller's colleagues in 1942, Per Nyström (who also served as under-secretary of state from 1945 to 1950, and later became a professor of history), has sharply criticized Hirdman's account as follows:

> Möller was by no means guided by the theories of the social engineers, but rather by the ideas of K. K. Steinke, and by the Danish social reforms of 1933, which Steinke carried out. The program recommended by the social engineers never came to characterize Swedish welfare policy, in which general security measures dominated altogether.[19]

Wherever possible, then, Möller tried to organize social policy on the basis of specified rights. For those cases in which means-testing could not be avoided, on the other hand, Möller introduced an interesting innovation. This involved assigning the administration of the means-test to the very groups to whom the policy was directed (or, more strictly, to their democratically constituted organizations). Two examples of this type of approach may be cited: firstly, the organization of the enterprise associations, which were entrusted with the administration of assistance to

---

[16] These directives were issued upon the commission's appointment in 1937. SOU (1942: 56), p. 19.

[17] Ibid., p. 21.

[18] See, e.g., Möller (1926), p. 18; Möller (1920), p. 104. Cf. also Möller's speeches in the Riksdag: FK (Swedish acronym for *Första kammarens protokoll*, or *Minutes of the First Chamber's Proceedings*) (1919: 15), p. 32; FK (1923:21), pp. 85f.; FK (1926: 38), pp. 5f., and AK (Swedish acronym for *Andra kammarens protokoll*, or *Minutes of the Second Chamber's Proceedings*) (1926: 13), pp. 66f.; FK (1937: 24), pp. 50f.; AK (1937: 23), pp. 40f.; AK (1946: 42) (extraordinary session), p. 10; and AK (1953: 223), p. 153. See also the government bills submitted by Möller: (1926: 109), p. 80. In regard to unemployment policy, see Rothstein (1996), chapters 4, 6, and 9.

[19] Nyström (1991), pp. 188f.

small companies; and secondly, the role assigned to the officially recognized unemployment compensation funds, in which trade-union representatives had, and indeed still have, the difficult task of deciding who has the right to unemployment compensation. In both cases, Möller justified the chosen arrangement on the grounds that an increase in the power of state officials over citizens could be thereby avoided.[20] What Möller did, in other words, was to make it possible for citizens to solve these intricate problems of implementation by way of their own, partially autonomous institutions. The object of this strategy was, among other things, to solve the problems occasioned by the incentives to cheating and over-utilization that can arise in such programs, by making it possible for citizens themselves, through their locally appointed representatives, to oversee the operations of these programs. In regard to this last point, there is cause to recall Elinor Ostrom's theory, presented in chapter 5, concerning solutions to the "tragedy of the commons," i.e., the over-utilization of common resources. The problems arising in connection with social insurance are identical to those Ostrom identifies in respect to the consumption of common resources; that is to say, individuals have an incentive to over-consume such resources, notwithstanding that their common interests demand that such over-exploitation be avoided (since otherwise the resources in question are soon exhausted, and everyone alike loses out). Ostrom describes the key features of successful solutions to these problems as follows:

> Most of the institutional arrangements used in the success stories were rich mixtures of public and private instrumentalities. If this study does nothing more than shatter the conviction of many policy analysts that the only way to solve CPR problems is for external authorities to impose full private property rights or centralized regulation, it will have accomplished one major purpose.[21]

The type of institution Möller created may be said to correspond to the success stories described by Ostrom, that is, a mixture of private organization and state regulation, in which the latter, through the creation of local institutions, enables citizens to solve the "tragedy of the commons" themselves should they so wish. By creating such local institutions, the state can contribute to the solution without needing to be involved in implementing it (i.e., in practice bureaucratizing it). Civil society, rather (if the expression be permitted), is given the

---

[20] On Möller's organization of the enterprise associations and unemployment compensation funds, see Rothstein (1992a).
[21] Ostrom (1992), pp. 182f.

possibility of organizing itself, so as to solve common problems on a local basis.[22]

If one seeks a reform clearly illustrating the difference between what Alva Myrdal *thought* and what Gustav Möller *carried out*, the program established for assisting needy families with children would be a good candidate. In brief, the approach favored by the Myrdals – which was termed "the in-kind line" – called for a selective targeting of assistance to families with children suffering from economic deprivation, and urged that such aid be distributed in the form of various goods. The needy mothers would receive clothing, shoes, vitamins, foodstuffs, etc., from municipal retail outlets. The authorities would see to the standardization of the quality of these goods. The argument for the in-kind line focused on the issues of targeting and quality. Means-testing would ensure that assistance went to the "truly needy," and that maximum efficiency in the use of tax monies was thereby achieved. The in-kind line made it possible, moreover, to guarantee that expenditures on behalf of needy families were converted into goods of the desired quality, for the consumption choices of recipients were directed.[23]

The selective, in-kind line lost out, in the end, to the idea of general, in-cash child benefits. Möller argued that the latter method would avoid the stigma associated with means-tests. Many other administrative problems arising in connection with means-tests would also be avoided thereby, and the need for a large bureaucracy – in order to ascertain who was entitled to support and who was not – would be obviated. Economically deprived families needed neither charity nor paternal instruction, but a cash increase in their household budget. One could, in Möller's view, trust the people themselves to make wise use of these monies.[24]

In his dissertation from 1967, *Planhushållningsdebatten* (*The Debate on Economic Planning*), Leif Lewin describes the Social Democratic ideology that developed after the reforms of the 1930s. Polemicizing against the "death of ideologies" thesis, Lewin argues that Social Democracy took the view that "the state authorities ought so to change society as to make it possible for the many to experience the feeling of freedom." This meant that, "with the aid of the coercive powers of the state, [the party] carries out structural changes," with the aim of "so altering social conditions that all enjoy equal prospects of experiencing the feeling of freedom and

---

[22] Cohen and Arato, among others, call attention to this possibility: (1993), ch. 10. See also Rothstein (1993b).

[23] Hatje (1974), p. 204. Police checks would be needed, in Alva Myrdal's view, to ensure that cash benefits were actually used on the children's behalf, and were not spent instead on "a new hat for the mother, or on spirits for the father."

[24] Hatje (1974), pp. 202ff.

of developing their potentialities."[25] To summarize thus far, it seems that Lewin's account – written twenty-seven years ago – of Social Democratic welfare ideology as it developed in the years following the Second World War, remains apposite today, and gives a more accurate picture than that proffered by Yvonne Hirdman and the Power Investigation.

It is true that Lewin's research did not concern family policy, but rather economic policy in general. Hirdman claims there was a difference between the two, and morever that the Social Democrats in general, and Gustav Möller in particular, were basically uninterested in the question of the state's relation to the family. Möller's interests rather lay, according to Hirdman, largely in the field of labor-market policy.[26] This is contradicted, however, by Möller's early involvement in social policy, an involvement which issued in the passage of such reforms – critical to the prospects of women and children – as maternity allowances, advance maintenance payments (i.e., the state acting as a "middleman" guaranteeing maintenance payment to single parents and taking care of securing payment from the parent that does not have custody), free maternity care, widows' pensions, free childbirth services, and a prohibition against discharging female employees on account of pregnancy or marriage.[27] A review of the social-policy reforms promulgated by the Ministry of Social Affairs during the years from 1933 to 1939 reveals that the greater number concerned children and mothers, and that they strengthened the autonomy of recipients as citizens, by granting them clearly specified rights. These reforms did not seek to put the lives of recipients "in order" by means of the discretionary disbursement of resources.[28]

Three elements permeated Möller's thinking on the subject of social policy. First, a passion for social justice. Not only his argumentation, but also his many and sometimes bitter struggles with finance ministers demonstrate the seriousness with which he took this question.[29] A second critical issue for Möller had to do with the prospects for strategic action, that is, what long-term alliances were possible for ensuring the reforms' passage and long-term survival. The broader (i.e., the more general) the

---

[25] Lewin (1967), pp. 77f.   [26] Hirdman (1990), p. 11.
[27] See Thullberg (1987).
[28] It is clear, from the scanty biographical material Möller left behind, that his efforts in the area of social policy were in a high degree inspired by the unkind fate that befell his mother. See Jönsson & Lindblom (1988), as well as Möller (1971).
[29] Thullberg (1987), and Jönsson & Lindblom (1988). Möller's decision to resign, following a series of controversies with Finance Minister Per-Evind Sköld on the subject of social policy, may be taken as evidence of his ideological convictions in this question.

design of the reforms, the more favorable the outlook for mobilizing sufficiently great electoral support on their behalf. Finally, Möller stressed the importance of correct procedures and justice in implementation. Social benefits should in the highest degree possible take the form of specified rights; they should not be favors for which the individual must petition, cap in hand. The idea was to replace discretionary poor relief with social policy as a right of citizenship.[30]

Möller sought by various means to immunize his reforms against both the abuse of power by bureaucrats and cheating on the part of recipients. Uniform and general cash benefits were of course an important method, as was his attempt to find functioning and reliable organizations to implement the reforms. Another clear example was his opposition to introducing income-graded classes into the system of sickness benefits. What Möller objected to was not the principle of income-related benefits,[31] but rather the invitation to fraud presented by a system in which citizens themselves would state their income class. The temptation to report overly high incomes would undermine the reform's legitimacy, and moreover would require a considerable apparatus of verification and control.

The Swedish welfare state and civil society

The purpose of this chapter has been to show that the construction of the Swedish welfare state was not based on any uniform paternalistic (or maternalistic) ideology of the sort that Yvonne Hirdman and the Power Investigation have claimed. The Myrdal line, which did in fact constitute a violation (to use Hirdman's language) of the integrity of citizens, met with determined resistance, and did not come to dominate the framing of Swedish social policy at this time. Behind the policy that was in fact implemented lay a wholly contrary vision, one asserting the need to remove the stigmatizing odor of poor relief from social policy, and the importance of replacing it with specified and as far as possible universal rights, that is, with Dworkin's idea of "equal concern and respect." And, in those cases in which means-testing could not be avoided, locally based, partially autonomous institutions would be created to administer the policy.

[30] Möller (1952). The receipt of poor relief entailed, until 1945, the reduction of the recipient to the status of a minor, as expressed in the loss of voting rights. Möller got the idea of framing social policy on the basis of rights from two Danish politicians active in the area of social policy: C. V. Bramsnaes and K. K. Steinke. See Nyström (1983).

[31] Cf. Rothstein (1993c).

I do not mean by this to deny that ideological tendencies of the type identified by Hirdman have characterized other social policies, especially those planned and implemented at a later date, that is, public child care, or the means-tested and treatment-oriented social-assistance program. A strong planning and managerial optimism, which could indeed take a rather paternalistic form, emerged within welfare policy in the late 1960s. One important fact should be weighed in the balance, however: planning and managerial optimism was by no means an isolated Swedish phenomenon at this time. On the contrary, as shown in chapter 3, this current was extremely prominent in the larger part of the Western world, and characterized political thinking not just in Sweden but also in the United States, the former West Germany, and the United Kingdom, to name just a few countries.[32] It can scarcely be derived, therefore, from any specifically Swedish or Social Democratic reform ideology. Hirdman's strongly historical approach, and correspondingly low comparative ambition, has led her astray in the matter of casual analysis.

I wish to argue, then, that the claim that Swedish social policy has impoverished the relations of civil society is not confirmed by an investigation into the character of the predominant ideology inspiring this policy. Two leading theorists of civil society, Jean L. Cohen and Andrew Arato, allow, moreover, that universal welfare programs cannot be seen as subversive of civil society. In their voluminous book on the political theory of civil society, for example, they write (in an endnote!) as follows:

> We fail to see how social security, health insurance, job training programs for the unemployed, unemployment insurance, and family supports such as day care or parental leave create dependency rather than autonomy, even if the particular administration of such programs as AFDC (such as the man-in-house-rule) do create dependency and are humiliating. But these are empirical questions. The theoretical issue behind such questions is the extent to which social services and social supports are symbolically constituted as welfare for "failures" or as supports for all members of the community.[33]

Cohen and Arato accordingly perceive – in contrast to those who have introduced the theory of civil society into the Swedish debate – the fundamental distinction between universal and means-tested social policy measures, and they appreciate the value of analyzing these differences empirically.[34] It is indeed, as they argue, of fundamental importance

---

[32] For the United States, see Glazer (1988); for the former West Germany, see Offe (1986), chs. 4 and 10.
[33] Cohen & Arato (1993), p. 664.   [34] Arvidsson & Berntson (1990).

whether social-policy measures are means-tested or universal, as far as judging the impact of such measures on citizen autonomy is concerned. This distinction was very well known, historically, to Swedish social policy-makers and commentators, who emphasized the difference between the violation of integrity characteristic of poor relief and the rights-based structure of social insurance. Accordingly, Karl Höjer writes as follows in his book, from 1952, reviewing the history of Swedish social policy:

> It has since earliest times been the case that, if one could not support oneself and sought help from society therefore, one lost one's rights and freedoms in great measure thereby . . . One was taken care of and ordered about the authorities saw fit . . . It is against this background, among other things, that one should see the satisfaction and gratitude with which even a meager social insurance system was greeted . . . It paid out sums in cash and left people in peace.[35]

Autonomy or violation – what do the data say?

How do the facts in the case look? That is, what kind of program creates dependency, and what kind increases the autonomy of citizens? The research seems for once to give an unambiguous answer: means-tested social programs create long-term dependency, and require recipients to submit to bureaucratic demands to put their lifestyle patterns in order.[36] Universal programs appear to produce exactly the opposite effect, that is, they increase the autonomy of citizens. One way to investigate this question is to see how countries with selective social policy systems compare to those with universal social policies, as regards their success in eliminating poverty and dependence on means-tested social assistance.[37] Such a comparison has in fact been recently done, at the Joint Center for Political and Economic Studies in Washington D.C., under the direction of Roger Lawson, Katherine McFate, and William Julius Wilson. This project has compared the type of selective social policy pursued in the United States with the more universal form prevailing in Northern Europe. (The study compares the United States, Canada, the United Kingdom, the former West Germany, the Netherlands, France, and

---

[35] Höjer (1952), p. 358.
[36] Empirical findings of this sort may be found in, among other places, Sunesson (1985).
[37] The argument is based on the idea that to be poor is also to lack autonomy. This could of course be questioned, but in a capitalist market economy, there is a least some relation between being poor and lacking autonomy.

Table 7.1. Percentage of households in poverty in the mid-1980s.

Country/year	All households	All families with children	All single-provider families with children
United States (1986)	18.1	23.8	53.3
Canada (1987)	13.9	15.7	48.4
United Kingdom (1986)	12.5	16.8	18.0
West Germany (1984)	6.8	7.9	8.9
The Netherlands (1987)	7.6	7.3	7.5
France (1984)	9.9	10.4	15.8
Sweden (1987)	8.6	5.1	5.5

Source: McFate, Smeeding, & Rainwater (1995), p. 53. Data taken from the Luxembourg Income Data Study
Note: Poverty is here defined as households with less than 50 percent of the adjusted median household income. This is roughly equivalent, in the US case, to the official poverty line. Those households are excluded in which the "head of household" is over fifty-five years of age. The term "head of household" is not to be found in the Swedish language. It may be noted that it was thanks to Möller, and not Alva Myrdal, that in-cash benefits were sent directly to mothers – which is probably why the concept "head of house-hold" never became established in Swedish social policy.

Sweden, and is based to a great extent on the Luxembourg Income Data Study.)

The findings of this project include the following: Despite the fact that, up through the mid-1980s, the United States has had a higher and more stable rate of economic growth than most of the European countries included in the survey, and a lower rate of unemployment besides, the percentage of American households that were poor (defined as those households receiving less than 50 percent of the median national income) was more than twice as high as that in any of the European countries. The theory that general economic growth cures poverty seems, in sum, no longer to be valid.

One should bear in mind, moreover, that the United States and Sweden lead the pack in the proportion of single-provider families. We may therefore conclude from the table above that these two countries also occupy the polar extremes when it comes to the effects of their (very differently structured) social policies on the situation of such families. The risk run by a single-provider family with children of living in poverty is twelve times higher in the United States than in Sweden. Social policy

Table 7.2. Percentage of poor households (before taxes and benefits) lifted out of poverty as a result of taxes and transfers

United States 1979	0.03
United States 1986	−0.5
Canada 1981	18.3
Canada 1987	20.1
United Kingdom 1980	33.6
United Kingdom 1986	46.1
West Germany 1981	20.3
West Germany 1984	36.4
The Netherlands 1983	61.6
The Netherlands 1987	61.8
France 1979	46.2
France 1984	51.5
Sweden 1981	58.7
Sweden 1987	43.8

Source: McFate, Smeeding, & Rainwater (1995), p. 53. Those households are excluded in which all members are over fifty-five years of age.

in the two countries also diverges greatly with respect to its ability to lift families of this type out of poverty. The effectiveness of social policy in "helping the poor," then, varies greatly between the systems. (The Dutch arrangement is the most efficacious.) The big difference, however, is that between the mainly selective systems on the one hand and the largely universal systems on the other. The most selective system, that is, that which according to its ideology taxes the rich and gives to the poor, is also that system which helps the poor least, in fact not at all. Indeed, if there is any change, it seems to be in a negative direction (note the US figure for 1986). That is, the poor got even poorer as a result of the selective social policy. We are, therefore, now able to answer the question often put forward about universal welfare policy: is it really worth the price fetched by this policy – higher taxes for everyone – in order to remedy a small number of difficulties? It is not even necessary to take issue with the normative premises of this question, since there is a clear empirical answer to his question: the other method available – the selective approach – does not seem to help the poor at all, but tends rather to worsen their situation.

It is not merely that economic growth seems no longer to be any help against poverty as a general social problem. In addition, those left in poverty by the selective social policy pursued in the selective systems have

Table 7.3. Percentage of households with children depending on public
support for at least half of their income

	United States (1986)	Canada (1987)	United Kingdom (1986)	Former West Germany (1984)	Nether- lands (1987)	France (1984)	Sweden (1987)
All families	10.0	8.2	23.2	5.6	14.4	7.2	9.7
All single-parent families	37.6	38.8	74.9	39.7	70.4	25.4	32.6
All two-provider families	4.4	4.9	15.6	4.1	8.3	5.8	6.7

Source: McFate, Smeeding, & Rainwater (1995), p. 52.

much less of a chance of escaping their condition than do their counterparts in the more universal welfare states. It is hard to avoid making a
connection here between the stigmatizing effects of selective social policy
and the difficulty of escaping poverty, even if this connection obviously
cannot be directly deduced from table 7.2. (It is scarcely possible, after all,
to quantify such a concept as "stigmatization.")

Another explanation offered for the marked variations in the size of
the poverty-stricken population is that benefit levels are so high in the
universal welfare states, and that citizens receive such a large proportion
of their income from public sources. This thesis as well, however, lacks
support in the data as shown in table 7.3. Families with children are not,
as a general rule, more dependent on public assistance in the universal
welfare states than in the selective ones. The differences between countries
in regard to the situation of single-parent families are probably rooted in
the varying extent to which single women with children find gainful
employment. Let us recall here the explanation discussed in the previous
chapter. In a country that follows a selective social policy, the typical
situation of a single woman with children to support is characterized by
the following: to begin with, she lacks gainful employment, since there is
no subsidized child care. She does not, therefore, pay taxes, that is, she
does not (1) contribute according to ability. And since she receives her
income from means-tested programs, there is a strong suspicion
throughout of (2) deficiencies in procedural justice (i.e., cheating).
Stigmatization follows thereby – not just because she receives means-

tested assistance, but also because she finds herself, on account of her lack of gainful employment, outside the natural fellowship of society. Accordingly, the (3) overarching and universal justice of the social policy may called into question.

In a universal system, by contrast, a woman with a similar family situation lives under otherwise very dissimilar conditions: To begin with, she has gainful employment, that is, she (1) contributes according to ability, among other things because subsidized child care is available. Furthermore, she can usually manage well enough without resort to means-tested social assistance, by combining her wage with the universal social benefits to which she is entitled, that is, the public support she receives (2) meets the requirements of procedural justice. The different manner in which households of this type are regarded in a universal system is evident, that is, the social policy can be justified by reference to (3) overarching and universal principles of justice. Further comment is superfluous as regards the greatly differing implications – for the personal autonomy enjoyed by citizens of this category – of the two systems under review.

In the Swedish debate on the welfare state, some commentators have sought to portray the public sector as structurally opposed to "civil society," as if the two arenas were communicating vessels: the larger the public sector, the smaller and weaker the civil society.[38] Substantive analysis has all too often given way, in this discussion, to ambitions of an ideological character.[39] This criticism of the welfare state has its point of departure in an analysis of the political system that prevailed in the former Soviet bloc. This coupling of social liberalism with totalitarian communism – as variations on a common theme – is somewhat far-fetched, to put it mildly, and proponents of this thesis have largely failed in their efforts to lay an intellectual basis for it. There is something fundamentally peculiar, for instance, about historiography in this genre. In my view, the criticism John Ely has aimed at Cohen and Arato's *magnum opus* is altogether pertinent here: "Cohen and Arato overlook the fact that political freedom arises with the development of collective rationality and civic personality (the individual citizen) breaking down and opposing tradition and tutelage – something which originally developed in free city states."[40] It was precisely with the appearance of a *state* (the European city-state, in this case) that civil society, as we know it in Western Europe, could begin to blossom.

I have tried in this chapter to show, then, that state activity should not

---

[38] Karlsson (1993), ch. 3.   [39] Cf. Trägårdh (1993).
[40] Ely (1992), p. 184.

be regarded as bearing an inverse relation to the strength of civil society, so that an increase in the former leads automatically to a diminution of the latter. Certain types of state measures can indeed undermine the vitality of civil society, but others can *increase* it. It all depends on what form the measures take; that is, do they help to increase the autonomy of citizens, or do they contribute, rather, to their subordination? To quote Cohen and Arato, "*certain* features of the welfare state fragment collectivities, destroy horizontal solidarities, isolate and render private individuals dependent on state apparatuses."[41] It is the word I have placed in italics that is critical here.

[41] Cohen & Arato (1993), p. 24. Their next sentence reads: "Unrestrained capitalist expansion, however, has the same destructive consequences."

8

The autonomous citizen and the future of the universal welfare policy

In the introductory chapter, one of the challenges facing the universal welfare state was said to be the increased individualism among its citizens. How would the increased demand for self-determination fit the standardized services provided by such a welfare state? To shed light on this problem, I will open this chapter with a story from the real life and times of the Swedish welfare state. It has to do with the welfare state's intervention in a process which can be technically complicated, unforeseeable, hard to manage politically, and dramatic. Powerful interests are involved – on the part of professional groups, politicians and administrators on a range of levels, and the citizens themselves. The process is, moreover, often ethically complex at the same time. It exhibits, in short, all the features of what in the methodological literature is called a "critical case," that is, it puts our hypotheses and theories to the severest test. For our example has to do with the public regulation and direction of how we come into this life – with the conditions of childbirth in the Swedish welfare state, in other words. Our case has to do, in other words, with the welfare state's management of citizens' lives even before they are placed in the cradle. It should be added that, contrary to for example, the situation in the United States, in Sweden it is professional midwives who are take care of the child-delivery process. Obstetricians are usually only called in when complications of some kind occur. So in all respects, this has very much been, and still is, a woman-to-woman affair and if there are any gender specific characteristics of the welfare state, they should be revealed in this case.

Our empirical case goes back twenty-five years, to the first half of the 1970s. At the time, Swedish public child-delivery services were organized

188

according to the following two principles: (a) the pregnant women's "municipal arrest," and (b) the absolute power of the public personnel over the process. The expectant mothers were subject to "municipal arrest" in that they were forbidden to leave the area of the most closely situated hospital during the four weeks prior to the planned date of delivery. If they did so nonetheless, and then ended up being forced to seek out another hospital in which to give birth, they could be charged for the entire cost of the delivery.

The virtually absolute power of the health-care staff (i.e., the midwives) was manifested in the fact that the mothers were, so to speak, objectified and processed on the conditions of the staff. The mothers had no opportunity, that is, to influence how the delivery would be done. One midwife, well known later on, described the conditions prevailing there around 1970 in the following words:

> The maternity ward was old and dilapidated, and two women often delivered in the same room . . . As late as in 1969, all the women were anesthetized with chloroform, whether they wanted it or not, . . . I began in a small way by getting the mothers to lift their head and look at the baby when it came out, instead of sleeping with chloroform over their nose . . . At the old maternity ward, a sign hung on the door to the infant room: "Entry forbidden." Shades hung on the door window. The mothers could not look in on their child when they wished. They could stand outside and press their noses up against the glass pane while the nurse looked after their child. "Plupp!" the sound went, and the shades came down right in front of their noses.[1]

In other words, the expectant mothers had neither the opportunity to influence how or where the delivery would take place, nor who would assist them in the process. The ideology prevailing at the time could be described as a sort of professionalized technocratism. In sum, even if the child-bearing citizens were perhaps treated with "equal concern" by the state, they were treated quite simply without any "respect" – as thinking, acting, and (according to the stories I have been told) feeling subjects.[2]

At the start of the 1970s, the midwife quoted above (Signe Jansson), traveled to France to learn about new methods of bringing children into

---

[1] Jansson (1988), p. 20 and p. 39.
[2] This account builds on Hogg, Jansson, & Stiege (1988), ch. 1. According to these authors, the expectant mothers were denied even the physical right to their own body, inasmuch as they (a) were forced to give birth in a lying position, and were not allowed to touch (b) their newborn child, or (c) their own lower abdominal area. I have been told, however, that more humane principles were introduced already in the early 1960s at a maternity ward in Stockholm.

this world. She discovered in that country that this task could be accomplished by means altogether different from that which, in Sweden, was regarded as the only way. This is not the place to go into the technicalities of the case, however interesting. My purpose is rather to highlight the critical respect in which the method used in Paris differed from that usually applied in Sweden at the time. The crux of the matter may be expressed in a single phrase: *giving birth on the woman's terms.*

The idea, as I understand it, was brilliant in its simplicity. Instead of regarding the childbearing citizen as a passive object to be processed through a professional structure – the details of which had already been decided in advance, and the shape of which said citizen could not influence – the expectant mother was instead regarded as a consciously *acting subject.* This meant assuming, to begin with, that she was capable of participating in and contributing to the process actively, and therefore also of shaping it (at least in part). In addition, it meant accepting her right to place demands and impose conditions on the manner in which the process was organized. By respecting the woman's desires, and by actively seeking out her involvement, the entire process could be made more humane, less painful, and less technified for everyone (the expectant mother, the medical staff, and, I believe, the child).

What the matter concerned more precisely was the following: teaching the expectant mother certain techniques for facilitating the delivery.[3] It was not just a question of technique, however. It also expressed a new view of the relation between the mother and the medical staff, such that the former was ensured enough knowledge of the process of child delivery as to feel capable of participating in the process, or even of taking control of it.

However, when Signe Jansson tried to put these lessons learned in France to use at Malmö General Hospital, she met with the solid resistance of the rest of the staff. It was the other (female) midwives most especially (not, as one might have expected, the male physicians) who opposed the changes. Jansson describes the course of events as follows:

> an enormous queue arose of parents wanting to take part in the pilot project. My colleagues were forced to receive telephone calls from expectant mothers who wanted me to assist them in delivering their child. They viewed this as a questioning of their working methods. This meant the conflict with my colleagues was deepened, and I was frozen out from the section . . . The pilot project went on for eleven months, and was brought to an end on account of the hard opposition of my colleagues. I

---

[3] It was a question, concretely speaking, of various breathing techniques for handling pain. See Hogg, Jansson, & Stiege (1988).

returned to my position as department director, and it was decided that I would continue with the psycho-prophylaxis courses until the queue was gone. The conflict with the midwives had not been solved. On account of it, many parents who came in and practiced "breathing" for child delivery were subjected to harrassment. The expectant parents dared not say they had been at a course with me.[4]

It was instead at a small hospital about forty miles away from Malmö that Signe Jansson got the opportunity, in the mid-1970s, to begin applying this approach (whereby the expectant mothers – not the state – set the conditions of child delivery). Gradually, as the process was developed and became known, women from outside the hospital district began contacting the program to ask whether it was possible to break the rules of "municipal arrest," and to give birth at Ystad Hospital's maternity ward. Formally speaking, it was not possible at all, but with a little ingenuity of various kinds (like false registration), and for a variety of reasons, a growing number of mothers from outside the hospital district began giving birth at the maternity ward in Ystad. Since it proved problematic, from a purely legal-technical standpoint, to demand payment from all of these women, the principle of "municipal arrest" soon collapsed, and full freedom of choice was instituted in all County Councils (which in Sweden are the authorities that have the responsibility for providing public health care).

After having been met at first with great skepticism by the dominant forces within the midwives' profession, the principle of "giving birth on the woman's terms" gradually won general acceptance and became, I believe one can say, the dominant ideology within this part of the public sector. The foremost reason for this was the great appreciation women showed for the new system of child delivery. Another was the good medical results achieved. In the second half of the 1980s, nearly 50 percent of the deliveries performed at Ystad Hospital were for women from outside the hospital's own district. This captured great attention within the profession. Signe Jansson, who had set the whole process in motion, concluded her working life as an employee of the County Council charged with teaching the method to the maternity wards of other hospitals. The maternity clinics which failed to bring themselves into line with the new method found the demand for their services so reduced that they were threatened with closure.

Today, the childbearing citizens in Sweden make full use of their right to choose between different clinics. In the Stockholm County Council area, for instance, as many as 25 percent drop the "assigned" maternity

---

[4] Jansson (1988), p. 41.

clinic in favor of another.[5] It need hardly be said that the model developed in Ystad has been copied. The producers have quite simply had to adapt themselves to the demands of women and parents for autonomy – to be treated with respect, instead of being objectified and left to the more or less discretionary power of the staff. Maternity wards unable to meet these demands have had to discontinue their operations.[6] Everything from giving birth while standing or under water or while hanging from ropes, with music (rock or classical), etc., is on offer. In the publications catering to this category of citizen, one can regularly read synopses of the services offered by different clinics (pools, home-like arrangements, ropes from the ceiling, musical arrangements, double beds, or what have you). Expectant mothers are no longer treated as objects in the hands of others who perform the delivery of their child. It is instead not unusual (as one midwife has put it) that they want to "direct" the whole show.[7]

A great deal more could be said about this change in respect to the duties of the state at the dawn of life, but the above account should suffice to illustrate the essential issues here: firstly, the significance of the fact that the last two decades have seen a sharp increase in the capabilities and knowledge commanded by citizens, and a corresponding rise in their demands for freedom of choice and self-determination as well;[8] secondly, that interesting things happen to an implementing organization when it can no longer take the demand for its services for granted; and thirdly, that variation and freedom of choice in the public services can be achieved within the framework of the universal welfare policy. I shall develop each of these themes below.

Individualism and solidarity

This matter of changes in social values is not altogether easy; indeed, it is one of the most difficult areas in social science. Nevertheless, it seems there is much to indicate that demands for autonomy among Swedish citizens have sharply increased. The Power Study's final report strongly emphasizes this change. It claims that a partly new type of citizen has emerged – one endowed with greater knowledge and capabilities. The

---

[5] Saltman & von Otter (1992).   [6] Saltman (1992), p. 63.
[7] From what I understand, this sometimes leads to a certain disappointment among the women, for this sort of process is characterized too by a far-reaching Clausewitzian "uncertainty" and "friction" as regards the possibility of predicting the course of events. A certain adaptive faculty is probably, according to my own experience (or participatory observation, shall we say), to be recommended.
[8] For a survey of developments within other branches of health care as well, see Saltman (1992), ch. 2.

report claims that citizens' demands for differentiation in services creates difficulties for universalistic and standardized solutions, and that their higher educational level makes it possible for them to call the judgments of experts into question.[9] For example, the Power Study's investigation of citizens' attitudes showed that the virtue held most highly by Swedish citizens was the ability to form one's own views independently of others.[10] At the same time, this investigation revealed that many citizens felt they lacked influence over the public services they use (above all schools and health care).

Some changes over time can also be confirmed. The proportion of citizens deeming themselves able to write a letter appealing against an authority's decision increased from 45.1 to 68.5 percent between 1968 and 1987. Moreover, an evaluative study done by Thorlief Pettersson within the framework of a larger European study supplies evidence for the proposition that the citizen of 1990 was substantially more individualistic than his counterpart of ten years earlier. Pettersson describes the content of the concept of individualism as follows:

> individualism means that the individual person becomes the goal and measure for different aspects of his life-view. The self-realization and well-being of the individual are prioritized, partly at the expense of such duties and commitments as had earlier prevailed, both in the family and in social life generally. The individual person's judgement of what is right and wrong, good and evil, takes precedence over traditional norms and values; the individual finds it harder to accept various impositions and restrictions on individual means of expression.[11]

According to this investigation, a sharp increase in the sort of values associated with individualism took place between 1981 and 1990. The index used to measure this rose from -23 to $+23$. At the same time, citizens' confidence in "the institutions of power and order" declined from $+15$ to -15.[12] These are clearly the greatest changes in value

---

[9] SOU (1990: 44), ch. 11.
[10] Petersson, Westholm & Blomberg (1989), p. 262. See also Petersson (1992), pp. 328–331.
[11] Pettersson (1992), p. 51.
[12] Ibid, p. 45. A high value on the individualism index reflects answers indicating that the respondent desires a greater emphasis on individual development, less scope for authorities, and greater scope for personal initiative at work; does not think that employees should automatically follow the instructions of their supervisors, tries to influence and convince others, and considers himself to enjoy considerable freedom of choice in his own life. The index indicating confidence in "the institutions of power and order" measures confidence in the armed forces, the police, and the courts. These changes are by no means restricted to Sweden, see ibid., p. 55.

patterns measured in the study. In the case of those values which are termed "social morals" in the study – which have to do with the degree of tolerance for cheating on taxes, benefit fraud, theft, the use of hashish, bribing, etc. – the index went from +9 to − 8. The other indexes – which register such things as post-materialist values and faith in democracy – changed but marginally.[13]

One might think this change in value patterns is limited to the highly educated middle class. It is true that individualistic attitudes are most marked in that social group. The interesting thing, however, is that it was only among the investigative category of blue-collar workers that any palpable change took place between 1981 and 1990; both high-level and low-level white-collar employees, by contrast, remained largely at their earlier high levels when it came to embracing individualistic values.[14] Accordingly, the proportion of workers with a individualistic viewpoint in general increased from 39 to 53 percent between 1981 and 1990, and in regard to working life, the share expressing an individualistic outlook rose from 17 to 43 percent.[15]

In regard to public services,[16] the Swedish welfare model has been built according to what we may call the "high-quality standard solution." The underlying idea was to make the quality of public services so high that no demand for better options arose. Both a normative and a strategic principle lay behind this ambition. Gustav Möller gave expression to the normative principle with the words: "only the best is good enough for the people." Public services were not to be a second-rate alternative reserved for those of lesser means; rather, the principle of universalism was to prevail. This normative principle was joined to a strategic one: better-off social groups would be more willing to support the universal welfare policy if the public services on offer satisfied them as well.

---

[13] Ibid.

[14] Pettersson & Geyer (1992), p. 13. The investigation defines a generally individualistic attitude as one marked by the possession of at least three of the following four characteristics: (1) recommending personal freedom over economic equality; (2) being inclined often to hold firm and to try to convince others; (3) desiring a stronger emphasis on individual development; and (4) wishing no greater respect for authorities.

[15] Ibid. Having an individualistic view of working life means that one embraces at least three of the following four statements: (1) it is fair that a more efficient secretary earns more; (2) employees should only follow their supervisors' instructions when they accord with their own convictions; (3) it is important to be able to take personal initiative on the job; (4) it is important to be able to take responsibility on the job.

[16] Or, if one insists on putting it this way, the continued colonization of their life-world.

The concept of a "standard solution" meant the services in question would be the same everywhere and for everyone, and organized in accordance with central directives of a political and professional character.[17] Allowing any freedom of choice in such a system is pointless, of course, for the services are the same for everyone everywhere. Freedom of choice has thereby come to be associated, in an automatic and unreflecting manner, with injustice.

In a society where citizens accept centrally prescribed models, where cultural differences are small, where demands for individually adapted services are as good as nonexistent, and where "alternative" lifestyles are scarcely to be met with – in such a society, the "high-quality standard solution" can work rather well. In the present situation, however, cultural differences are increasing, growing numbers of citizens view their life as an individually planned project and their lifestyle as a matter of individual choice, and citizens' level of knowledge is high and their capacity to safeguard their interests advanced. In such a society, the "high-quality standard solution" risks becoming more of a problem than a solution.

To return to a topic discussed earlier: three problems are occasioned by the increase in demands for autonomy and freedom of choice. The first is analytical: how can a state with far-reaching ambitions to furnish citizens with *basic capabilities* in the form of benefits and services manage to do this while safeguarding the principle of *equal concern and respect,* if the demands of individual citizens to influence the character of these basic capabilities are sharply increasing at the same time? Is it possible to realize both of these ideas under conditions of increasing individualism? Or does this rather mean we must sacrifice either the idea that the state should supply citizens with certain politically determined basic capabilities, or the idea that this should be done with equal concern and respect?

The second problem is normative. As we saw in chapter 4, centrally placed officials and politicians are largely unable to manage services of this sort, at least in significant aspects. What actually takes place when the citizen encounters the implementing organization – in the classroom, for example, or in the treatment room at the local care center, or in the child-care group – is largely impossible to influence from the center. The conditions of legitimation and organization thus become central for "what the state can do." Here, the attitudes, ambitions, and outlook of the field personnel play the decisive role in determining whether these programs exhibit the qualities we consider most important. In a system of the Swedish type, in which citizens traditionally have not enjoyed the right to choose between different service producers, the result has been to

---

[17] Petersson (1991).

create a "black hole" in the democratic process.[18] This is especially serious when the services in question are of critical importance for the life situation of citizens, and indeed this is often the case, since the whole idea behind the universal welfare state has been that services of just this type should be publicly produced. If physically handicapped persons, for instance, are not able to select (and reject) their personal assistants themselves, but are rather forced to accept those offered by the central administration, the result is to expose them to an unchecked exercise of power. Power and responsibility drift apart, which undermines the legitimacy of public policy. This point cannot be put better than Signe Jansson has done:

> I used to say in the parents' groups: "Remember that you pay a lot of money so that child delivery and health care will work. Now when at last you are in the situation of needing these resources, you have the right to put demands" . . . For we are in fact paid by them so that the delivery will go well. We must not forget that. It is one of the institutional problems with the health care structure we have that people do not pay directly for the services they get. They do not "see" that they pay and that we should give them service. We easily forget this, we who work in the care sector. We are afraid of parting with our knowledge, and this knowledge becomes a means of power.[19]

Our example of child-delivery services makes it clear that the viewpoint expressed by some Swedish feminists to the effect that freedom of choice in these services is something only men are interested in, while women (with their different psychological disposition) are interested in an understanding dialogue and not in choosing between different producers – this viewpoint does not hold good empirically. Since it remains the case, despite everything, that only women bear children, our example demonstrates that the desire to choose, at any rate, is *not* a factor distinguishing the sexes.[20] We may profit here from Susan Moller Okin's theory of the relation between gender and justice. Okin stresses that, when one cannot refuse to participate in an institution, or when the costs for so doing are very high, the result is to undermine one's capacity to express internal criticism as well, that is, to make one's voice heard. The inability to exit, then, weakens one's voice. The citizen who is unable to drop one service producer in favor of another ends up getting the worst of it in this dialogue, for the producer occupies a monopoly position.

---

[18] Cf. Le Grand & Bartlett (1993) discussion of the "purchaser–provider" split.
[19] Jansson (1998), p. 40, cf. Le Grand & Bartlett (1993), p. 7.
[20] This has been argued by Swedish feminists, see e.g., the editor of *Pockettidingen R*, Gunilla Thorgren, in *Aftonbladet,* 03–01–90.

Expressing criticism, in such a situation, of a kind that is regarded as serious is a course of action involving great risks.[21] The right to choose another producer is *not* incompatible with a dialogue between equals. It is rather the case that the risk of not being chosen furnishes producers of this type of service with a strong incentive to be particularly sensitive in their dialogue with citizens. Okin is very likely right when she observes that, for the contracting parties in an institution to be able to take part in a dialogue between equals, they must be equivalent in power and status. One way of achieving this is to ensure that they have chosen each other on a voluntary basis.[22]

The third problem with the new individualism is electoral, that is, it has to do with the universal welfare policy's political support. What happens if a large number of well-off and individualistic citizens start to take the view that the discrepancy has grown too great between, on the one hand, their demands on the public service producers – in regard to program design, self-determination, and personal autonomy – and, on the other, the service producers' ability and/or willingness to meet these demands? The probable political scenario is that this group of citizens will then choose to obtain these services outside the public sphere, and to defray the expenses thereof on their own. Let us further assume that, in a very high degree, this will not be a question just for high-income but also for middle-income groups. A likely course of development is that, following such a choice, these citizens will very soon put the question to themselves of why they should pay twice – first for the specialized service they desire, and then for the public standard variant they themselves do not use, but which instead goes to "the others," that is, those lacking the means to purchase such services on their own. Their willingness to contribute economically and electorally to the public sector will probably dramatically diminish.[23] As Saltman has argued, the future of the publicly run health-care system looks anything but bright if this problem is not solved by furnishing patients with more "corrrective power" (such as the possibility of dropping care-givers with whom they are not satisfied in favor of others).[24]

---

[21] Ladberg (1986), who has studied this practice at Swedish day-care centers, maintains that parents who express such criticism risk having their children treated worse than the others.

[22] Okin (1989). Okin's example is of the situation of women in the family, but the model is generally applicable, in her view.

[23] A great deal of empirical support for this supposition can be found in what has happened to large parts of the public school system in the United States. See, e.g., Chubb & Moe (1990).

[24] Saltman (1992), p. 51.

As noted in chapter 6, the universal welfare state requires that a sufficiently broad political alliance – one including middle-income earners – can be created on its behalf. In all likelihood it is very difficult, perhaps impossible, to maintain an electoral majority for the solidaristic financing of public services in a situation in which a great many middle-income earners – and perhaps others as well – turn their backs on the public services.[25]

The solution to all of these problems can be found, as ought to be evident, in our introductory example. Firstly, by guaranteeing citizens the right to choose between different service options, we solve the dilemma between treating them with *equal concern and respect,* and supplying them with *basic capabilities* (because we respect their choice of service producer).[26] By means of this freedom of choice, secondly, we deal with *democracy's black hole,* which is otherwise so serious in these programs. Citizens are ensured the right to drop service producers who do not satisfy their demands. Since the usual electoral procedures are not applicable in this area – we do not vote for those who take care of our children at day-care centers, and those for whom we vote cannot direct a large part of what occurs in these processes – citizens must be given the opportunity of "voting with their feet." Thirdly, we solve the electoral problem – there is no group with any reason for abandoning its support for the collective financing of these services. To return to our introductory example: the number of privately financed maternity wards in Sweden is, as far as I know, zero.

One might assume, perhaps, that the new individualism will necessarily undermine the idea of a solidaristic and collective financing of these programs. However, the individualistically minded citizen with whom we are faced is *not* the same as the egoistic citizen. On the contrary, it appears that the value dimensions of collectivism/individualism, on the one hand, and of altruism/egoism, on the other, are different from (and largely independent of) each other. Accordingly, Pettersson and Geyer write that the new individualists do not hold the values neo-liberals have assumed they do:

Compared with the less individualistically inclined, moreover, they do *not*

---

[25] The historical connection has to do with how the Social Democrats, at the end of the 1950s, designed the system of supplementary pensions strategically – as a way of creating such an alliance between blue-collar workers and white-collar employees. See Svensson (1994).

[26] This is not to say that all demands can be met, but it is a question of establishing a sufficiently strong economic demand, rather than of politically determined standard variants. The criticism of inadequate variation in the services on offer does not strike the political system in the former case.

show any stronger interest in increasing today's wage differentials, they do *not* evidence any greater tendency to view the poor with a "they-just-have-themselves-to-blame" attitude, they do *not* show any stronger tendency to regard their fellow beings in less of a spirit of trust and fellowship . . . They are neither the irrepressible entrepreneurs imagined by the neo-liberals nor the selfish egoists supposed by the social democrats.[27]

(Nor are these largely younger and highly educated citizens more critical of the universal welfare policy than their more collectivistically-minded brothers and sisters.[28])

At the Institute for Future Studies, an investigation of the values of youth has recently been presented. The result shows that those born in the 1970s hold individual responsibility in high esteem, but that this is "not a question of a take-care-of-yourself-and-the-devil-take-the-hindmost view of the world."[29]

One could say that what these studies show is the appearance not of an egoistic but of a solidaristic individualism, if such an expression be permitted. This solidaristic individualism may be seen as expressive of the following attitude: citizen X demands that the public services be supplied in a manner appropriate to his own situation and needs, but is prepared at the same time to support citizen Y's demand to obtain services matching his own altogether different situation, *provided this support is mutual,* that is, that it fulfills the requirement of the just distribution of costs that is part of the theory of contingent consent. One can, furthermore, see the demand for freedom of choice and individualized treatment in the public services as an expression of the requirement of procedural justice presented in connection with the theory of contingent consent. That is to say, to the degree that the production of public services fulfills, in its concrete organization, the demands for freedom of choice and individual adjustment – and rubs out "democracy's black hole" thereby – citizens will be willing to contribute solidaristically to defraying its costs.

Ronald Inglehart is perhaps the most prominent scholar, internation-

---

[27] Pettersson & Geyer (1992) pp. 28f. Italics in last sentence removed. That these are two different dimensions is demonstrated by Goul Andersen (1993) as well. Survey research on voters and elections has shown that the hypothesis that voters vote according to self-interest has weak empirical support. Researchers point instead to the presence of different value dimensions. The "solidaristic individualists" most closely resemble what in voting studies are called "sociothropic" voters. For an overview, see Lewin (1991), pp. 57–80.

[28] Pettersson & Geyer (1992), p. 28f.

[29] Andersson, Fürth, & Holmberg (1993), p. 180.

ally speaking, when it comes to studying shifts in values. In his latest book, he speculates a great deal about what the new individualism will mean for the welfare state. On the one hand, he argues that those societies which give the greatest scope to creativity and individual initiative will be those best equipped to meet the future. The problem, however, is that these factors cannot be planned into existence, but are genuinely unforeseeable, and are therefore beyond the politically manageable. On the other hand, he claims that "the dismantling of the welfare state is not in the cards," and points out that Reagan's and Thatcher's attempts in this direction "ran into a brick wall of political resistance." Inglehart concludes that "the future lies with those societies that can strike an effective balance between individual autonomy and central authority." The citizens of the Western world, who earlier were willing to sacrifice their individual autonomy for economic and physical security, are less and less willing to do this. Increasingly, they take such security for granted, and instead place a higher value on "self-expression both in their work and in political life." Whether this should be interpreted in left-wing or right-wing political terms depends, in Inglehart's view, on whether or not one regards increased state power as a progressive left-wing project in itself. For his part, and here I would like to concur, Inglehart argues that, to the extent matters develop in line with a society offering increased leeway for "self-realization, the new trends seems progressive. What is crucial is the result, not the means by which it is reached."[30]

Market and state: competition, responsibility, and efficiency

One of the lessons of our introductory example is that interesting things happen to service producers when they can no longer take customers for granted. This is the classical argument for market solutions, that is, that competition forces through more efficient production, adaptation to customers' wishes, and respect for customers. Producers are forced, both before themselves and before others, to scrutinize their behavior critically and to justify it. The question of market versus public solutions is one of the most debated and, I would claim, most misunderstood questions in the debate over what the state can and should do. A very common feature of the debate, even on an advanced level, is the so-called Nirvana assumption. Representatives of the one side compare the ideal picture of the market or state with its actually existing opposite; unsurprisingly, the result is given from the start.[31] Defenders of the public sector, for

---

[30] Inglehardt (1990), pp. 10f, cf. Le Grand & Bartlett (1993) pp. 9.
[31] See, e.g., Savas (1981) and Wolf (1993).

	Market	State
Nirvana assumption	Efficiency	Justice
	Freedom of choice	Democracy
	Creativity	Equal treatment
Actually existing problems	Segregation	Bureaucracy
	Cartel-formation	Corruption
	Monopolies	Queues

Figure 8.1   Pictures of the market and of the state.

instance, compare its ideal justice with such problems of actually existing markets as segregation and the formation of cartels. Neither markets nor the public sector are in the habit, however, of behaving in accordance with the ideal picture; we must look instead at how the two systems function within different areas in practice (see figure 8.1).

The question of market solutions or political direction turns on a simple thing: how to select an appropriate managerial system for the implementing organization. There is a virtually endless literature on the management of organizations, public as well as private. After having wrestled with a large part of this literature for nearly fifteen years now, I am prepared at last to summarize it in a single sentence:

Organizations which do not receive one sort of signal when they do something right, and another sort of signal when they do something wrong, will in the long run do more wrong things than right.

The reason for this is not, or at least not necessarily, that the responsible staff lack knowledge, resources, or interest in doing the right thing. The problem lies rather in the signal system – the staff simply do not know what the right thing is, because they do not get one sort of signal when they do something right, and another sort when they do something wrong. The chances, moreover, of doing the wrong thing are almost always much greater than the chances of doing the right thing.

As chapter 4 made clear, it is extraordinarily difficult, by means of the parliamentary-democratic chain of command, to design functioning signal systems for the type of public activities under examination here.

The uncertainty in the policy theory means that the need for situational adjustment is altogether too great in most cases for any such signal system to be possible. It is necessary to use management by goals and framework laws instead; this gives the frontline personnel great discretionary power over implementation, and thus creates a "black hole" in parliamentary democracy. As the Power Study puts it: "Framework legislation is based ultimately on the idea that harmony prevails between the state and the citizens. The authorities are assumed to know what is best for the citizens."[32] This is right, and yet wrong, since framework legislation can be combined with other methods for enabling citizens to hold the relevant officials responsible.

Instead of trying desperately to design, on paper, new and ever more sophisticated systems of central management and evaluation,[33] another possibility exists, as indicated by the case we have examined here. That is, we can "manage from below," by using the choices of the citizens themselves as a signal system, or in other words, to use "quasi-markets."[34] The advantage of this method lies above all in its clarity; it is hard for the responsible producers to disregard a diminishing demand for their services (when citizens take their custom elsewhere). It sends a clear signal – both to the responsible politicians and to the producing organization and its staff – that something is not as it should be, that the "right thing" is not being done. There are thus very good reasons, from both a normative and efficiency-furthering standpoint, to allow some form of competition between different service producers.

With this said as our point of departure, however, all the appropriate reservations should be listed. For it is not always the case that market solutions, or market-like solutions, are suitable for activities of this sort. Again, the IDO-principle applies, and in this case, fortunately, we can also say something about what It Depends On. To quote John Donahue:

> There is a large element of nonsense in the privatization debate. Proponents are fond of invoking the efficiency that characterises well run companies in competitive markets and then, not troubling with any intervening logical steps, trumpeting the conclusion that private firms will excel in *public* undertakings as well. To go from the observation that private companies tend to do what they do better than public agencies, to the assertion that companies should take over the agencies' duties, is

---

[32] SOU (1990: 44), p. 238.
[33] The list of such attempts is long, and they are all marked by the law of flagging enthusiasm. See Gorpe (1978) and Lundquist (1992), chs. 3 and 4.
[34] Le Grand & Bartlett (1993).

rather like observing that the clients of exercise spas are healthier, on average, than the clients of hospitals, and concluding from this that workout coaches should take over from doctors. Public tasks are different and, mostly, harder.[35]

The first analytical problem we face is that, in practice, we never encounter pure markets free from public regulation. Every functioning market system must, if it is not to degenerate into corruption or other types of pathological problems of collective action, be embedded in a series of public institutions (such as a functioning legal system for dealing with ownership rights and contract provisions). A functioning market must be created by means of politically fashioned institutions. Certainly, these regulations may be of various kinds; economists generally distinguish, for instance, between market-conforming and non-market-conforming regulations.

Moreover, as Donald Kettl has shown in his study of the conditions prevailing in this area in the United States, a curious discrepancy between theory and empirical evidence characterizes this discussion. On the one hand, market solutions are generally held out as better and more efficient than any attempts on the state's part to produce anything. Unlike the state, the market is productive, allows freedom of choice, furthers innovation, drives inefficient producers out of business, and so on. The state, on the other hand, just tends to grow and grow, without regard for available resources. In the United States, it is even forbidden for the state to compete directly with the citizens if the products demanded are available on the market. Nevertheless, this enthusiasm for market solutions has not always had its counterpart in practice. In Kettl's report the text reads as follows:

> Despite the enthusiasm for entrepreneurial government and privatization, the most egregious tales of waste, fraud, and abuse in government programs have often involved greedy, corrupt, and often criminal activity by the government's private partners – and weak government management to detect and correct these problems.[36]

The reason for this, Kettl shows, is that in many of the areas in which the state might wish to contract the provision of a public service out to

---

[35] Donahue (1992), p. 208, Cf. Le Grand & Bartlett (1993). From a game-theoretical perspective, the problem is that the state as a purchaser of the goods is not likely to have anything near "perfect information", cf. G. Miller (1992).

[36] Kettl (1993a), p. 5. See also J. Jacobs (1992), who has called attention to the moral disasters that can occur when the norm-systems of the market and the political system are confused.

competing private entrepreneurs, textbook market conditions do not exist. In particular, "arm's-length transactions among a large number of buyers and sellers for relatively undifferentiated goods" are not to be found.[37] This problem partly reflects the fact that the products the state wishes to purchase are not of such a character as to permit textbook market conditions. For one thing, the state is often the only buyer; for another, the products in question often are not standardized, but rather highly specialized. Moreover, it is sometimes difficult or even impossible to specify exactly what it is the state wants. Or, put another way, the good or service in question is so special, and its delivery must take place under such varying and unforeseeable conditions, that it is impossible to frame the contracts with sufficient precision (so that they function in an authoritative fashion).[38] This applies, according to Kettl, not least in the social area:

> The very nature of social services, with their fuzzy objectives and uncertain technologies, makes it difficult for governments to write crisp, enforceable, contracts. Contractors naturally resist goals that are too specific or that hold them to levels of performance they doubt they can achieve. Governments cannot prescribe in advance exactly what outcomes they want or, if they know the outcomes, they cannot explain how to get there.[39]

Market solutions can only meet the demands put on them if such demands can be clearly and distinctly expressed. There is always the risk that providers will engage in what is called "opportunistic behavior," that is, to try to cut corners to increase profits.[40] As I pointed out earlier, efficiency is not the only goal for which the state should strive. Others include: (1) the rule of law, that is, that the procedures applied are correct; (2) the treatment of all citizens with "equal concern and respect"; and (3) responsibility, that is, that citizens are assured the possibility of passing retrospective judgment on the efforts of the elected politicians. This means that market solutions involving the assignment of public tasks to private, profit-making enterprises must be handled with caution.

---

[37] Kettl (1993a), p. 15.
[38] Donahue (1992) reviews a couple of interesting failures from the United States. The one concerns private prisons, where it has not been possible to specify exactly how the detainees are to be handled and treated in different situations. The other has to do with labor market training, where it has not proved possible to deal with the private training entrepreneurs' incentive to accept only applicants with the best prospect of (a) succeeding in the training itself, and (b) finding work afterwards.
[39] Kettl (1993a), p. 173.
[40] Le Grand & Bartlett (1993), p. 25.

Production	Private	Private	Private	Private	Public	Public	Public	Public
Regulation	Private	Private	Public	Public	Private	Private	Public	Public
Financing	Private	Public	Private	Public	Private	Public	Private	Public

Figure 8. 2   Different public, private and mixed alternatives.

Studies done of health-care provision, for example, point to the import-ance of strict public regulation and quality control if competition is not to have undesirable effects.[41] Economic incentives furnish a powerful managerial instrument, but they are also hard to handle.

It is not the case, in practice, that we must choose here between "public" and "private." For every productive activity involves *three* different aspects, each of which opens up different opportunities for influencing the activity in question. They include (a) regulation: who sets the rules for the activity and sees to it that they are followed? (b) Financing: how are the expenses defrayed? And (c) production: who bears the direct responsibility for the activity, and disposes thereby of the operative means of control?[42] If we cross-tabulate these dimensions, we end up not with two but with eight different variations on the public/private theme. It is thus possible, as shown in figure 8.2, to mix "public" and "private" elements in a considerable variety of ways.[43]

Let us return now to our introductory example – that of child-delivery services. We find, first of all, that it is publicly financed. Many aspects of this activity are publicly regulated, moreover, and in a number of different ways. For instance, the professionals working in this area (physicians and midwives) must be licensed; in addition, they are held publicly responsible through the system of control exercised by the National Board of Social Affairs. The production of child-delivery services is public as well, even if the element of "private" initiative seems to have been considerable and competition between different public care-givers has taken place. Swedish examples of systems combining private pro-duction with largely public financing and regulation include the system of national dental insurance and school vouchers.

---

[41] Cf. Jonsson (1993).
[42] Lundqvist (1991); cf. Montin (1992).
[43] Lundqvist (1991), p. 213, cf. Le Grand & Bartlett (1993), ch. 1.

It is interesting to compare Sweden with Denmark in this respect. Denmark is in many ways very similar to Sweden, yet it differs in some striking ways. Elsewhere I have argued that Danish welfare policy exhibits a less authoritarian and more liberal cast than its Swedish counterpart. In Denmark, which has had a "free" school system (i.e., a system with school choice but public finance) since the interwar period, it is the parties on the left that have defended the principle that parents should enjoy the right to choose between schools, and that this choice should be financed largely by public means.[44] For a long time, moreover, Danish citizens have enjoyed the right to choose a "house doctor." The attitudes of Danish citizens towards the public services has been investigated recently in a large interview-study, which put the same questions as those contained in the citizen survey done as part of the Swedish Power Study. The results show that Danish citizens consider themselves to enjoy substantially greater influence within the areas of education and health care than their Swedish counterparts consider themselves to have. Danes also expressed greater satisfaction than did Swedes. Jens Hoff, who carried out this study, draws the following conclusion:

> these results appear to indicate that the areas of education and day-care in Denmark are special: characterized by active users and participation-oriented or receptive institutions.[45]

The interesting conclusion we can draw from this is the following: it is *not* the case, according to this study, that the right of Danish citizens to select and to reject, on the one hand, and their willingness to offer criticism and to participate actively, on the other, can be seen as alternative strategies. The right to select and to reject does *not* diminish the discursive process; rather, these different avenues of influence stand out as *complementary* strategies. Expressed in more classical political scientific terms – the opportunity of protesting by means of "exit," on the one hand, and the opportunity of remaining within the organization and trying through argumentation and "voice" to change things, on the other, are not mutually exclusive. On the contrary, the right to "exit" strengthens the influence one can exercise with one's "voice."[46] The reason for this, I believe, is that a service organization which runs the risk that its clients will "vote with their feet" has powerful cause to be sensitive.

What general conditions must be fulfilled, then, for it to be suitable to assign the performance of public tasks to private or other non-state

[44] Lindbom (1995).   [45] Hoff (1993), p. 93.   [46] Ibid., p. 94.

organizations? Those researchers who have tried (without ideological blinders) to compile empirical results on the effects of privatization have come to the conclusion that the following conditions are decisive:[47]

1 That the contract between the state and the producer can be specified precisely.
2 That the state has the resources to evaluate the producers (so that it can cancel unfulfilled contracts, for example) and to assess the quality of services rendered.
3 That a functioning competition between different producers can be created.

The first condition is based on on the principle that, if one cannot indicate what it is one wants, one should not be surprised to get something other than what one expects. As mentioned earlier, this poses varying degrees of difficulty in different areas. The second condition above is pretty obvious as a theoretical matter, but it places partly different demands on the state than those applying today. It would rather be a state that represents the interests of the citizens against the producers of public services than a state which is synonymous with the producers.[48]

The third condition is especially interesting. It turns out that there is no real point in privatizing a public program from the standpoint of cost. What is interesting is whether a functioning competition can be introduced (which, incidentally, is often easier said than done). Such competition can take place between public and private producers, but also between exclusively public or exclusively private producers.[49] If these conditions can be fulfilled, there are no obstacles in principle to asigning the production of public services to private entrepreneurs, because the

---

[47] Kettl (1993a), p. 8; Donahue (1992), pp. 210ff, Le Grand & Bartlett (1993), ch. 1. This research has warned, furthermore, of two problems that can arise in connection with the privatization of public tasks. The one is that, in view of what we know about how the political process works, we may expect the risk to be great that privatization will be introduced in precisely those areas where it is least suitable, while public production will be retained in just those areas in which the introduction of competition would be most beneficial. The reason for this this is that those groups within the public sector who have the most to lose from the introduction of competition will also be those able to resist it most effectively. And the converse danger also applies: hordes of private entrepeneurs will try to land public contracts in exactly those areas where (a) they believe they will be able to work with imprecise contracts, (b) such contracts cannot be evaluated, and (c) where they see possibilities of establishing a monopoly position. See Donahue (1992), ch. 9.
[48] Cf. Phillips (1993), pp. 41f.
[49] Donahue (1992), p. 211.

political system retains control over the operation of services in those respects which are primary – those touching on "equal concern and respect."[50]

It is not at all necessary, however – from the standpoint of the theoretical and normative concerns forming the basis of this study – that private producers take charge of public programs. This is a question of suitability, to be decided from case to case according to the criteria above. Empirical research has revealed cases in which privatization has failed in a spectacular fashion, since it has been applied to activities which are so complex, and which work with such an uncertain policy theory, that it has proved impossible to write the contract precisely.[51] When this contractual condition can be fulfilled, moreover, the critical thing is not privatization, but rather the introduction of competition between different service alternatives, so that the corrective power exercised by citizens is increased.

There is, in sum, every reason to be pragmatic in the choice of who supplies services for the public reckoning. That citizens are to be furnished with certain *basic capabilities* says nothing about who should produce these. There may be reason to recall here that such public transfers as child allowances do not involve any public production at all. Citizens enjoy full freedom of choice in choosing the uses to which these monies are put.

In those cases (and they are many), in which the citizen collective takes the view that, by basic capabilities, something other than money must be meant (i.e., health care, education, etc.), it is appropriate – under certain specific conditions – to make over the delivery of these services to competing producers who may be private, semi-private, or public. Competition is a powerful instrument both for creating efficiency and freedom of choice, and for meeting the demands of citizens for autonomy. That it can change the staff's attitudes and readiness to satisfy the wishes of citizens would not seem to be a matter over which there can be any doubt. We can take the following statement of the physician Sven Britton as an example: "Even so I must observe, to my disappointment, that market adjustment has led to a better feeling for service among the staff in Huddinge. Competition sets powerful forces in motion."[52] At the same time, there are many areas in which this obviously is not appropriate, or where only a limited competition between different public service producers should be allowed.

---

[50] Cf. Wetterberg (1991), pp. 192ff.
[51] Donahue (1992), chapters 6 and 8.
[52] In *Företag & Samhälle* (1993), no. 2, p. 48.

There is cause here once again to stress the critical importance of implementation in this context. It is clear, as far as the relation of freedom of choice to the univesal welfare policy is concerned, that various combinations are possible. For it is not true that increased freedom of choice leads necessarily to the abandonment of the universal welfare policy, nor is it the case that a universal welfare policy must exclude freedom of choice. The consequences of freedom of choice for the universal welfare policy – for whether or not it can be carried out in accordance with "equal concern and respect" and a just distribution of "basic capabilities" – depend on how the implementation of the freedom of choice program is structured. Everything depends, in other words, on how the implementation process is organized. In an article summing up the experiences of various countries with market strategies in the educational area, William Lowe Boyd writes as follows:

> School choice plans have both great promise and real perils. Citizens and policy-makers concerned about improving their community and nation's schools will want to weigh these matters carefully. If choice plans are to be adopted, it is essential that they be carefully designed and monitored to ensure that they produce desirable outcomes . . . Choice plans may promote, but will not, by themselves, guarantee widespread school improvement.[53]

Freedom of choice, competition, and the universal welfare policy

In summary thus far, we may say that the universal welfare policy runs some serious risks that may imperil its future. The greatest risk lies in the fact that the earlier idea of centralized and standardized solutions is no longer accepted by large segments of the population. Traditional misgivings about introducing competition and freedom of choice have focused on the danger of segregation – that a society would be created in which the strong could utilize all the advantages of freedom of choice at the expense of the weak, and that the principle of universalism would be undermined thereby.

Let us take the question of social segregation first.[54] This is an undeniable danger of a system featuring a high degree of freedom of choice. It should not be exaggerated, however; one should not measure this real-world danger against a nirvana assumption. Schools, for instance, are already strongly segregated as a result of segregated housing

---

[53] Boyd (1993), p. 26.
[54] For a review of this problem, see Olsson-Hort (1992).

patterns.[55] If comparisons are to be made, realities must be set alongside realities. One should not simply assume, moreover, that citizens possessed of modest economic resources would be less competent than their fellow citizens at making choices of this kind, were they granted the economic opportunity of choosing. For in that case one would also have to argue, in the name of consistency, against universal cash child allowances and pensions of the type launched by the Swedish Social Democrats.

The empirical situation is unclear here, however. Some studies from the United states, for instance, show that the introduction of vouchers has not increased segregation but, on the contrary, reduced it.[56] Other studies show the opposite. The Swedish Agency for Administrative Development has recently evaluated various freedom of choice models applied by Swedish municipalities in the areas of child care, education, old-age care, and health care. This investigation does not reveal any tendencies toward social segregation, but the authors enter the reservation that freedom of choice is still very new, and that it is impossible as yet to foresee its impact over the long term.[57]

What, then, are the conditions – as based on the normative principles guiding this account – that must be fulfilled for it to be possible to combine the universal welfare policy with the demands for freedom of choice using some form of "blocked currency" like vouchers? How, in other words, should the above-mentioned contract between the state and the producer in general terms look? Tentatively the conditions are four.

Firstly, that all service producers – whether private, cooperative, or public – follow the same basic rules in respect to quality and standards. As for which "basic capabilities" the state should furnish all citizens with – this is a question the citizens themselves must decide, through the democratic process.

All variation in the services on offer must take place above the democratically determined level of "basic capabilities." The reason for this is that not everything will do, that is, obviously not just any activity can be accepted as a public concern (even when it is carried out by non-public producers). If a service is paid for with public monies, then it must be implemented according to the principles adumbrated above, for the simple reason that activities which are financed, at least in part, by public revenues are a common political concern.[58] The determination of what

---

[55] Olsson-Hort (1992), ch. 6.
[56] Chubb & Moe (1990), pp. 111ff and pp. 248ff. Some education researchers warn, however, that the introduction of vouchers can contribute to increased segregation. See, e.g., Lennart Grosin, "Ytterligare skolsegregation blir följden," *Svenska Dagbladet* (10–31–91). See also Boyd (1993), pp. 21–26.
[57] SOU (1993:47).   [58] G. Miller (1992).

constitutes "basic capabilities" cannot be left to the discretion of the producers. In addition, there is particular reason in just these areas to protect the consumer/citizen, who is often in an exposed position when it comes to services of this type.[59] From the standpoint of efficiency, moreover, it bears stressing that these conditions ensure fair competition between the various alternatives offered on the market. Thus, competition can only be introduced in areas in which it is possible to achieve sufficient precision in the framing of contracts, and in which the state can verify that the contract is indeed fulfilled (and take corrective measures if it is not). One can also put this point as follows: competition must take place on equal terms in respect to the quality of services furnished.

Secondly, non-public service producers must refrain from charging fees which (other than insignificantly) exceed those charged by public producers. All citizens must, financially speaking, be treated with "equal concern and respect." The requirement of equal treatment cannot be disregarded if this principle is to apply. Otherwise, the result will be to introduce stigmatizing means-testing "through the back door," and the principle of universalism will break down. Fulfilling this second condition would seem to be fairly uncomplicated. The terms of competition must be equal in an economic sense as well.

Thirdly, all service producers must assume their fair share of the costly and difficult cases. If this is not done, means-testing comes in through the back door again. If service producers whose costs are defrayed wholly or in part with public funds are allowed to choose among citizens, the principle of "equal concern and respect" is set at nought. Some freedom-of-choice romanticists tend to forget that, in a market, both buyer and seller can decide whether to enter a contract or not, that is, one can be both selected and rejected. If the hard cases fall solely to the public producers, they will not be able to compete on equal terms, and will gradually become an inferior alternative.[60] Again, competition must take place on equal terms. This is one of those cases in which the requirements of justice and efficiency seem to go hand in hand.

Fourthly, all citizens must enjoy access to these services on the basis of the principle of "equal concern and respect." Accordingly, producers cannot be allowed to discriminate among customers on grounds of race, religion, gender, social status, etc. Public services must be accessible to all on equal terms, regardless of who produces the service in question. Of course, demand will sometimes exceed the supply available from indi-

---

[59] Jonsson (1993), p. 64.
[60] Boyd (1993) reaches this conclusion after reviewing the results of market solutions in various school systems.

vidual producers, but access cannot be allocated in such cases on discriminatory grounds such as those listed above.[61]

It may be possible to meet each of these four conditions, although the third may sometimes be difficult or even impossible to fulfill. In certain areas, such as care of the elderly and handicapped, there may be cause to be extra careful, since the incentive to "skim off the cream" can be exceedingly strong.[62]

These four conditions imply, however, a state which in certain ways differs from the present one. Functions such as evaluation, inspection, and control of the producers (public and/or private) become more important than before. Studies done of the concrete consequences of assigning public tasks to private companies stress that it is critical that the roles are held apart – that the officials charged with framing the contract and seeing to it that its provisions are fulfilled are wholly free and independent of the organs responsible for the production itself. The loyalty of these officials to the public good must be beyond question.[63] We observe here two different kinds of competence, and two sorts of norm-system as well. It is one thing to specify the public tasks to be performed, and to verify that they are in fact carried out in accordance with prevailing rules; it is another to carry out the tasks themselves, in a (heavily regulated) market under conditions of competition.[64] In this way, then, a clear division can be established between the production of services and the performance of duties peculiar to the state.

It is often forgotten in the privatization debate that the problems involved in framing contracts – that is, in specifying what the tasks to be performed are, and verifying that they are performed in fact – do not vary in character according to whether the local implementing organization is public or private. For the governing organs, that is, regulating "free schools" and private local care centers, differ in degree but not in kind from regulating public schools and public local care centers.

Implementation researchers speak plainly here, for once, when they point out the serious managerial problems that can arise in this area. To

---

[61] This excludes, as I see it, the allocation of public revenues to confessional schools in the degree that the confessional affiliations of pupils have a bearing on their admission.

[62] Olsson-Hort (1992), pp. 121ff.

[63] Donahue (1992); Kettl (1993a), ch. 1 and ch. 9.

[64] Cf. J. Jacobs (1992). I believe, however, that Jacobs is wrong in claiming that only two different moral systems exist – those of the market and the political sphere. These areas are general, i.e., entry is open to all. If we broaden the focus, however, to include spheres to which entry is restricted, we discover that two further moral spheres exist: that of the family/clan/ local community, and that prevailing in the associational/organizational sphere. See Rothstein (1992a), ch. 1.

be sure, public producing organizations do not have motives of profit for fiddling with contract provisions; nevertheless, the staff of such organizations have interests differing from those of the responsible politicians and of the citizens as well. For one who is disrespectfully or otherwise badly treated, it is of little moment whether this is done for reasons of profit or because the staff do not consider his demands worth taking seriously. Contract specification and evaluation/control should therefore be as strictly applied to public service producers as to their private counterparts. We should therefore regard both public and private day-care centers, schools, local care centers, etc. – when they are financed wholly or in part with public monies – not as arms of the state, but rather as partially autonomous organs which perform public tasks on their own responsibility, and which are duty-bound to answer to the state and the citizens concerning how they carry out their duties. As pointed out in chapter 4, a triangular drama is played out here between the state, the producer, and the citizen.

The task of the producing organizations – to perform public tasks on their own responsibility – entails undertaking to fulfill the contract in the general terms stipulated above, that is, to follow the rules concerning quality and to refrain from discriminating in regard to admission. This also entails a responsibility to operate the program according to prevailing ethical and professional criteria. The survival of such organizations depends on their fulfillment of these conditions, which means they must be capable of learning and of foreseeing, and that they must be flexible.[65] Autonomous organizations must take the responsibility for these things themselves.

As mentioned earlier, this involves returning to the more classical state duties – setting rules, inspecting, evaluating – tasks we know the state can competently carry out. By means of such a change, in which we distinguish the state in this narrower sense from the organs responsible for providing public services, we can establish a double signal system. To begin with, a central system, which sends clear signals to producers in regard to whether or not the services they provide meet the politically determined criteria. Secondly, a decentralized system built on the signals sent by citizens when they select some producers and reject others. A double pressure can thereby be put on the implementing organizations, whether they are public or private. They must live up to the centrally determined criteria, and they must be sufficiently sensitive to the wishes

---

[65] I.e., the three factors which the military historians Cohen & Gooch (1990, p. 26) identify as critical for the ability of organizations to avoid disasters.

of citizens as to attract their custom. Again, they must behave as flexible, knowledge-seeking, and foreseeeing organizations.

The local organizations charged with implementation – schools, day-care centers, hospitals, universities – are thus not, according to this approach, so obviously a part of the state. They are, rather, partially autonomous institutions of civil society, for they carry out their duties on their own responsibility. It is not the citizens, either collectively or individually, who stand at the disposal of these institutions. It is the latter, rather, that exist for the pleasure of the citizens.

Conclusions

The conclusion thus far seems clear: citizens' increased demands for freedom of choice and self-determination by no means spell the end of the universal welfare policy. Freedom of choice has, for some reason, been associated with neo-liberalism, an ideology which does not embrace the principle of the state's duty to furnish citizens with any welfare services at all, and which calls into question the right of democratic majorities to impose taxes on citizens for the purpose of financing such activities. This is just part of the matter, however. For every democratic system must strike a balance between a collectivist/communitarian and an individualistic/autonomistic ideal of democracy. Exactly where this balance should be struck is a critical question of values; my purpose here is to argue that, if a far-reaching change in citizens' values takes place in the direction of individualism, the balance between collectivist and individualist democratic ideals must – for democracy's continued legiti-macy – be shifted in the same direction as well.

Thus, we can view freedom of choice as a negation not of democracy, but rather of just its collectivist and communitarian form. As Richard Saltman has pointed out, the opportunities of citizens to choose within this policy area may be seen

> as an exercise of democratic rather than commercial rights. By this second approach, the patient's opportunity to choose becomes a mechanism by means of which individual persons exercise more influence over what happens to them in a publicly run system of care, and acquire more control over their living conditions thereby – a fundamental principle of democratic theory generally.[66]

One may, accordingly, view freedom of choice in this context as a "basic resource" with which the state is obliged to furnish citizens. The

---

[66] Saltman (1992), p. 54.

opportunity to choose here becomes a way for citizens to exercise their democratic rights, and to ensure that they are treated with *equal concern and respect*. It furnishes a way, that is, to avoid falling into democracy's *black hole*.

It would seem to be clear that the new individualism places much heavier demands on the organizations responsible for producing public services. These must be prepared, in a clearer fashion than before, to adapt themselves to the demands of individual citizens, and to try to fulfill the goals stated in the general contract. They must, in other words, become autonomous institutions.

The usual approach in the ideological and party-political debate is to set an equals sign between those advocating less collective and public responsibility for the well-being of citizens, on the one hand, and those wishing to introduce freedom of choice and competition, on the other. Logically, however, there is no connection between these things. How extensive the public commitment to the well-being of citizens should be is an altogether distinct question from whether or not the services following on this commitment should be produced by organizations which are publicly owned. One could, for example, propose heavy increases in child allowances – as an expression of the idea that the state should assume an increased responsibility for the well-being of families with children – without this in itself leading to the employment of a single new public official. And the converse also applies: neo-liberals may wish to see a much smaller state than the present one, yet they typically recommend that all of the tasks undertaken by such a state – police, defense, prisons, courts, debt collection, etc. – be performed by publicly employed persons. There seems, finally, to be good evidence for the proposition that, if a controlled competition were introduced into the public services, a substantial increase in output could be achieved for the same level of taxes.[67] It would therefore seem reasonable for advocates of an extensive public welfare commitment – those holding a broad notion of basic capabilities – to express very strong interest in the introduction of such competition.

[67] Donahue's estimate – which seems cautious and very well-grounded empirically – is that savings of 20 percent can be achieved with unimpaired quality. But see also Rothstein (1993b).

Toward a constructive theory of public policy

The question posed in the introductory chapter was whether constructive theory of the state and its policies is possible. The argument put forward here is that it is possible to cross the boundary between "is" and "ought". It is not that we can in any way prove our normative premises, but that we can – on the basis of a few basic principles over which there can be widespread agreement – reason our way to certain rules which should govern the concrete design of our political institutions. What has made this enterprise possible is the use of institutional theory, for *political institutions are both empirical and normative orders*. This is not the place to repeat the results of the analysis in full, but rather to highlight a few major principles.

Firstly, according to some important new work in game theory, it seems impossible to explain why self-interested, utility-maximizing, and rational individuals ever chose to cooperate on a large scale. As, for example, Mark Irving Lichbach has shown, every explanation presented so far on how the problem of collective action can be solved, presupposes that it has already been solved.[1] According to this literature, the only way to understand why large-scale political cooperation occurs, is to point at the political institution (i.e., the State) that existed before the game about choosing to cooperate or not ever got started.[2] The character of this meta-institution may explain why large-scale cooperation exists, because

---

[1] Lichbach (1995), cf. Biccieri (1993), Bianco & Bates (1990), Hechter (1992), Bendor & Mookherje (1987).

[2] In a very different research approach, this has been labeled as "bringing the state back in," cf. Skocpol & Finegold (1982).

it can influence the expectations of the actors in three ways. One is that they can install a feeling of trust that others will cooperate. Second, those responsible for the meta-institution (in this case the state leaders) can put forward a moral argument that what is to be achieved by this cooperation is a morally just cause. Lastly, they may be successful in showing that the institution that is going to be responsible for the implementation of this morally good cause is a "just institution."

This means that institutions not only change what individuals conceive to be rational and as lying in their own well-considered interest. They also influence what they regard as right and just, that is, as "fair play." That these social norms are significant was already clear, but now – by means of institutional analysis – we can also establish where these norms come from and why, at an aggregate level, they vary between societies. In this way, then, we turn the current view of preferences within social science – where they come from and how they should be explained – upside down. Instead of focusing on various factors in the surrounding society (classes, history, culture), we have pointed to *political* institutions as the central explanation for variations in social norms (on an aggregate level). We can thereby both shake off the narrow self-interest straitjacket thrust on political science by economistic methods of analysis, and liberate ourselves from the structural determinism originating in sociology. Politics, understood as the conscious design of political institutions and programs, is not just something to be explained by the surrounding society; it has its own explanatory power. The design given to political institutions governs the notions of morality and justice prevailing in society.

An exception among political philosophers as regards the importance of articulating a constructive theory is Barry Gross. In an article analyzing the responsibility of the state for ensuring equality of educational opportunity, he argues that such a normatively based standpoint is meaningless:

> We are often told that we are morally obligated to produce equal opportunity for all. Therefore, it seems, we should examine what power we have to produce that desired state. For it would be nonsense to say that we are required to provide what is beyond our power to provide. When we examine this question, we find our power limited by two sets of constraints upon the idea itself of equal opportunity. We cannot do the logically impossible. The other set comprises limits upon our ability to produce the directed socio-economic change, getting known outputs for known inputs.[3]

---

[3] Gross (1987), p. 121.

Our analysis in this book indicates that the pessimism expressed by Gross (and many others) about the possibilities of politics is without foundation, or in any case exaggerated. The relevant part of the chart – where empirical and philosophical state theory intersect – is by no means empty. It has been possible to specify things which the state both should and can do.

Based on the principle of *equal concern and respect,* we have argued against means-testing and for universalism. This principle has, furthermore, supplied the basis for our claim in regard to public services that citizens should be granted freedom of choice as between different producers. If we wish to treat citizens in this way, we cannot tolerate any black holes in the democratic process, nor can we expose citizens to treatment of a stigmatizing or integrity-violating character.

The other principle concerns *what* the state should do, namely the idea of *basic capabilities.* If citizens are to be able to act as autonomous individuals in the face of political, economic, and social structures, they must have the right to certain basic capabilities enabling them to make well-considered choices. The determination of which capabilities should be considered basic, and of how extensive these capabilities should be – this must be made according to the principle that citizens are to be enabled to function as autonomous individuals capable of making well-considered choices in an independent fashion. Just what these capabilities should be, and exactly what amount should be deemed sufficient, naturally cannot be answered by political philosophy, but must rather be decided in the political process. The point is not, as some have feared, to render the political process superfluous with political-philosophical argumentation. The purpose is instead a more limited one – to establish what the point of departure should be for the political discussion of what the state should do.

The same applies to the principle of citizens' autonomy we have endorsed. A universal welfare state does not prescribe to citizens which life projects are better than others. We have been forced to modify the principle of neutrality somewhat, however, and to accept that the state should try to prevent citizens from choosing life projects which, we can on very good grounds assume, have not been chosen autonomously. Clear cases include mental illness or social incapacity (on account of long and persistent drug abuse, for instance). Of course, exactly where these boundaries should be drawn (especially where minors are concerned) is a question as delicate as it is difficult, and it is not altogether easy to offer any answers founded on principle. The purpose of our argument, however, has been to place the burden of proof where it belongs: on those who adopt a maternalist position – who wish to employ the coercive power of the state to dictate that certain life projects be followed (or rather to obstruct certain such projects, actually).

It has proved possible to combine the two principles we have derived from the domain of political philosophy with a more empirical analysis of what the state can do. This especially applies in the case of universal cash benefits. Basic pensions, other social-insurance benefits, and child allowances are things the state can competently provide; they fit together nicely, moreover, with the normative principles of basic capabilities and equal concern and respect. The price we must pay for these good things is a relatively broad targeting of public policy, that is, a rather anti-perfectionist policy (for which there are other good arguments besides). We have highlighted the managerial paradox – that the more precisely targeted the legislating body wants a public program to be, the less power it has over how the program is implemented. We have particularly stressed the difficulties of intervening in dynamic societal conditions in a precise manner. Sometimes we must recognize that there are things we want the state to do that it is simply unable to do.

A more problematic issue concerns the public production of services. Problems of management easily become complicated here, and in some cases the state is forced to try to solve problems for which no effective counter-measures are known. It is essential, however, not take a pathological or hyper-critical attitude towards this, as so many implementation researchers have done. Many public programs fail to reach the goals set out for them, but that does not mean such programs are in vain or that we would wish to see them undone. The uncertainty in the policy theory – that is, that central political organs do not always know what should be done or how – can be compensated for. It does not in itself pose insurmountable problems for state capacity. By devoting special attention to the quality of organization, and to the creation of legitimacy for measures taken in the stage of implementation, the state can deal properly even with areas characterized by the problems mentioned above. To this may be added that the ethics of public officials can be strengthened on the basis of the requirement that they treat all citizens with "equal concern and respect."

Furthermore, we have called attention to the importance of guaranteeing citizens the right to choose between different service producers. Organizations which produce public services must, however, meet certain definite conditions if their operations are to accord with our two basic principles. These conditions, briefly summarized, are that they accept certain centrally prescribed norms of quality, and that they refrain from discriminating among citizens in their admission procedures. Citizens can thus be given the opportunity to "manage from below," by exercising their right to choose between different service producers. Also here, however, we have indicated the possibility of solving the problems of legitimacy within the framework of the universal welfare policy – in a society marked, moreover, by more individualistic citizens than earlier.

This entails, however, a partly new view of the organizations charged with executing public tasks. Independently of conditions of ownership, these bodies must operate as partially autonomous organizations attempting, on their own responsibility, to fulfill the conditions of the contract applying in their area. Consequently, their capacity to learn, to handle uncertainty, and to adapt to new conditions becomes decisive for their long-term survival. They must, in other words, anchor the legitimacy of their activities both in the citizenry as a whole (by living up to "the contract"), and among individual users as well (by making their services sufficiently attractive as to be in demand).

We can now say more about the various challenges to the universal welfare policy presented in the first chapter. In respect of the economic and fiscal problems of the welfare state today, we have not suggested any solutions; we have, however, noted a number of restrictions that should be placed on the pure analysis of economic efficiency. In addition, when it comes to the prospects for securing sufficient support – both financially and electorally – for the existing system, the theory of contingent consent should be of great value. Again, citizens are likely to support a welfare state if they believe its goals to be just, if they believe its implementation processes to be fair, and if they have reason to trust that most other citizens will loyally pay their taxes and not cheat the system.

We have further found that the critique fastening on the welfare state's presumed displacement of the relations of civil society suffers from serious deficiencies, both in its internal logic and in the empirical evidence it presents. There is nothing to suggest that a universal welfare policy, as we have defined it here, entails a colonization of civil society by the state. On the contrary, there are good arguments for the contrary proposition – that a welfare state built on the principle of "basic capabilities" and "equal concern and respect" furthers citizens' prospects of realizing their autonomously chosen life projects. Indeed, if the organizations charged with public tasks are enjoined to undertake them on their own responsibility, in the manner that has been detailed here (and much suggests that developments are moving in this direction), the result will be to anchor these organizations more in civil society than in the state.

Nor does the palpable development of more individualistic value

	Scope	
	Small	*Large*
Orientation *Communitarian/ Perfectionist*	Fostering state	Paternalistic welfare state
Neutral/Liberal	Night-watchman state	Non-paternalistic welfare state

Figure 9.1   The state's scope and orientation

patterns – and the demands associated with them for freedom of choice and individualized treatment in the public services – necessarily constitute a fatal blow to the idea of a universal welfare policy. The development of a much more differentiated (and efficient) production of services can very well be accomplished, as we have shown, within the framework of the universal welfare policy. Individual and egoism do not, we have discovered, together constitute a uniform dimension. The new citizen seems rather to hold an outlook we have tentatively denoted *solidaristic individualism.*

Not the least importantly, we have found that the arguments for changing over to a more selective welfare policy can be called into question on other than economic grounds. There is simply no possibility of combining means-testing with the principle of equal concern and respect – that part of the chart is empty.

How, then, shall we characterize this state which, on the one hand, takes a far-reaching solidaristic responsibility for the well-being of its citizens, and on the other, considers their choice of life project to be a private affair with which the majority should not concern itself? If we cross-tabulate these dimensions, the following four types of state result (see figure 9.1). I have found the designation *non-paternalistic welfare state* fitting for our case.[4] Regarding future prospects, our argumentation has proceeded in three steps. Firstly, that social norms and not just rationalistic forces are important for explaining why welfare state ambitions vary between countries. Secondly, that the moral principles embraced by citizens are not, or at least not only, structurally given. They are instead the product of the legitimacy of public policy. Thirdly, that this legitimacy is determined by how the institutions deciding over public policy and implementing it are structured. I shall not repeat the argument

---

[4]   I got this idea from Hampton (1997), p. 175.

here, but shall rather highlight another aspect. For the political institutions we have portrayed as decisive are immune neither to change nor to influence. They are tenacious structures, certainly, but historically it has proved possible – at any rate in certain situations – to create and to change them consciously.

As a study of the future of the universal welfare model, this analysis has not sought to extrapolate from current trends. For most societal processes are not linear but dynamic. We have sought rather to define the relation between the institutions of the welfare state and its prospects for attracting sufficient support. In other words, the future of welfare policy lies in how it functions internally, rather than in surrounding factors. If it is true that the shape of welfare policy is decided by the social norms established among citizens, and if these norms in turn are determined by the type of political institutions we have analyzed, then the future of the welfare state of whatever type is something that lies in the hands of its political leaders and citizens, since they decide whether they want to change our political institutions or not. If the history that has led to the great variation in welfare systems among the Western capitalist countries is to be understood as path-dependent, then what has caused history to start off on these different paths is what matters. If each case has its own specific history, then the actions by political leaders at the time when the historical path turns in its specific direction, what I have called the *formative moment* is the crucial factor. In other words, the initial design of the political institutions of the welfare state is what matters.

The good news, if I may exaggerate a little, is that in designing our political institutions, we also in large part determine the normative attitudes citizens hold about welfare policy. If citizens regard the prevailing welfare programs as designed in accordance with principle of justice, if they consider the implementation of such programs to be fair, and if they believe all citizens (or almost all of them, at least) pay their due share of the costs incurred, then the political support for the universal welfare policy will in all likelihood endure. Otherwise not.

Bibliography

Åberg, Rune. 1990. "Värderingsförändringar och samhällsutveckling," in Rune Åberg (ed.). *Industrisamhälle i omvandling. Människor, arbete och social liv i en svensk industristad från femtiotal till åttiotal.* Stockholm. Carlssons Förlag

Åström, Karsten. 1988. *Socialtjänstlagen i politik och förvaltning.* Lund. Lund University Press

Ackerman, Bruce C. 1980. *Social Justice and the Liberal State.* New Haven. Yale University Press

Adler, Michael & Asquith, Stewart. 1981. "Discretion and Power," in same authors (eds.). *Discretion and Welfare.* London. Heineman

Agell, Jonas. 1992. "Det svenska skattesystemet," in Bo Södersten (ed.). *Den offentliga sektorn.* Stockholm. SNS Förlag

Agell, Jonas, Lindh, Thomas, & Ohlsson, Henry. 1994. "Tillväxt och offentlig sektor". *Ekonomisk Debatt* 22

Ahlbäck, Shirin. 1995. "Politikermakt eller tjänstemannavälde?" *Statsvetenskaplig tidskrift* 98

Aldrich, Howard E. 1979. *Organizations and Environments.* Englewood Cliffs, N.J. Prentice-Hall

Algotsson, Karl-Göran. 1993. *Lagrådet, rättsstaten och demokratin under 1900-talet.* Stockholm. Norstedts Juridik

Anderson, Charles W. 1990. *Principled Pragmatism.* Chicago. Chicago University Press

Andersson, Åke E., Fürth, Thomas, & Holmberg, Ingvar. 1993. *70-talister om värderingar förr, nu och i framtiden.* Stockholm. Natur och Kultur

Antman, Peter (ed.). 1993. *Systemskifte. Fyra folkhemsdebatter.* Stockholm. Carlssons

Arvidsson, Göran. 1991. "Korsbefruktning företag/förvaltningar," in Göran
    Arvidsson & Rolf Lind (eds.). 1991. *Ledning av företag och förvaltningar*.
    Stockholm. SNS Förlag
Aristotle. *Politics* 1.
Arneson, Richard J. 1990a. "Primary Goods Reconsidered," *NOÛS* 24
    1990b. "Liberalism, Distributive Justice, and Equal Opportunity for
    Welfare," *Philosophy and Public Affairs* 19
Aron, Raymond. 1983. *Clausewitz. Philosopher of War*. London. Routledge
    and Kegan Paul
Arvidsson, Håkan and Berntson, Lennart, 1990. *Det civila samhället*.
    Stockholm. Timbro
Axberg, Mikael. 1993. "Rättvisa och personligt ansvar," working paper at the
    Department of Government, Uppsala University
Axelrod, Robert. 1984. *The Evolution of Cooperation*. New York. Basic Books
Baldwin, Peter. 1990. *The Politics of Social Solidarity: Class Bases of the
    European Welfare State 1875–1975*. Cambridge. Cambridge University
    Press
Bardach, Eugene. 1977. *The Implementation Game*. Cambridge, Mass. MIT
    Press
Barry, Brian. 1965. *Political Argument*. London. Routledge and Kegan Paul
    1989. *Theories of Justice*. London. Harvester-Wheatsheaf
    1990. "The Welfare State versus The Relief of Poverty," *Ethics* 91
    1995. *Justice as Impartiality*. Oxford: Oxford University Press
Barry, Norman P. 1981. *An Introduction to Modern Political Theory*. London.
    Macmillan
Bates, R. H. 1988. "Contra contractarianism. Some Reflections on the New
    Institutionalism," *Politics and Society* 18
Beck, Ulrich. 1992. *Risk Society. Towards an New Modernity*. London. Sage
Beetham, David. 1985. *Max Weber and the Theory of Modern Politics*.
    Cambridge. Polity Press
Beiner, Ronald. 1992. *What's the Matter with Liberalism*. Berkeley. University
    of California Press
    1996. "What Liberalism Means," *Social Philosophy and Policy* 13
Bell, John. 1985. "The Basis of Rights in a Welfare State," in Jan M.
    Broekman, *et al.* (eds.). *Social Justice and Individual Responsibility in the
    Welfare State*. Archiv Für Rechts- und Sozialphilosophie, Beiheft 24,
    Stuttgart. Franz Steiner Verlag
Bendor, Jonathan & Mookherje, Dilip. 1987. "Institutional Structure and the
    Logic of Ongoing Collective Action," *American Political Science Review*
    81
Bennich-Björkman, Li. 1991. *Statsstödda samhällskritiker. Författarautonomi
    och statsstyrning i Sverige*. Stockholm. Tiden
Benson, J. Kenneth. 1982. "A Framework for Policy Analysis," in D. L. Roger

and D. A. Whetter (eds.). *Interorganizational Coordination. Theory, Research, Implementation.* Ames. Iowa State University Press

Bergqvist, Christina. 1990. "Myten om den universella välfärdspolitiken," *Statsvetenskaplig tidskrift* 91

Bergström, Hans. 1991. "Sweden's Politics and Party System at the Crossroads," *West European Politics* 14

Berman, Paul. 1980. "Thinking about Programmed and Adaptive Implementation. Matching Strategies to Situations," in Helen M. Ingram & Dean E. Mann (eds.). *Why Policies Succeed or Fail.* Beverly Hills. Sage

Berthu, Georges & Lepage, Henri. 1988. *Äganderätt ger välstånd.* Stockholm. Ratio

Beuchamp, Tom L. 1980. "Distributive Justice and the Difference Principle," in H. Gene Blocker & Elisabeth H. Smith (eds.). *John Rawls' Theory of Social Justice – An Introduction.* Athens, Ohio. Ohio University Press

Bianco, William T. & Bates, Robert H. 1990. "Cooperation by Design. Leadership, Structure and Collective Dilemmas," *American Political Science Review* 84

Bicchieri, Christina. 1993. *Rationality and Coordination.* Cambridge. Cambridge University Press

Birgersson, Bengt-Owe & Westerståhl, Jörgen. 1985. *Den svenska folkstyrelsen.* Stockholm. Liber

Björklund, Stefan. 1977. *Den uppenbara lösningen. Om möjligheten till en objektiv ståndpunkt i politiska värdefrågor.* Stockholm. Aldus/Bonniers

Björnberg, Ulla. 1992. "Tvåförsörjarfamiljen i teori och verklighet," in Joan Acker, *et al. Kvinnor och mäns liv och arbete.* Stockholm. SNS Förlag

Bobbio, Norberto. 1990. *Liberalism and Democracy.* London. Verso

Borg, Anders E. 1992. *Generell välfärdspolitik. Bara magiska ord?* Stockholm. City University Press

Boyd, William Lowe. 1993. "Parental Choice of Schools. An International Movement," in Gary Miron (ed.). *Toward Free Choice and Market-Oriented Schools: Problems and Promises.* Stockholm. Skolverket

Brand, Donald. 1988. *Corporatism and the Rule of Law.* Ithaca. Cornell University Press

Brunsson, Nils. 1989. *The Organization of Hypocrisy.* Chichester. John Wiley
1990. "Reformer som rutin," in Nils Brunsson and Johan P. Olsen (eds.). *Konsten att reformera.* Stockholm. Carlssons Förlag

Brunsson, Nils & Olsen, Johan P. (eds.) 1990. *Makten att reformera.* Stockholm. Carlssons Förlag

Buchanan, James M. & Tullock, Gordon. 1962. *The Calculus of Consent.* Ann Arbor. The University of Michigan Press

Campbell, Tom. 1990. *Justice.* Atlantic Highlands, N.J. Humanities Press International

Carlsson, Alan. 1990. *The Swedish Experiment in Family Politics: The Myrdals and the Interwar Population Crisis.* New Brunswick. Transaction Books

Carlsson, Bo & Isaksson, Åke. 1989. *Hälsa, kommunikativt handlande och konfliktlösning.* Lund. Bokbox

Carlsson, Per, Garpenby, Peter, & Bonair, Ann. 1991. "Kan sjukvården styras." Report from the Centrum för utvärdering av medicinsk teknologi, University of Linköping, no. 15

Castles, Francis G. (ed.). 1989. *The Comparative History of Public Policy.* Cambridge. Polity Press

Castles, Francis & Mitchell, Deborah. 1992. "Identifying Welfare State Regimes: The Link Between Politics, Instruments and Outcomes," in *Governance* 5

Cerych, Ladislav & Sabatier, Paul A. 1986. *Great Expectations and Mixed Performances: The Implementation of Higher Education in Europe.* Stoke-on-Trent. Trentham Books

Chase, Gordon. 1979. "Implementing a Human Services Program. How Hard Will it Be?" *Public Policy* 27

Chubb, John E., & Moe, Terry M. 1990. *Politics, Markets, and America's Schools.* Washington D.C. The Brookings Institution

von Clausewitz, Carl. 1836/1984. *On War.* Princeton. Princeton University Press

Cohen, Eliot A. & Gooch, John. 1990. *Military Misfortunes: The Anatomy of Failure in War.* New York. The Free Press

Cohen, Gerald. 1989. "On the Currency of Equalitarian Justice," *Ethics* 99

Cohen, Jean L. & Arato, Andrew. 1993. *Civil Society and Political Theory.* Cambridge, Mass. MIT Press

Coleman, James S. 1990. *Foundations of Social Theory.* Cambridge, Mass. Harvard University Press

Cook, Karen S. 1987. "Toward a More Interdisciplinary Research Agenda: The Potential Contributions of Sociology," *Social Justice Research* 1

Cook, Karen Schweers & Levi, Margaret (eds.). 1990. *The Limits of Rationality.* Chicago. The University of Chicago Press

Culpitt, Ian. 1992. *Welfare and Citizenship: Beyond the Crises of the Welfare State?* London. Sage

Dandeker, Christopher. 1990. *Surveillance, Power and Modernity.* Cambridge. Polity Press

Davidson, Alex. 1989. *Two Models of Welfare.* Uppsala. Statsvetenskapliga föreningen

Demchak, Chis C. 1991. *Military Organizations, Complex Machines, Modernization in the U.S. Armed Services.* Ithaca. Cornell University Press

Dewes, Peter. 1987. *The Logics of Disintegration.* London. Verso

Dionne E. J. Jr. 1991. *Why Americans Hate Politics.* New York. Simon and Schuster

Dogan, Mattei. 1988. "Crisis of the Welfare State," in same author (ed.). *Comparing Pluralist Democracies. Strains on Legitimacy.* Boulder. Westview Press

Donahue, John D. 1992. *The Privatization Decision. Public Ends, Private Means.* New York. Basic Books

Douglas, Mary. 1988. *How Institutions Think.* London. RKP

Dryzek, John. 1990. *Discursive Democracy.* Cambridge. Cambridge University Press

Dunleavy, Patrick. 1991. *Democracy, Bureaucracy and Public Choice: Economic Explanations in Political Science.* New York. Harvester Wheatsheaf

Dworkin, Gerald. 1988. *The Theory and Practice of Autonomy.* Cambridge. Cambridge University Press

Dworkin, Ronald. 1977. *Taking Rights Seriously.* London. Duckworth

1981a. "What is Equality? Part 1. Equality of Welfare," *Philosophy and Public Affiars* 10

1981b. "What is Equality? Part 2. Equality of Resources," *Philosophy and Public Affairs* 10

1985. *A Matter of Principle.* Cambridge, Mass. Harvard University Press

1989. "Liberal Community," *California Law Review* 77

Edwards, John. 1988. "Justice and the Bounds of Welfare," *Journal of Social Policy* 17

Eklund, Klas. 1993. *Hur farligt är budgetunderskottet?* Stockholm. SNS Förlag

Elliot, Maria. 1992. "Medborgerlig tillit och misstro," in Sören Holmberg & Lennart Weibull (eds.). *Perspektiv på krisen.* Göteborg. Göteborgs Universitet

Elmore, Richard F. 1978. "Organizational Models of Social Program Implementation," *Public Policy* 26

1983. "Social Policymaking as Strategic Intervention," in Edward Seidman (ed.). *Handbook of Social Intervention.* Beverly Hills. Sage

Elster, Jon. 1986. "The Market and the Forum: Three Varieties of Political Theory," in Jon Elster & Aanund Hylland (eds.). *Foundations of Social Choice Theory.* Cambridge. Cambridge University Press

1987. "On the Possibility of Rational Politics," *Archives Européennes de Sociologie* 38

1989. *The Cement of Society.* Cambridge. Cambridge University Press

1991. "Rationality and Social Norms," *Archives Européennes de Sociologie* 31

1992. *Local Justice: How Institutions Allocate Scarce Goods and Necessary Burdens.* New York. Russell Sage Foundation

1993. *Political Psychology.* Cambridge. Cambridge University Press

Ely, John. 1992. "The Politics of Civil Society," *Telos* 93

Eriksen, Erik Oddvar. 1993. *Grenser for staten?* Oslo. Universitetsforlaget

Esping, Hans. 1994. *Ramlagarna i förvaltningspolitiken*. Stockholm. SNS Förlag

Esping-Andersen, Gøsta. 1990. *The Three Worlds of Welfare Capitalism*. Cambridge. Polity Press

1996. "After the Golden Age? Welfare State Dilemmas in a Global Economy," in Gøsta Esping-Andersen (ed.). *Welfare States in Transition. National Adaptions in Global Economies*. London. Sage

Etzioni, Amitai. 1988. *The Moral Dimension: Towards a New Economics*. New York. The Free Press

Falkemark, Gunnar. 1992. "Rudolf Kjellén – vetenskapsman eller humbug," in Gunnar Falkemark (ed.). *Statsvetarporträtt. Svenska statsvetare under 350 år*. Stockholm. SNS Förlag

Ferejohn, John. 1991. "Rationality and Interpretation: Parliamentary Elections in Early Stuart England," in Kirsten Renwick Monroe (ed.). *The Economic Approach to Politics: A Critical Reassessment of the Theory of Rational Choice*. New York. HarperCollins

Fischer, Frank. 1980. *Politics, Values and Public Policies: The Problem of Methodology*. Boulder, Col. Westview Press

1983. "Ethical Discourse in Public Administration," in *Administration and Society* 15

1995. *Evaluating Public Policy*. Chicago. Nelson Hall

Fischerman, Ethan. 1991. "Political Philosophy and the Policy Studies Organization," in *PS. Political Science and Politics* 24

Fishkin, James S. 1975. "Justice and Rationality: Some Objections to the Central Argument in Rawls' Theory," *American Political Science Review* 69

1983. "Can There Be a Neutral Theory of Justice?" *Ethics* 93

1992. *The Dialogue of Justice: Toward a Self-Reflective Society*. New Haven. Yale University Press

Fisk, Milton. 1989. *The State and Justice: An Essay in Political Theory*. New York. Cambridge University Press

Fox, Charles J. 1987. "Biases in Public Policy Implementation Evaluation," *Policy Studies Review* 7

Frank, Robert H., Gilovich, Thomas, & Regan, Dennis T. 1993. "Does Studying of Economics Inhibit Cooperation?" *Journal of Economic Perspectives* 7

Friedman, Kathie V. 1981. *Legitimation of Social Rights and the Western Welfare State*. Chapel Hill. The University of North Carolina Press

Fritzell, Johan. 1991. *Icke av marknaden allena. Inkomstfördelningen i Sverige*. Stockholm. Stockholms Universitet, Institutet för Social Forskning

Frolich, Norman & Oppenheimer, Joe A. 1990. "Choosing Justice in Experimental Democracies with Production," *American Political Science Review* 84

1992. *Choosing Justice: An Experimental Approach to Ethical Theory.*
Berkeley. California University Press

Garrett, Geoffrey. 1997. *Partisan Politics in the Global Economy.* Cambridge.
Cambridge University Press

Garrett, Geoffrey & Weingast, Barry. 1991. "Ideas, Interests and
Institutions." Paper, Department of Political Science, Stanford
University

Gauthier, David. 1986. *Morals by Agreement.* Oxford. Clarendon Press

George, Robert P. 1993. *Making Men Moral. Civil Liberties and Public
Morality.* Oxford. Oxford University Press

Giddens, Anthony. 1979. *Central Problems in Social Theory: Action, Structure
and Contradiction in Social Analysis.* London. Macmillan

Gilligan, Carol. 1982. *In a Different Voice: Psychological Theory and Women's
Developments.* Cambridge, Mass. Harvard University Press

Glazer, Nathan. 1988. *The Limits of Social Policy.* Cambridge, Mass. Harvard
University Press

Goggin, Malcolm L. 1986. "The 'Too Few Cases/Too Many Variables'
Problem in Implementation Research," *Western Political Quarterly* 39

Goggin, Malcolm L., Bowman, Ann, Lester, James P., & O'Toole, Laurence J.
Jr. 1990. *Implementation Theory and Practice. Toward a Third
Generation.* Glenview, Ill.: Scott Foresman/Little Brown

Goldman, Alan H. 1980. "Responses to Rawls from the Political Right," in
H. Gene Blocker & Elizabeth H. Smith (eds.). *John Rawls' Theory of
Social Justice – An Introduction.* Athens Ohio. Ohio University Press

Goodin, Robert E. 1982. *Political Theory and Public Policy.* Chicago. The
University of Chicago Press

1988. *Reasons for Welfare: The Political Theory of the Welfare State.*
Princeton. Princeton University Press

Goodin, Robert E., Le Grand, Julian, and associates. 1987. *Not Only the Poor:
The Middle Class and the Welfare State.* London. Allen and Unwin

Gorpe, Peter. 1978. *Politikerna, byråkraterna och de nya styrningformerna.*
Stockholm. Liberförlag

Gortner, Harold F., Mahler, Julianne, & Nicholson, Jeanne Bell. 1987.
Organization Theory: A Public Perspective. Chicago. The Dorsey Press

Goul Andersen, Jørgen. 1993. "Samfundsind og egennytte," *Politica* 25

Grafstein, Robert. 1992. *Institutional Realism: Social and Political Constraints
on Rational Actors.* New Haven. Yale University Press

Gray, John. 1993. *Beyond the New Right: Markets, Governments and the
Common Environment.* London. Routledge

Green, Donald P. & Shapiro, Ian. 1994. *Pathologies of Rational Choice Theory:
A Critique of Applications in Political Science.* New Haven. Yale
University Press

Grosin, Lennart. 1992. *Skolklimat, prestation och uppförande i åtta högstadieskolor*. Department of Pedagogy, Stockholm University, report no. 53

Gross, Barry. 1987. "Real Equal Opportunity," *Social Philosophy and Policy* 4

Gutman, Amy. 1990. "Introduction" in same author (ed.). *Democracy and the Welfare State*. Princeton. Princeton University Press

Gutman, Amy & Thompson, Dennis. 1990. "Moral Conflict and Political Consensus," in R. Bruce Douglass, Gerald M. Mara, & Henry S. Richardsson (eds.). *Liberalism and the Good*. New York. Routledge

Habermas, Jürgen. 1987. *The Philosophical Discourse of Modernity*. Cambridge, Mass. MIT Press

1990. *Moral Consciousness and Communicative Action*. Cambridge, Mass. MIT Press

Hadenius, Axel. 1986. *A Crisis of the Welfare State?* Uppsala. Almqvist and Wiksell

Halleröd, Björn. 1991. *Den svenska fattigdomen*. Lund. Arkivs förnämliga avhandlingsserie

Ham, Christopher & Hill, Michael. 1984. *The Policy Process in the Modern Capitalist State*. Brighton. Wheatsheaf

Hampton, Jean. 1997. *Political Philosophy*. Boulder: Westview Press

Handel, Michael B. 1986. *Clausewitz and Modern Strategy*. London. Frank Cass

1989. *War, Strategy and Intelligence*. London. Frank Cass

Hanf, Kenneth & Scharpf, Fritz W. (eds.). 1978. *Interorganizational Policy Making: Limits to Coordination and Central Control*. London. Sage

Hansson, Ingemar. 1993. "Århundradets skattereform och århundradets utgiftsreform," in Klas Eklund (ed.). *En "skattereform" för socialförsäkringarna*. Stockholm. Publica

Hansson, Sven-Ove. 1989. "Introduktion," in *Idéer om rättvisa*. Stockholm. Tidens Förlag

Hardin, Russell. 1982. *Collective Action*. Baltimore. Johns Hopkins Press

1996. *One for All: the Logic of Group Conflict*. Princeton. Princeton University Press

Harrington, Michael. 1962. *The Other America*. New York. Macmillan

Hart, H. L. A. 1979. "Between Utility and Rights," in Alan Ryan (ed.). *The Idea of Freedom: Essays in Honour of Isaiah Berlin*. Oxford. Oxford University Press

Hasenfeld, Yeheskel & Brock, Thomas. 1991. "Implementation of Social Policy Revisited," *Administration and Society* 22

Hatje, Ann-Katrin. 1974. *Befolkningsfrågan och välfärden*. Stockholm. Allmänna förlaget

Hechter, Michael. 1987. *Principles of Group Solidarity*. Berkeley. University of California Press

1992. "The Insufficiency of Game Theory for the Resolution of Real-World Collective Action Problems," *Rationality and Society* 4

Heclo, Hugh and Madsen, Henning. 1987. *Policy and Politics in Sweden: Principled Pragmatism*. Philadelphia. Temple University Press

Held, David. 1987. *Models of Democracy*. Cambridge. Polity Press

Held, Virginia. 1984. *Rights and Goods: Justifying Social Action*. Chicago. The University of Chicago Press

Hermansson, Jörgen. 1990. *Spelteorins nytta. Om rationalitet i politik och vetenskap*. Uppsala. Statsvetenskapliga Föreningen

1993. *Politik som intressekamp. Parlamentariskt beslutsfattande och organiserade intressen i Sverige*. Stockholm. Norstedts Juridik

1995. "Hur kan demokratin rättfärdigas," in Anders Sannerstedt and Magnus Jerneck (eds.). *Den moderna demokratins problem*. Lund. Studentlitteratur

Herméren, Göran. 1972. *Värderingar och objektivitet*. Lund. Studentliteratur

Hill, Michael J. 1972. *The Sociology of Public Administration*. London. Weidenfeld and Nicolson

Hirdman, Yvonne. 1987. "Makt och kön," in Olof Petersson (ed.). *Maktbegreppet*. Stockholm. Carlssons Förlag

1989. *Att lägga livet tillrätta*. Stockholm. Carlssons Förlag

Hjern, Benny. 1983. "Förvaltnings- och implementeringsforskning. En essä," *Statsvetenskaplig tidskrift* 86

Hjern, Benny & Porter, David O. 1981. "Implementation Structures: A New Unit of Administrative Analysis," *Organization Studies* 2

Hoff, Jens. 1993. "Medborgerskab, brugerrolle og makt," in Johannes Andersen, *et al. Medborgerskab. Demokrati og politisk deltagelse*. Herning. Systime

Hogg, Beatrice, Jansson, Signe, & Stiege, Kärsti. 1988. *Att föda på kvinnans villkor*. Stockholm. Prisma

Höjer, Karl J. 1952. *Svensk socialpolitisk historia*. Stockholm, P. A. Norstedts and Söner

Hollander, Anna. 1985. *Omhändertagande av barn*. Stockholm. Aktuell Juridik

Hook, Sidney. 1980. *Philosophy and Public Policy*. London. Pfeffer and Simons

Howard, Michael. 1983. *Clausewitz*. New York. Oxford University Press

1985. "Men Against Fire: The Doctrine of the Offensive in 1914," in Peter Paret (ed.). *Makers of Modern Strategy from Machiavelli to the Nuclear Age*. Princeton. Princeton University Press

Howe, Roger E. & Roemer, John. 1981. "Rawlsian Justice as the Core of a Game," *American Economic Review* 71

Hydén, Håkan. 1984. *Ram eller lag? Om ramlagstiftning och samhällsorganisation*. Stockholm. Civildepartementet

1988. "Reflexiv rätt och reglering," in Asmund Born (ed.). *Refleksiv ret.* København. Nyt fra samfundsvidenskaberne

Immergut, Ellen M. 1993. *Health Politics.* New York. Cambridge University Press

Inghe, Gunnar & Inghe, Maj-Britt. 1967. *Den ofärdiga välfärden.* Stockholm. Tidens Förlag

Inglehart, Ronald. 1990. *Culture Shift in Advanced Industrial Society.* Princeton. Princeton University Press

Ingraham, Patricia W. 1987. "Toward More Systematic Consideration of Policy Design," *Policy Studies Journal* 15

Ingram, Helen. 1990 "Implementation: A Review and a Suggested Framework," in Naomi B. Lynn and Aaron Wildavsky (eds.). *Public Administration: The State of the Discipline.* Chatham, N.J. Chatham House

Isaksson, Anders. 1992. *När pengarna är slut. Välfärden efter välfärdsstaten.* Stockholm. Brombergs

Jacobs, Jane. 1992. *Systems of Survival: A Dialogue on the Moral Foundations of Commerce and Politics.* New York. Random House

Jacobs, Mark D. 1986. "The End of Liberalism in the Administration of Social Case-work," *Administration and Society* 18

Jacobsson, Bengt. 1989. *Konsten att reagera.* Stockholm. Carlssons Förlag

Janoski, Thomas. 1990. *The Political Economy of Unemployment: Active Labor Market Policy in West Germany and the United States.* Berkeley. The University of California Press

Jansson, Signe. 1988. "Mitt liv, mitt yrke och uppbyggnaden av Ystad BB," in Beatrice Hogg, Signe Jansson, & Kärsti Stiege (eds.). *Att föda på kvinnans villkor.* Stockholm. Prisma

Jencks, Christopher. 1992. *Rethinking Social Policy.* Cambridge. Harvard University Press

Johnston Conover, Pamela, Crewe, Ivor, & Searing, Donald. 1990. *Conceptions of Citizenship Among British and American Publics: An Exploratory Analysis.* Colchester: Dept. of Government, University of Essex

1992. "Does Democratic Discussion Make Better Citizens?" Paper presented at the 1992 Annual Meeting of the American Political Science Association, Chicago, September 1–4, 1992

Jonsson, Ernst. 1993. *Konkurrens inom sjukvården. Vad säger forskningen om effekterna?* Stockholm. SPRI

Jönsson, Nine Christine & Lindblom, Paul. 1988. *Politik och kärlek. Gustav Möller och Else Kleen.* Stockholm. Tiden

Karlsson, Nils. 1993. *The State of State.* Uppsala. Acta Universitatis Upsaliensis

Katz, Michael B. 1989. *The Undeserving Poor: From the War on Poverty to the War on Welfare.* New York. Pantheon Books

Kaufmann, Franz-Xavier, Majone, Giandomenico, & Ostrom, Vincent, with the assistance of Wolfgang Wirth. 1986. *Guidance, Control, and Evaluation in the Public Sector*. Berlin–New York: Walter de Gruyter

Kaufman, Herbert. 1960. *The Forest Ranger*. Baltimore. John Hopkins Press

Keegan, John. 1976. *The Face of Battle*. London. Penguin Books

Kelman, Steven. 1984. "Using Implementation Research to Solve Implementation Problems," *Journal of Policy Analysis and Management* 4

Kelsen, Hans. 1945. *General Theory of Law and State*. Cambridge, Mass. Harvard University Press
1992. *General Theory of Norms*. Oxford. Clarendon Press

Kettl, Donald F. 1993a. *Sharing Power: Public Governance and Private Markets*. Washington D.C. The Brookings Institution
1993b. "Public Administration: The State of the Field", in Ada W. Finifter (ed.). *Political Science: The State of the Discipline II*. Washington D.C. American Political Science Association

King, Desmond & Rothstein. Bo. 1993. "Institutional Choices and Labor Market Policy: A British–Swedish Comparison," *Comparative Political Studies* 26

King, Desmond S. & Waldron, Jeremy. 1998. "Citizenship, Social Citizenship and the Defence of Welfare Provision," *British Journal of Political Science* 18

Kjellström, Svenåke & Lundberg, Olle. 1984. "Hälsa och vårdkonsumtion," in Robert Eriksson and Rune Åberg (eds.). *Välfärd i förändring. Levnadsvillkor i Sverige 1968–1981*. Stockholm. Prisma

Knudsen, Tim. 1991. "Planering" in Bo Rothstein (ed.). *Politik som organisation. Förvaltningspolitikens grundproblem*. Stockholm. SNS Förlag

Knudsen, Tim & Rothstein, Bo. Forthcoming. "State-Building in Scandinavia," *Comparative Politics*

Korpi, Walter. 1980. "Social Policy and Distributional Conflict in the Capitalist Democracies," *West European Politics* 3
1981. *Den demokratiska klasskampen*. Stockholm. Tidens Förlag
1997. "Eurosclerosis and the Sclerosis of Objectivity," *The Economic Journal* 107

Korpi, Walter and Palme, Joakim. 1993. "Socialpolitik i kris och reformer. Sverige i internationell belysning," appendix 17 to SOU 1993:16, *Nya villkor för ekonomi och politik*. Stockholm. Allmänna förlaget

Kreps, David M. 1990. "Corporate Culture and Economic Theory," in James Alt & Kenneth Shepsle (eds.). *Perspectives on Positive Political Economy*. Cambridge. Cambridge University Press

Kuhnle, Stein & Solheim, Liv. 1991. *Velfersstaten – vekst og omstillning*. Oslo. Tano

Kymlicka, Will. 1989. *Liberalism, Community and Culture.* Oxford.
    Clarendon Press
    1990. *Contemporary Political Philosophy.* Oxford. Clarendon Press
Ladberg, Gunnilla. 1986. *Daghem och föräldrar.* Stockholm. Prisma
Langton, Rae. 1991. "Whose Right? Ronald Dworkin, Women and
    Pornographers," *Philosophy and Public Affairs* 20
Larmore, Charles. 1987. *Patterns of Moral Complexity.* Cambridge.
    Cambridge University Press
Larsson, Tor. 1984. *Industrins furirer.* Stockholm. Almqvist and Wiksell
Lau, Richard R. 1992. "Book Reviews" (review of Leif Lewin's *Self-Interest
    and Public Interest in Western Politics*), *American Political Science Review*
    86
Laurin, Urban. 1986. *På heder och samvete. Skattefuskets utbredning och
    orsaker.* Stockholm. Norstedts
Le Grand, Julian & Bartlett, Will (eds.). 1993. *Quasi-markets and Social
    Policy.* London. Macmillan
Lehning, Percy B. 1990. "Liberalism and Capabilities: Theories of Justice and
    the Neutral State," *Social Justice Research* 4
Levi, Margaret. 1987. *Of Rule and Revenue.* Berkeley. University of California
    Press
    1990. "A Logic of Institutional Change," in Karen Schweers Cook &
    Margaret Levi (eds.). *The Limits of Rationality.* Chicago. The University
    of Chicago Press
    1991. "Are There Limits to Rationality?" *Archives Europeénnes de Sociologie*
    31
    1993. "The Construction of Consent," Administration, Compliance and
    Governability Program, Working Paper No. 10, Research School of
    Social Sciences, Australian National University
    1997. *Consent, Dissent, and Patriotism.* New York: Cambridge University
    Press (in press)
Levin, M. A. & Ferman, B. 1985. *The Political Hand. Policy Implementation
    and Youth Employment Programs.* New York. Pergamon Press
Lewin, Leif. 1967. *Planhushållningsdebatten.* Stockholm. Almqvist and Wiksell
    1970. *Folket och eliterna. En studie i modern demokratisk teori.* Stockholm.
    Almqvist and Wiksell
    1984 (1992). *Ideologi och strategi. Svensk politik under 100 år.* Stockholm.
    Norstedts.
    1988. *Det gemensamma bästa. Om egenintresset och allmänintresset i
    västerländsk politik.* Stockholm. Carlssons Förlag
    1990. *Upptäkten av framtiden.* Stockholm. Carlssons
    1991. *Self-Interest and Public Interest in Western Politics.* Oxford. Oxford
    University Press
Lewis, David. 1984. "Conclusion: Improving Implementation," in David

Lewis and Helen Wallace (eds.). *Policies into Practice: National and International Case Studies in Implementation*. London. Heinemann

Lichbach, Mark I. 1994. "Rethinking Rationality and Rebellion," *Rationality and Society* 6

1995. *The Rebel's Dilemma*. University of Michigan Press

Lidström, Anders. 1991. *Discretion: An Art of the Possible*. Umeå. Umeå University, Department of Political Science

Lindbeck, Assar. 1993. *The Welfare State*. Aldershot, Hants. Edward Elgar

Lindblom, Charles. 1977. *Politics and Markets: The World's Political-Economic Systems*. New York. Basic Books

Lindbom, Anders. 1995. *Medborgarskapet i välfärdsstaten : föräldrainflytande i skandinavisk grundskola*. Stockholm. Almqvist and Wiksell International

Lindensjö, Bo. 1987. "Den politiska maktens gränser," in Olof Petersson (ed.). *Maktbegreppet*. Stockholm. Carlssons

Linder, Stephen H. & Peters, B. Guy. 1990. "Research Perspectives on the Design of Public Policy: Implementation, Formulation, and Design," in Dennis J. Palumbo & Donald J. Calista (eds.). *Implementation and the Policy Process: Opening up the Black Box*. New York. Greenwood Press

Lindley, Richard. 1986. *Autonomy*. London. Macmillan

Lipsky, Michael. 1980. *Street-level Bureaucracy: Dilemmas of the Individual in Public Services*. New York. The Free Press

Lister, Ruth. 1995. "Dilemmas in engendering citizenship," *Economy and Society* 24

Ljunggren, Stig-Björn. 1992. *Folkhemskapitalismen. Högers programutveckling under efterkrigstiden*. Stockholm. Tiden

Lowi, Theodore J. 1972. "Four Systems of Policy, Politics and Choice," *Public Administration Review* 32

1984. "Ronald Reagan – Revolutionary?" in Lester M. Salamon and Michael S. Lund (eds.). *The Reagan Presidency and the Governing of America*. Washington, D.C. The Urban Institute

Luhman, Niklas. 1969. *Legitimation durch Verfahren*. Neuwied. Luchterhands

1979. *Trust and Power*. Chichester. John Wiley

Lundberg, Lars. 1982. *Från lag till arbetsmiljö*. Malmö. Liber

Lundquist, Lennart. 1986. *Implementation Steering: An Actor-Structure Approach*. Lund. Studentlitteratur

1988. *Byråkratisk etik*. Lund. Studentlitteratur

1991. *Förvaltning och demokrati*. Stockholm. Norstedts

1992. *Förvaltning, stat och samhälle*. Lund. Studentlitteratur

1993. *Det vetenskapliga studiet av politik*. Lund. Studentlitteratur

Lundqvist, Lennart J. 1991. "Privatisering. Varför och varför inte?" in Bo Rothstein (ed.). *Politik som organisation. Förvaltningspolitikens grundproblem*. Stockholm. SNS Förlag

Lundström, Mats. 1993. *Politikens moraliska rum. En studie i F. A. Hayeks politiska filosofi*. Uppsala. Almqvist and Wiksell International

Lundström, Tommy. 1993. *Tvångsomhändertagande av barn*. Stockholm. Stockholms Universitet, Socialhögskolan

McFate, Katherine, Smeeding, Timothy, & Rainwater, Lee. 1995. "Markets and States: Poverty Trends and Transfer System Effectiveness in the 1980s," in Katherine McFate, Richard Lawson, & William Julius Wilson, (eds.): *Poverty, Inequality and the Future of Social Policy: Western States in the New World Order*. New York. Russell Sage

MacIntyre, Alasdaire. 1981. *After Virtue*. Notre Dame. University of Notre Dame Press

Majone, Giandemenico & Gretschmann, Klaus. 1986. "Analyzing the Public Sector: Shortcomings of Current Approaches," in Franz-Xavier Kaufmann, Giandomenico Majone, & Vincent Ostrom, with the assistance of Wolfgang Wirth (eds.). *Guidance, Control, and Evaluation in the Public Sector*. Berlin–New York. Walter de Gruyter

Malnes, Raino. 1992. "Philosophical Argument and Political Practice: On the Methodology of Normative Theory," *Scandinavian Political Studies* 15

Mansbridge, Jane J. 1990. "The Rise and Fall of Self-Interest in the Explanation of Political Life," in Jane J. Mansbridge (ed.). *Beyond Self Interest*. Chicago. The University of Chicago Press

March, James B. & Olsen, Johan P. 1986. *Ambiguity and Choice in Organizations*. Bergen. Universitetsforlaget

1989. *Rediscovering Institutions: The Organizational Basis of Politics*. New York. The Free Press

Margalit, Avishai. 1996. *The Decent Society*. Cambridge, Mass. Harvard University Press

Margolis, Howard. 1984. *Selfishness, Altruism and Rationality*. Chicago. University of Chicago Press

Mason, H. L. 1988. "Implementing the Final Solution: The Ordinary Regulation of the Extraordinary," *World Politics* 40

Matland, Richard E. 1995. "Synthesizing the Implementation Literature: The Ambiguity–Conflict Model of Policy Implementation," in *Journal of Public Administration Research and Theory* 7

Mayhew, Bruce. 1980. "Structuralism vs. Individualism. Part 1. Shadowboxing in the Dark," *Social Forces* 59

Maynard, Alan. 1993. "Jämlikhet och effektivitet vid fördelning av resurser i hälso- och sjukvård," in Göran Arvidsson, Bengt Jönsson and Lars Werkö (eds.). *Prioriteringar i sjukvården – Etik och ekonomi*. Stockholm. SNS Förlag

Mayntz, Renate. 1975. "Legitimacy and the Directive Capacity of the Political

System," in Leon N. Lindberg (ed.). *Stress and Contradiction In Modern Capitalism.* Lexington, Mass. D. C. Heath

Mazmanian, Daniel A. & Sabatier, Paul A. (eds.). 1981. *Effective Policy Implementation.* Lexington, Mass. D. C. Heath

1983. *Implementation and Public Policy.* Glenview, Ill. Scott Foresman and Company

Michelman, Frank. 1976. "Constitutional Welfare Rights and A Theory of Justice," in Norman Daniels (ed.). *Reading Rawls: Critical Studies of A Theory of Justice.* New York. Basic Books

Mill, John Stuart. 1861/1972. *Considerations on Representative Government.* London. Dent and Sons

1863/1910. *Utilitarianism, Liberty, Representative Government.* London. J. M. Dent

Miller, David. 1978. "Democracy and Social Justice," *British Journal of Political Science* 8

1987a. "Justice," in David Miller (ed.). *The Blackwell Encyclopedia of Political Thought.* London. Blackwell

1987b. "Political Theory," in David Miller (ed.). *The Blackwell Encyclopedia of Political Thought.* London. Blackwell

1990. "Equality," in G. M. K. Hunt (eds.). *Philosophy and Politics.* Cambridge. Cambridge University Press

1991. "Recent Theories of Social Justice," *British Journal of Political Science* 21

1992. "Distributive Justice: What the People Think," *Ethics* 102

Miller, Gary. 1992. *Managerial Dilemmas. The Political Economy of Hierarchy.* Cambridge. Cambridge University Press

Mintzberg, Henry M. 1979. *The Structuring of Organization.* Englewood Cliffs, N.J. Prentice-Hall

Misztal, Barbara. 1996. *Trust in Modern Societies.* Cambridge. Polity Press

Moene, Karl Ove & Wallerstein, Michael. 1996. "Self-Interested Support for Welfare Spending." Paper presented at the Annual Meeting of the American Political Science Association, San Francisco, Aug. 29–Sept. 1, 1996

Montin, Stig. 1992. "Privatiseringsprocesser i kommunerna," *Statsvetenskaplig tidskrift* 95

1993. *Svenska kommuner i omvandling.* Örebro. Novemus, Högskolan i Örebro

Moon, John D. 1990. "The Moral Basis of the Democratic Welfare State," in Amy Gutman (ed.). *Democracy and the Welfare State.* Princeton. Princeton University Press

Mucciaroni, Gary. 1990. *The Political Failure of Employment Policy 1945–1982.* Pittsburgh. University of Pittsburgh Press

Mulhall, Stephen &Swift, Adam. 1992. *Liberals and Communitarians*. Oxford. Blackwell

Murray, Charles A. 1984. *Loosing Ground: American Social Policy 1950–1980*. New York. Basic Books

Myrdal, Gunnar. 1969. "Den mjuka staten i underutvecklade länder," in *U-hjälp i utveckling*. Stockholm. Wahlström and Widstrand

1970. *Objektivitetsproblemet i samhällsforskningen*. Stockholm

Möller, Gustav. 1920. "Socialiseringsproblemet," *Tiden* 12

1926. *Arbetlöshetsförsäkringen jämte andra sociala försäkringar*. Stockholm. Tidens Förlag

1952. "Svensk socialpolitik," *Tiden* 44

1971. "Hågkomster," in Åke Wedin (ed.). *Arbetarrörelsens Årsbok*. Stockholm. Prisma

Nagel, Thomas. 1987. "Moral Conflicts and Political Legitimacy," *Philosophy and Public Affairs* 16

Nakamura, Robert T. & Smallwood, Frank. 1980. *The Politics of Policy Implementation*. New York. St Martins Press

Niklasson, Lars. 1992. *Bör man lyda lagen. En undersökning av den offentliga maktens legitimitet*. Uppsala. Acta Universitatis Upsaliensis

Nilsson, Lennart. 1991. "Den offentliga sektorn under åtstramning och omprövning," in Sören Holmberg and Lennart Nilsson (eds.). *Trendbrott? Samhälle, Opinion, Massmedia*. Göteborg. Göteborgs Universitet

Norell, Per-Ola. 1989. *De kommunala administratörerna. En studie av politiska aktörer och byråkratiproblemet*. Lund. Studentlitteratur

North, Douglas, 1990. *Institutions, Institutional Change and Economic Performance*. Cambridge. Cambridge University Press

Nove, Alec. 1983. *The Economics of Feasible Socialism*. London. Allen and Unwin

Nozick, Robert. 1974. *Anarchy, State and Utopia*. New York. Basic Books

1989. *Examined Life: Philosophical Meditations*. New York. Simon and Schuster

Nussbaum, Martha. 1990. "Aristotelian Social Democracy," in R. Bruce Douglass and Gerald M. Mara and Henry S. Richardsson (eds.). *Liberalism and the Good*. New York. Routledge

Nyström, Per. 1983. "Välfärdsstatens styrningsmekanismer," in Anders Björnsson (ed.). *I folkets tjänst*. Stockholm. Ordfront

1991. "Hur man löser ett skenproblem – enligt logikens lagar," *Tiden* 83

Öberg, Per-Ola. 1994. *Särintresse och allmänintresse: korporatismens ansikten*. Stockholm. Almqvist & Wiksell International

Offe, Claus. 1986. *Disorganized Capitalism: Contemporary Transformations of Work and Politics*. Cambridge. Polity Press

1988. "Democracy Against the Welfare State? Structural Foundations of

Neoconservative Political Opportunities," in J. Donald Moon (ed.). *Responsibility, Rights, and Welfare: The Theory of the Welfare State.* Boulder, Col. Westview Press

O'Higgins, Michael. 1987. "Egalitarians, Equalities, and Welfare Evolution," *Journal of Social Policy* 16

Okin, Susan Moller. 1989. *Justice, Gender and the Family.* New York. Basic Books

Olofsson, Gunnar. 1979. *Mellan klass och stat.* Lund. Arkiv avhandlingsserie

Olsen, Johan P. 1990. *Demokrati på svenska.* Stockholm. Carlssons

1993. "Utfordringar for offentlig sektor og for statsvitenskapen," *Norsk statsvitenskapelig tidsskrift* 9

Olsen, Johan P. & Peters, B. Guy. 1996. *Lessons from Experience. Experimental Learning in Administrative Reforms in Eight Democracies.* Oslo. Scandinavian University Press

Olson, Mancur C. 1965. *The Logic of Collective Action.* Cambridge, Mass.. Harvard University Press

Olsson, Sven E. 1990 (1993). *Social Policy and Welfare State in Sweden.* Lund. Arkiv

1991. "När makten lades tillrätta," in Sven E. Olsson and Göran Therborn (eds.). *Vision möter verklighet. Om social styrning och faktisk samhällsutveckling.* Stockholm. Allmänna förlaget

Olsson-Hort, Sven E. 1992. *Segregation – ett svenska dilemma.* Appendix 9 to Långtidsutredningen 1992. Stockholm. Allmänna förlaget

Ordeshook, Peter C. 1986. *Game Theory and Political Theory.* Cambridge. Cambridge University Press

Orloff, Ann Shola. 1993. *The Politics of Pensions: A Comparative Analysis of Britain, Canada and the United States 1880–1940.* Madison. The University of Wisconsin Press

Osborne, David and Gaebler, Ted. 1993. *Reinventing Government.* New York. Penguin

Oskarsson, Maria. 1994. *Klassröstning i Sverige. Rationalitet, lojalitet eller bara slentrian?* Stockholm. Nerenius och Santérus Förlag

Ostrom, Elinor. 1992. *Governing the Commons: The Evolution of Institutions for Collective Action.* Cambridge. Cambridge University Press

O'Toole, Laurence J. Jr. 1983. "Interorganizational Co-operation and the Implementation of Labour Market Training Programs," *Organizational Studies* 4

1986. "Policy Recommendations for Multi-Actor Implementation. An Assessment of the Field," *Journal of Public Policy* 6

Ottomeyer, Klaus. 1977. *Människan under kapitalismen.* Göteborg. Röda Bokförlaget

Palm, Thede. 1981. *Nederlagets män och andra essäer.* Stockholm. Militärhistoriska Förlaget

Palumbo, Dennis J. 1987. "Implementation: What Have We Learnt and Still
    Need to Know," *Policy Studies Review* 7
Palumbo, Dennis J. & Calista, Donald J. (eds.). 1990. *Implementation and
    the Policy Process: Opening Up the Black Box.* New York. Grennwood
    Press
Pedersen, Mogens N. 1977. "Om det rette brug av historiske materialer i
    statskundskaben," in *Festskrift till Erik Rasmussen.* Aarhus. Politica
Pedersen, Peter A. 1985. *Monash as a Military Commander.* Carlton, Vic.
    Melbourne University Press
Perrow, Charles 1986. *Complex Organizations: A Critical Essay.* New York.
    Random House
Petersson, Olof. 1987a. "Introduktion" in same author (ed.). *Maktbegreppet.*
    Stockholm. Carlssons Förlag, 1987
    1987b. *Metaforernas makt.* Stockholm. Carlssons Förlag
    1989. *Makt i det öppna samhället.* Stockholm. Carlssons Förlag
    1991. "Democracy and Power in Sweden," *Scandinavian Political Studies* 14
    1992. *Svensk politik.* Stockholm. Publica
Petersson, Olof, Westholm, Anders, & Blomberg, Göran. 1989. *Medborgarnas
    makt.* Stockholm. Carlssons Förlag
Pettersson, Thorleif. 1992. "Välfärd, värderingsförändringar och
    folkrörelseengagemang," in Sigbert Axelsson and Thorleif Pettersson
    (eds.). *Mot denna framtid.* Stockholm. Carlssons Förlag
Pettersson, Thorleif & Geyer, Kalle. 1992. *Värderingsförändringar i Sverige.
    Den svenska modellen, individualismen och rättvisan.* Stockholm.
    Brevskolan
Phillips, Anne. 1993. *Democracy and Difference.* Oxford. Polity Press
Pierson, Paul. 1994. *Dismantling the Welfare State? Reagan, Thatcher and the
    Politics of Retrenchment.* Cambridge. Cambridge University Press
    1996. "Path Dependence and the Study of Politics." Paper presented at the
    Annual Meeting of the American Political Science Association, San
    Francisco Aug. 29 – Sept. 1, 1996
Porter, David O. &Olsen, Eugene A. 1976. "Some Critical Issues in
    Government Centralization and Decentralization," *Public
    Administration Review* 36
Premfors, Rune. 1989. *Policyanalys.* Lund. Studentlitteratur
    1993. "En postmodern demokrati?" in Björn von Sydow, Gunnar Wallin,
    & Björn Wittrock (eds.). *Politikens väsen. Idéer och institutioner i den
    moderna staten.* Stockholm. Tidens Förlag
Pressman, Jeffrey L. & Wildavsky, Aaron. 1973. *Implementation.* Berkeley.
    University of California Press
Przeworski, Adam. 1985. *Capitalism and Social Democracy.* Cambridge.
    Cambridge University Press

Przeworski, Adam & Sprague, John. 1986. *Paper Stones: A History of Electoral Socialism*. Chicago. The University of Chicago Press

Putnam Robert B. 1993. *Making Democracy Work: Civic Traditions in Modern Italy*. Princeton: Princeton University Press

Rapaport, Elizabeth. 1981. "Ethics and Social Policy," *Canadian Journal of Philosophy* 9

Rawls, John. 1971. *A Theory of Justice*. Oxford. Oxford University Press

1977. "The Basic Structure as a Subject," *American Philosophical Quarterly* 14

1980. "Kantian Constructivism in Moral Theory: The Dewey Lectures," *The Journal of Philosophy* 77

1982. "Social Unity and Primary Goods," in Amartya Sen and Bernard Williams (eds.). *Utilitarianism and Beyond*. Cambridge. Cambridge University Press

1985. "Justice as Fairness. Political not Metaphysical," *Philosophy and Public Affairs* 14

1987. "The Idea of an Overlapping Consensus," *Oxford Journal of Legal Studies* 7

1988. "The Priority of Rights and the Idea of the Good," *Philosophy and Public Affairs* 17

1993. *Political Liberalism*. New York. Columbia University Press

Raz, Joseph. 1986. *The Morality of Freedom*. Oxford. Clarendon Press

Regan, Geoffrey. 1987. *Great Military Disasters: A Historical Survey of Military Incompetence*. New York. M. Evans and Co

Renwick Monroe, Kirsten (ed.). 1991. *The Economic Approach to Politics: A Critical Reassessment of the Theory of Rational Choice*. New York. HarperCollins

Ricci, David. 1984. *The Tragedy of Political Science: Politics, Scholarship, and Democracy*. New Haven. Yale University Press

Riksrevisionsverket. 1991. *Priset för våra liv – en rapport från RRVs konferens om riskvärdering*. Stockholm. Riksrevisionsverket

Ripley, R. B. & Franklin, G. A. 1982. *Bureaucracy and Policy Implementation*. Homewood, Ill. The Dorsey Press

Rivière, Helene, 1993. *Mening var ju att hjälpa människorna, inte att ta ifrån dem ansvaret*. Stockholm. City University Press

Roemer, John E. 1985. "Equality of Talent," *Economy and Philosophy* 1

Rombach, Björn. 1991. *Det går inte att styra med mål*. Lund. Studentlitteratur

Rosanvallon, Pierre. 1988. "The Decline of Social Visibility," in John Keane (ed.). *Civil Society and the State: New European Perspectives*. London. Verso

Rorty, Richard. 1987. *Contingency, Irony, and Solidarity*. Cambridge. Cambridge University Press

1991a. *Objectivity, Relativism and Truth.* Cambridge. Cambridge
University Press
1991b. "The Priority of Philosophy to Democracy," *Philosophical Papers,*
Vol 1. New York. Cambridge University Press
1993. *Postmodernism and Democratic Theory.* Philadelphia. Temple
University Press
Rose, Richard & Peters, Guy B. 1978. *Can Governments Go Bankrupt?* New
York. Basic Books
Rothstein, Bo. 1983. "Folkhemmmets förverkligande eller den nya
Leviathan," *Zenit* 77
1985. "Managing the Welfare State: Lessons from Gustav Möller,"
Scandinavian Political Studies 8
1988. "Struktur-aktörsansatsen. Ett metodiskt dilemma," *Statsvetenskaplig
tidskrift* 97
1990. "Marxism, Institutional Analysis and Working Class Strength: The
Swedish Case," *Politics and Society* 18
1992a. *Den korporativa staten. Intresseorganisationer och statsförvaltning i
svensk politik.* Stockholm. Norstedts
1992b. "State Capacity and Social Justice," *Politics and Society* 20
1992c. "Labor Market Institutions and Working-Class Strength," in Sven
Steinmo, Kathleen Thelen, & Frank Longstreth (eds.). *Structuring
Politics: Historical Institutionalism in a Comparative Perspective.* New
York. Cambridge University Press
1993a. "The Crisis of the Swedish Social Democracy and the Future of the
Universal Welfare State," *Governance* 6
1993b. "Valfrihet kan bli dyrt," in Peter Antman (ed.). *Systemskifte. Fyra
folkhemsdebatter.* Stockholm. Carlssons
1993c. "Mera myt än verklighet," *Tiden* 2/93
1996. *The Social Democratic State: Bureaucracy and Social Reforms in
Swedish Labor Market and School Policy.* Pittsburgh. University of
Pittsburgh Press
Sabatier, Paul A. 1986. "Top-down and Bottom-up Approaches to
Implementation Research: A Critical Analysis and Suggested Synthesis,"
Journal of Public Policy 6
Sainsbury, Diane. 1991. "Analyzing Welfare State Variations: The Merits and
Limitations of Models Based on the Residual–Institutional Distinction,"
Scandinavian Political Studies 14
1996. *Gender Equality and the Welfare State.* Cambridge: Cambridge
University Press
Salomon, Lester M. (ed.). 1989. *Beyond Privatization: The Tools of
Government Action.* Washington D.C. The Urban Institute
Salonen, Tapio. 1993. *Margins of Welfare: A Study of Modern Functions of
Social Assistance.* Lund. Hällestad Press

Saltman, Richard B. 1992. *Patientmakt över vården*. Stockholm. SNS Förlag
Saltman, Richard B. and von Otter, Carsten. 1992. *Planned Markets and Public Competition: Strategic Reform in Northern European Health Systems*. London. Open University Press
Sandel, Michael. 1982. *Liberalism and the Limits of Justice*. New York. Cambridge University Press
Sannerstedt, Anders. 1996. "Implementering – hur politiska beslut genomförs i praktiken," in Bo Rothstein (ed.). *Politik som organisation. Förvaltningspolitikens grundproblem*. Stockholm. SNS Förlag
Sassen, Saskia, 1992. "To Them That Have Not," *Times Literary Supplement* 05–22–92
Savas, E. S. 1981. *Privatizing the Public Sector: How to Shrink Government*. Ottawa, Ill. Caroline House
Scanlon, Thomas M. 1982. "Contractualism and Utilitarianism," in Amartya Sen and Bernhard Williams (eds.). *Utilitarianism and Beyond*. Cambridge. Cambridge University Press
Scharpf, Fritz W. 1988. "Verhandlungssysteme, Verteilungskonflikte und Pathologien der Politische Steurung," in Manfred G. Schmidt (ed.). Staatstätigkeit, *Politische Vierteljahresschrift*, special issue 19
1989. "Decision Rules, Decision Styles and Policy Choices." *Journal of Theoretical Politics* 2
1990. "Games Real Actors Could Play," *Rationality and Society* 2
Schlytter, Astrid, 1987. *Barnomsorg och ramlag*. Stockholm. Nordiska institutet för samhällsplanering
Schmidt, Stephan. 1991. "Att agera eller reagera," *Tiden* 2/91
Seidman, Edward. 1983. "Introduction," in Edward Seidman (ed.). *Handbook of Social Intervention*. Beverly Hills. Sage Publications
Sen, Amartya. 1977. "Rational Fools: A Critique of the Behavioral Foundations of Economic Theory," *Philosophy and Public Affairs* 6
1982. *Choice, Welfare and Measurement*. Cambridge, Mass. MIT Press
1988. "Freedom of Choice," *European Economic Review* 32
1989. "Marknadens moraliska status," in *Idéer om rättvisa*. Stockholm. Tiden
Sharpe, Laurence J. 1986. "Intergovernmental Policy-Making: The Limits of Subnational Autonomy," in Franz-Xavier Kaufman, Giandomenico Majone, & Vincent Ostrom, with the assistance of Wolfgang Wirth (eds.). *Guidance, Control and Evaluation in the Public Sector*. Berlin–New York. Walter de Gruyter
Sheplse, Kenneth. 1989. "Studying Institutions: Some Lessons from a Rational Choice Approach," *Journal of Theoretical Politics* 1
Simon, Herbert A. 1955. *Administrative Behavior: A Study of Decision-Making Processes in Administrative Organizations*. New York. Macmillan

Sjunnesson, Jan. 1991. "Pragmatisk politik som liberalismens legitimitet,"
    Zenit 111
Sjöström, Kurt. 1974. Socialpolitiken i det kapitalistiska samhället. Inledning
    till en marxistisk analys. Stockholm. Arbetarkultur
Skocpol, Theda. 1987. "America's Incomplete Welfare State: The Limits of
    New Deal Reforms and the Origins of the Present Crisis," in Martin
    Rein, Gøsta Esping-Andersen, & Lee Rainwater (eds.). Stagnation and
    Renewal in Social Policy. Armonk, N.Y. M. E. Sharpe
    1991. "Targeting within Universalism: Politically Viable Policies to
    Combat Poverty in the United States," in Christopher Jencks and Paul
    E. Peterson (eds.). The Urban Underclass. Washington D.C. The
    Brookings Institution
    1995. Protecting Mothers and Soldiers. Cambridge, Mass.: Harvard
    University Press
Skocpol, Theda & Finegold, Kenneth. 1982. "State Capacity and Economic
    Intervention in the Early New Deal," Political Science Quarterly 97
Smart, J. C. C. 1978. "Distributive Justice and Utilitarianism," in J. Arthur
    and W. H. Shaw (eds.). Justice and Economic Distribution. Englewood
    Cliffs. Prentice-Hall
Södersten, Bo, 1992. "Är den offentliga sektorn för stor," in Bo Södersten
    (ed.). Den offentliga sektorn. Stockholm. SNS Förlag
Söderström, Hans Tson. 1977. "På jakt efter en rättvis fördelning av
    välfärden," Ekonomisk Debatt 6
    1988. Hur skall välfärden fördelas. Konjunkturrådets rapport 1988.
    Stockholm. SNS Förlag
Söderström, Hans Tson (ed.).1994. Välfärdsland i ofärdstid. Konjunkturrådets
    rapport 1994. Stockholm. SNS Förlag
Söderström, Lars. 1988. "The Redistribution Effects of Social Protection:
    Sweden," in Jean Pierre Jallade (ed.). The Crisis of Redistribution in
    European Welfare States. Stoke-on-Trent. Trentham Books
Soltan, Karol. 1987. The Causal Theory of Justice. Berkeley. The University of
    California Press
SOU (Statens Offentliga Utred) 1934:39. Betänkande med förslag till
    spridrycksförordning m.m. Stockholm
SOU 1942: 56. Socialvårdens organisation m.m. Stockholm
SOU 1990: 44. Demokrati och makt i Sverige. Stockholm. Allmänna Förlaget
SOU 1991: 46. Handikapp, Välfärd, Rättvisa. Stockholm. Almänna Förlaget
SOU 1993: 16. Nya villkor for ekonomi och politik. Stockholm. Allmänna
    Förlaget
SOU 1992: 52. Ett samhälle för alla. Stockholm. Allmänna Förlaget
SOU 1993: 47. Konsekvenser av valfrihet inom skola, barnomsorg, äldreomsorg
    och primärvård. Stockholm. Allmänna Förlaget
SOU 1993: 90. Lokal demokrati i utveckling. Stockholm. Allmänna Förlaget

SOU 1993: 93. *Vårdens svåra val*. Stockholm. Allmänna Förlaget
Steinmo, Sven. 1993. *Taxation and Democracy*. New Haven. Yale University Press
Steinmo, Sven & Thelen, Kathleen. 1992. "Historical Institutionalism in Comparative Politics," in Sven Steinmo, Kathleen Thelen, & Frank Longstreth (eds.). *Structuring Politics: Historical Institutionalism in a Comparative Perspective*. New York. Cambridge University Press
Stephens, John D. 1996. "The Scandinavian Welfare States: Achievements, Crisis and Prospects," in Gøsta Esping-Andersen (ed.). *Welfare States in Transition. National Adaptions in Global Economies*. London: Sage Publications
Stinchcombe, Arthur L. 1992. "Simmel Systematized," *Theory and Society* 21
Stjernquist, Nils & Magnusson, Håkan. 1989. *Kommunal självstyrelse och jämlika kommuner*. Stockholm. Civildepartementet
Sunesson, Sune. 1985. *Ändra allt. En uppmaning till socialarbetare*. Stockholm. Liber
Sunstein, Cass R. 1991. "Preferences and Politics," *Philosophy and Public Affairs* 20
Svallfors, Stefan. 1989. *Vem älskar välfärdsstaten?* Lund. Arkiv Förlag
1991. "The Politics of Welfare Policy in Sweden: Structural Determinants and Attitudinal Cleavages," *British Journal of Sociology* 42
1992a. "Den stabila välfärdsopinionen. Attityder till svensk välfärdspolitik 1986–92." Working report, Department of Sociology, Umeå University
1992b. "Dimensions of Inequality: A Comparison of Attitudes in Sweden and Britain," Working paper, Department of Sociology, Umeå University
1993a. "Policy Regimes and Attitudes to Inequality: A Comparision of Three European Nations," in Thomas P. Boje & Sven E. Olsson-Hort (eds.). *Scandinavia in a New Europe*. Oslo. Scandinavian University Press
1993b. "Om socialstatsprojektet," *Sociologisk forskning* 3/93
1996. *Välfärdsstatens moraliska ekonomi*. Umeå. Borea
Sveriges offentliga sektor i europeisk konkurrens – konsekvenser av EES-avtalet och medlemskap i EG/EU. 1993. Stockholm. Allmänna Förlaget
Svensson, Torsten. 1994. *Socialdemokratins politiska dominans*. Uppsala. Acta Universitatis Upsaliensis
Tarrow, Sidney. 1996. "Making Social Science Work Across Space and Time," *American Political Science Review* 90
Taylor, Michael. 1987. *The Possibility of Cooperation*. Cambridge. Cambridge University Press
Teubner, Günter. 1983. "Substantive and Reflexive Elements in Modern Law," *Law and Society Review* 18
Therborn, Göran, 1973. *Vad är bra värderingar värda*. Lund. Caverfors

1991. "Samhällelig styrning," in Sven E. Olsson & Göran Therborn (eds.). *Vision möter verklighet. Om social styrning och faktiskt samhällsförändring*. Stockholm. Allmänna Förlaget

Thigpen, Robert B. & Downing, Lyle A. 1983. "Liberalism and the Neutrality Principle," *Political Theory* 11

Thompson, Dennis, 1985. "Philosophy and Politics," *Philosophy and Public Affairs* 14

Thompson, Michael, Ellis, Richard, & Wildavsky, Aaron. 1990. *Cultural Theory*. Boulder, Col. Westview Press

Thorngren, Gunilla. "Valfrihet – men på männens villkor," in *Aftonbladet* 90-03-01

Thullberg, Per. 1987. "Gustav Möller," *Svenskt Biografiskt Lexikon* 127

Tilton, Tim. 1990. *The Political Theory of Swedish Social Democracy*. Oxford. Clarendon Press

Tingsten, Herbert. 1971. *Mitt liv*, part 1. Stockholm. Bonniers

Titmuss, Richard M. 1967. "Universal and Selective Social Services," *New Statesman* 1967-09-15, reprinted in Brian Abel-Smith & Kay Titmuss. (eds.). *Selected Writings of Richard M. Titmuss*. 1987. London. Allen and Unwin

1968. *Commitment to Welfare*. London. Allen and Unwin

1971. "Welfare 'Rights,' Law and Discretion," *Political Quarterly* 42

Trägårdh, Lars. 1993. "I strid med de tio budorden," in Peter Antman (ed.). *Systemskifte. Fyra folkhemsdebatter*. Stockholm. Carlssons

Tsebelis, George. 1990. *Nested Games: Rational Choice in a Comparative Perspective*. Berkeley. The University of California Press

Tullock, Gordon. 1983. *Economics of Income Redistribution*. Boston. Kluwer and Nijhoff

Tyler, Tom R. 1987. "Procedural Justice Research," *Social Justice Research* 1

1990. "Justice, Self-Interest and the Legitimacy of Legal and Political Authority," in Jane Mansbridge (ed.). *Beyond Self-Interest*. Chicago. University of Chicago Press

Tännsjö, Torbjörn. "Regeringen utfärdar yrkesförbud," *Dagens Nyheter* 1993-11-22 s. A4

Uddhammar, Emil. 1993. *Svensk statsdoktrin*. Stockholm. City University Press

Uddhammar, Emil (ed.). 1993. *Gemenskaparna* Stockholm. City University Press

Ullman-Margalit, Edna. 1977. *The Emergence of Norms*. Oxford. Clarendon Press

van Creveld, Martin. 1985. *Command in War*. Cambridge, Mass. Harvard University Press

Vedung, Evert. 1991. *Utvärdering i politik och förvaltning*. Lund. Studentlitteratur

Verba, Sidney, Nie, Norman H., & Kim, Jae-on. 1987. *Participation and Political Equality: A Seven-nation Comparison.* Chicago: University of Chicago Press
von Otter, Carsten & Saltman, Richard B. 1992. *Valfrihet som styrmedel.* Stockholm. Arbetslivscentrum
Walzer, Michael. 1983. *Spheres of Justice: A Defense of Pluralism and Equality.* New York. Basic Books
1990. "The Communitarian Critique of Liberalism," *Political Theory* 18
Weale, Albert. 1990. "Equality, Social Solidarity, and the Welfare State," *Ethics* 100
Weatherly, Richard. 1991. "Doing the Right Thing: How Social Security Clients View Compliance." Report no. 3 (1991), Research Program on Administration, Compliance and Governability, Research School of Social Sciences, Australian National University
Weber, Max. [1922] (1971). *Makt og byråkrati.* Oslo. Gyldendal
[1919] (1977). *Vetenskap och politik.* Göteborg. Korpen
Weir, Margaret. 1992. *Politics and Jobs: The Boundaries of Employment Policy in the United States.* Princeton, N.J. Princeton University Press
Weisbard, Alan. 1987. "The Role of Philosophers in the Public Policy Process," *Ethics* 97
Westerståhl, Jörgen. 1993. "Om statsvetenskapens förträfflighet," in Björn von Sydow and Gunnar Wallin and Björn Wittrock (eds.). *Politikens väsen. Idéer och institutioner i den moderna staten.* Stockholm. Tidens Förlag
Wetterberg, Gunnar. 1991. *Den nya samhället.* Stockholm. Tidens Förlag
Wildavsky, Aaron. 1979. *Speaking Truth to Power.* Boston. Little Brown
1987. "Choosing Preferences by Constructing Institutions: A Cultural Theory of Preference Formation," *American Political Science Review* 81
1991. "Can Norms Rescue Self-Interest?" *Critical Review* 5
Williams, Walter. 1976. "Implementation Analysis and Assessment," *Policy Analysis* 1
1982. "The Study of Implementation: An Overview," in Walter Williams *et al.* (eds.). *Studying Implementation: Methodological and Administrative Issues.* Chatham, N.J. Chatham House Publishers
1989. "Implementing Public Programs," in James L. Perry (ed.). *Handbook of Public Administration.* Jossey-Bass
Wilson, James Q. 1993. *The Moral Sense.* New York. The Free Press, 1993
Winter, Sören. 1990. "Integrating Implementation Research," in Dennis J. Palumbo & Donald J. Calista (eds.). *Implementation and the Policy Process: Opening up the Black Box.* New York. Greenwood Press
Wittrock, Björn & de Leon, Peter. 1985. "Beyond Organizational Design: Contextuality and the Political Theory of Public Policy," in Kenneth Hanf & T. A. J. Toonen (eds.). *Policy Implementation in Federal and Unitary Systems.* Dordrecht. Martinus Nijhoff

Wolf, Charles, Jr. 1993. *Markets or Governments: Choosing between Imperfect Alternatives.* Cambridge, Mass. MIT Press

Wolfe, Alan. 1989. *Whose Keeper? Social Science and Moral Obligation.* Berkeley. University of California Press

Wolman, Harold. 1980. "The Determinants of Program Success and Failure," *Journal of Public Policy* 1

Young, Ken. 1981. "Discretion as an Implementation Problem: A Framework for Interpretation," in Michael Adler & Stewart Asquith (eds.). *Discretion and Welfare.* London. Heinemann

Zald, Mayer N. 1981. "Trends in Policy Making and Implementation in the Welfare State," in H. D. Stein (ed.). *Organizations and the Human Services.* Philadelphia. Temple University Press

Zarefsky, David. 1986. *President Johnson's War on Poverty: Rhetoric and History.* Alabama. The University of Alabama Press

Zaremba, Maciej. 1992. *Minken i Folkhemmet.* Stockholm. Timbro

Zey, Mary (ed.). 1992. *Decision Making: Alternatives to Rational Choice Models.* Newbury Park. Sage Publications

Ziehe, Thomas. 1993. *Kulturanalyser. ungdom, utbildning, modernitet.* Eslöv. Symposion

Index

249